Für / For

Dido, Sabri & Luiz

Iwan Schumacher

1972—At Home and on the Way

Edition Patrick Frey

Nº 222

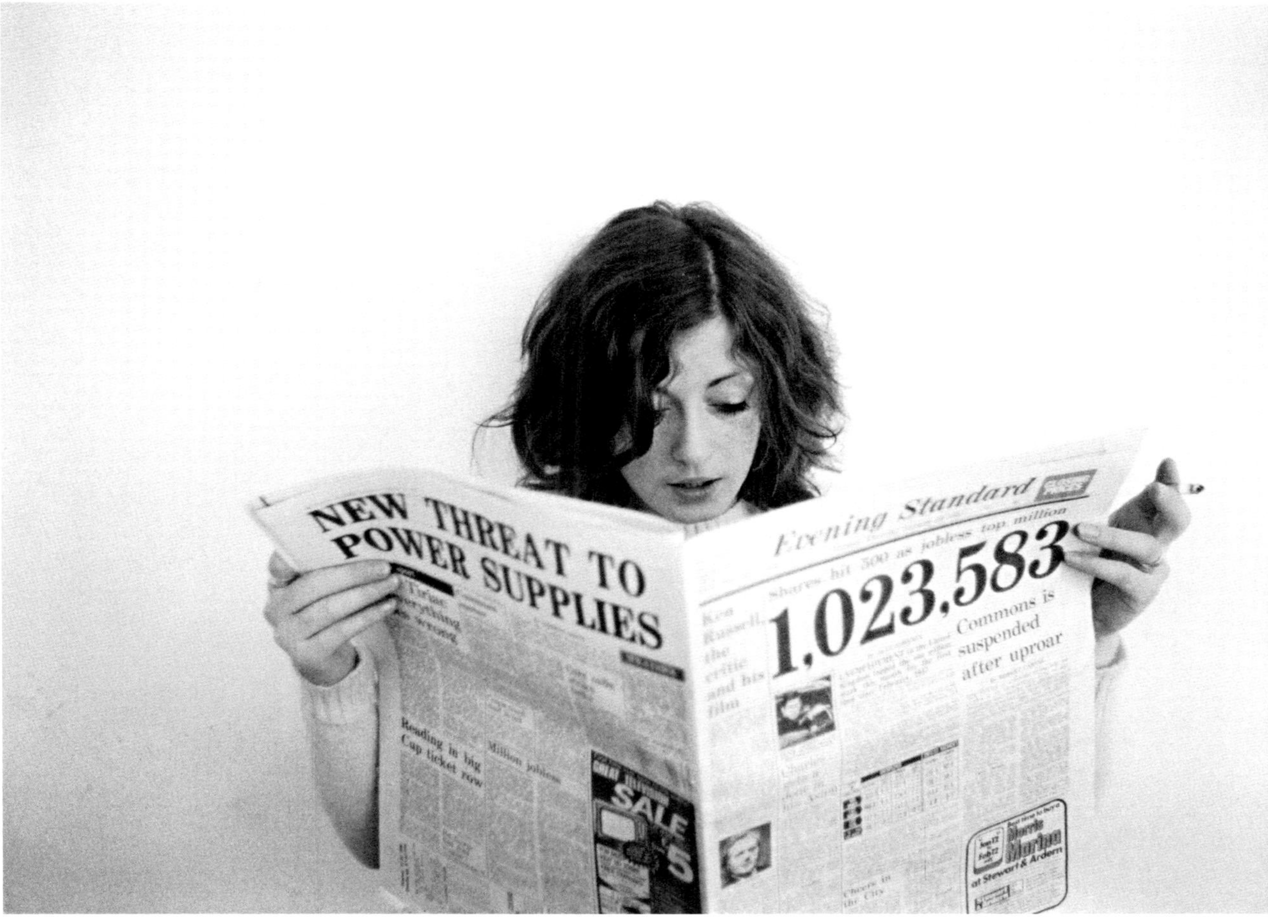
NEW THREAT TO POWER SUPPLIES
Evening Standard
Shares hit 500 as jobless top million
1,023,583
Commons is suspended after uproar
Ken Russell, the critic and his film
Reading in big Cup ticket row
Million jobless
SALE
at Stewart & Ardern

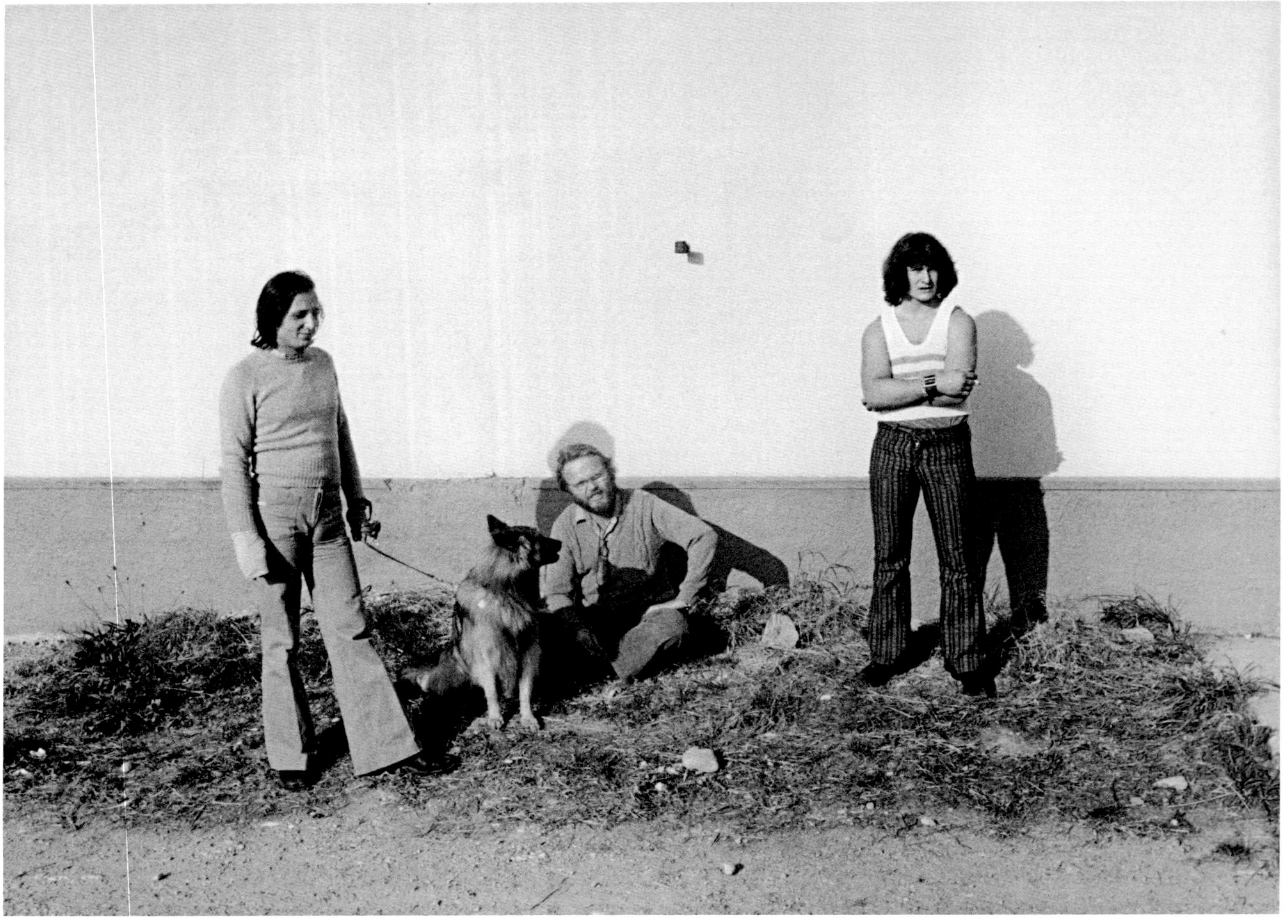

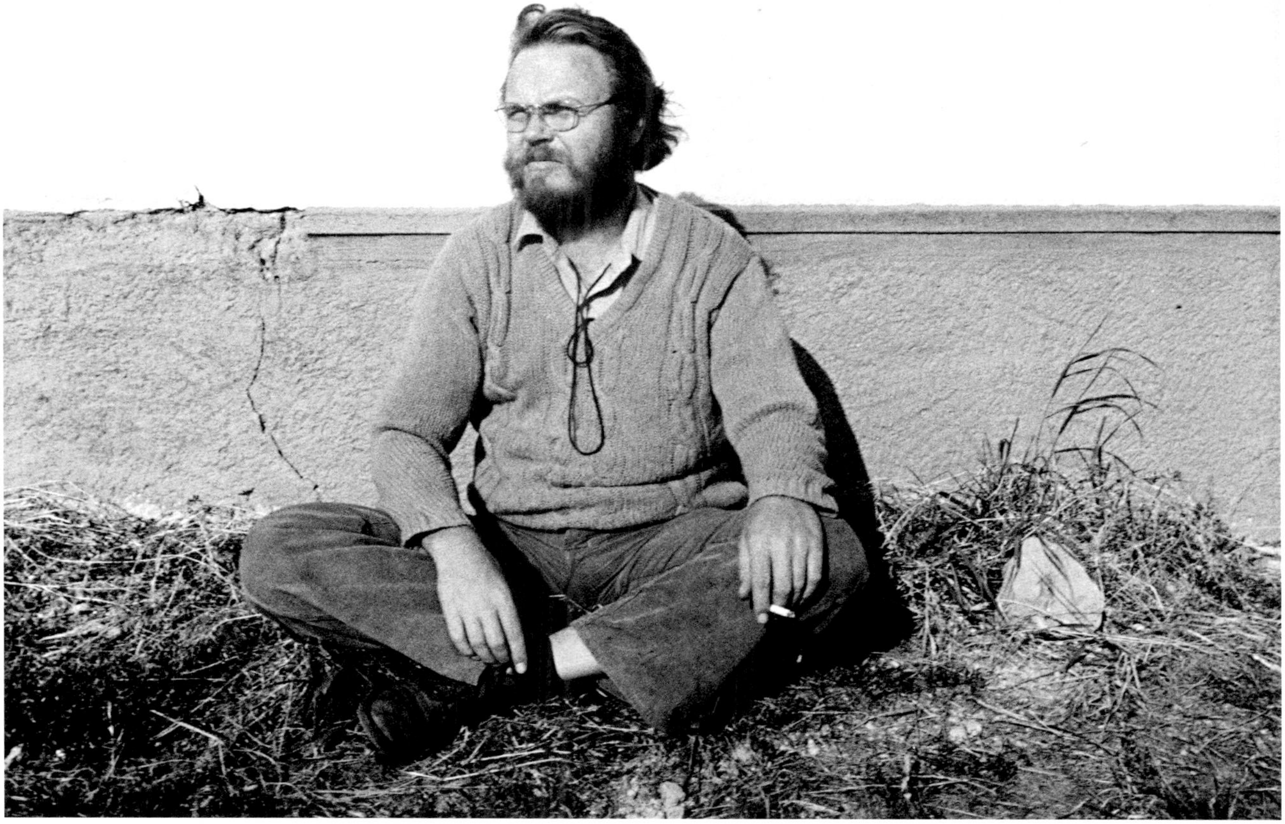

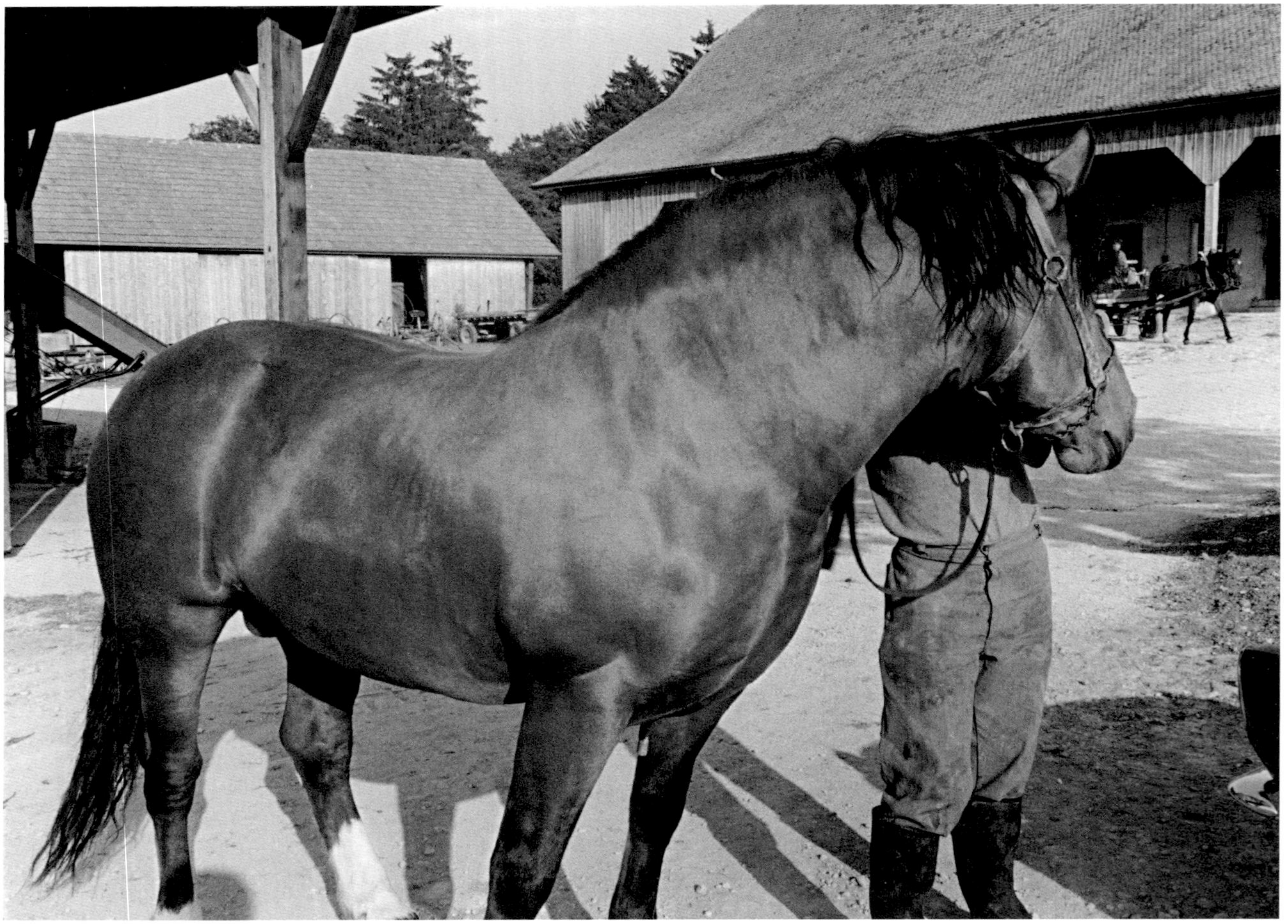

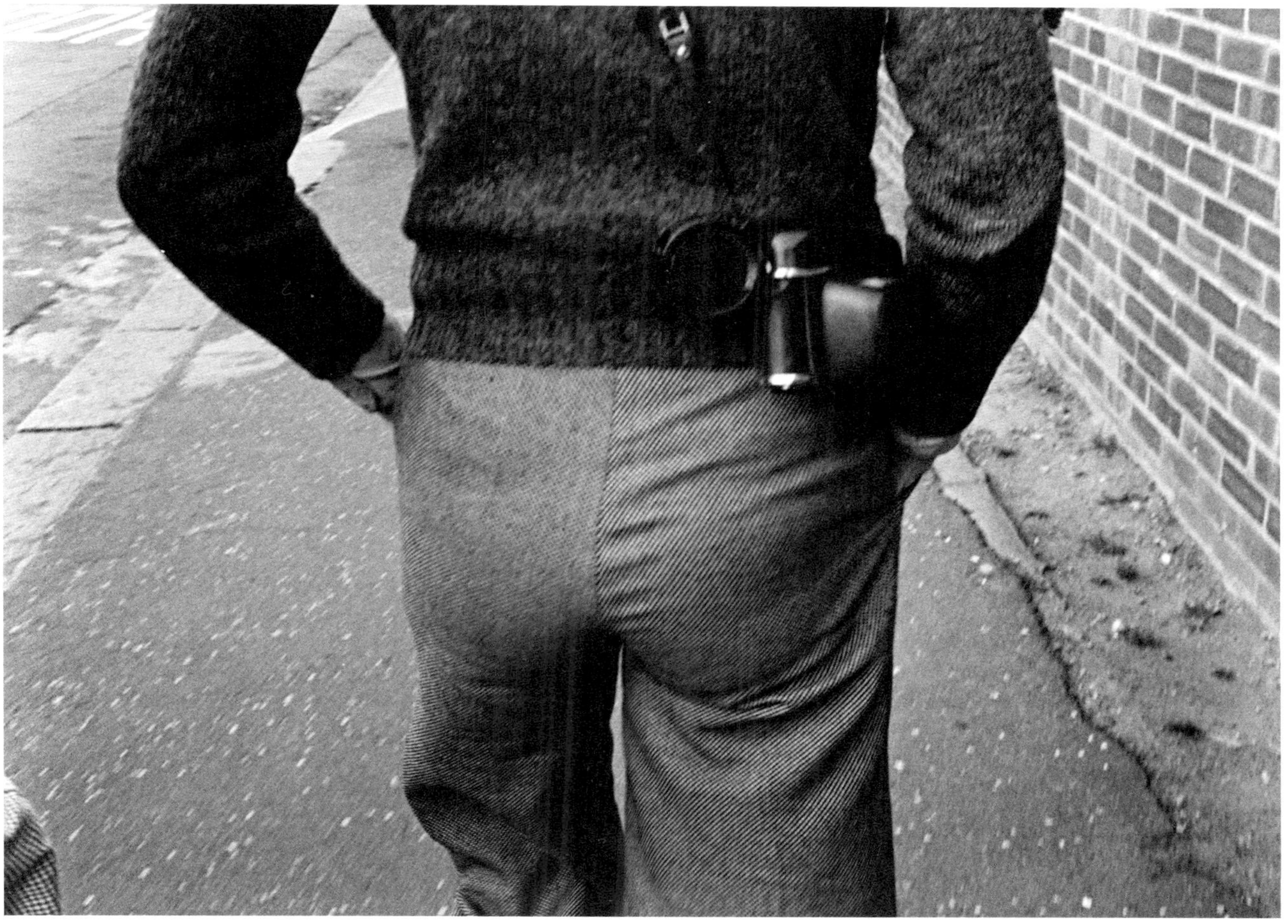

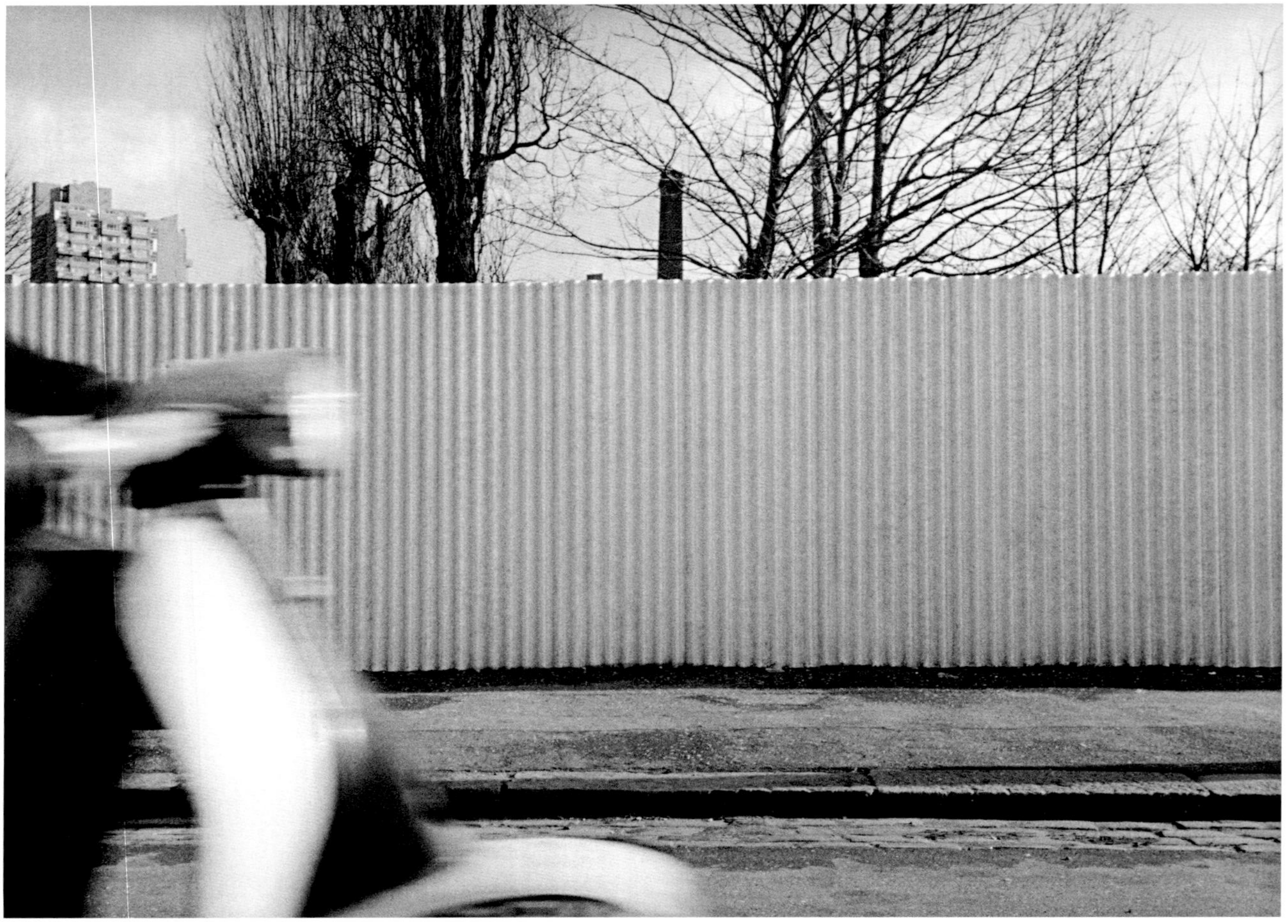

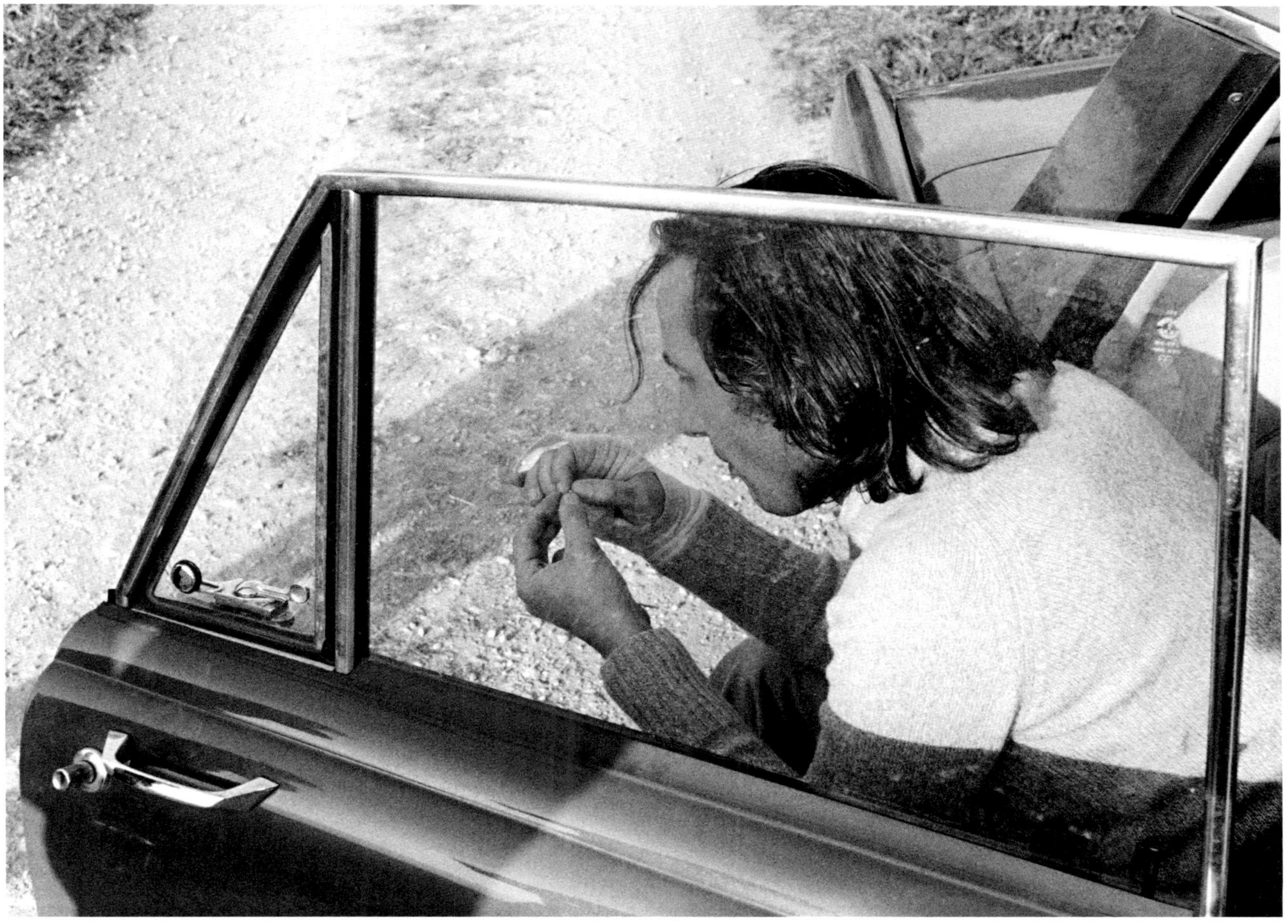

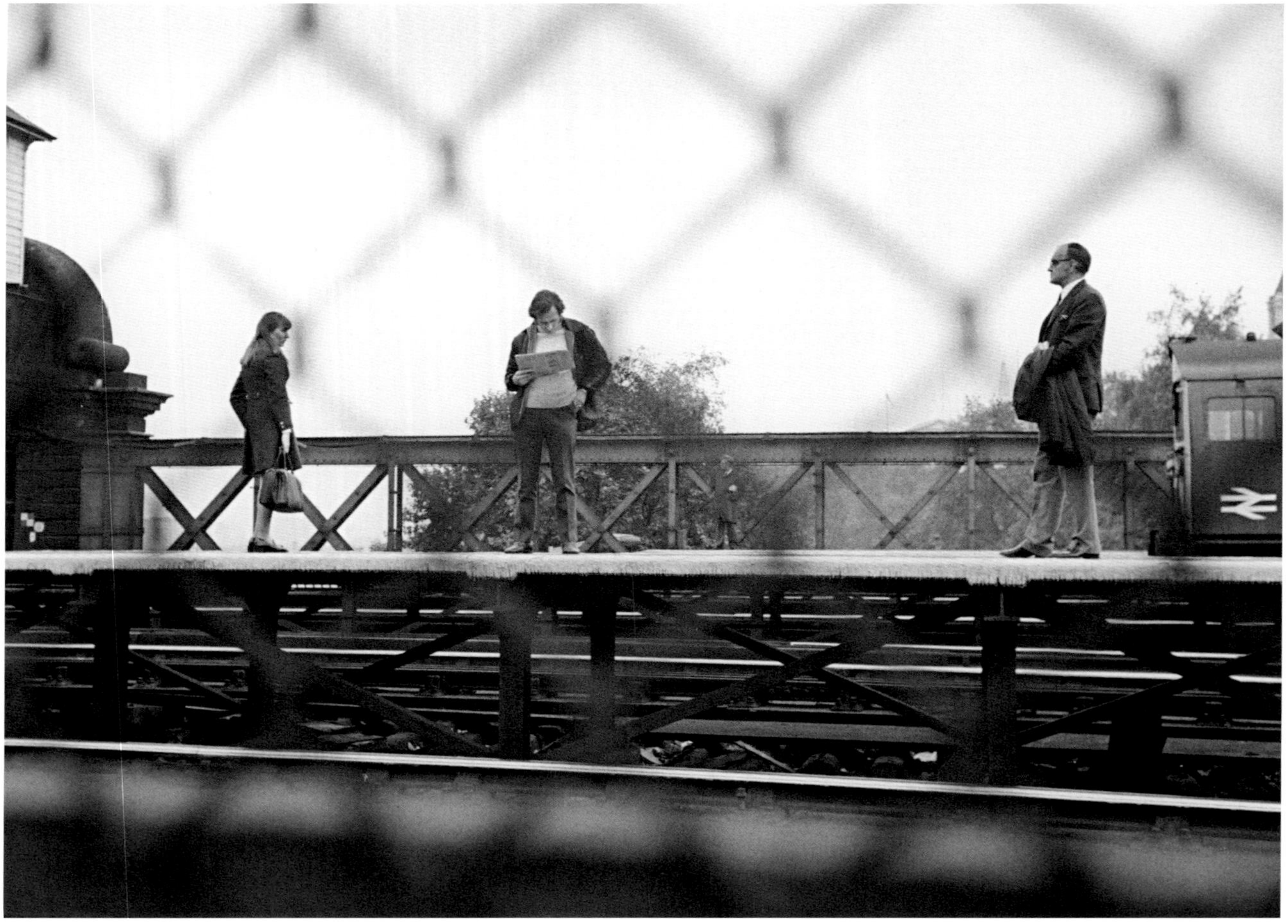

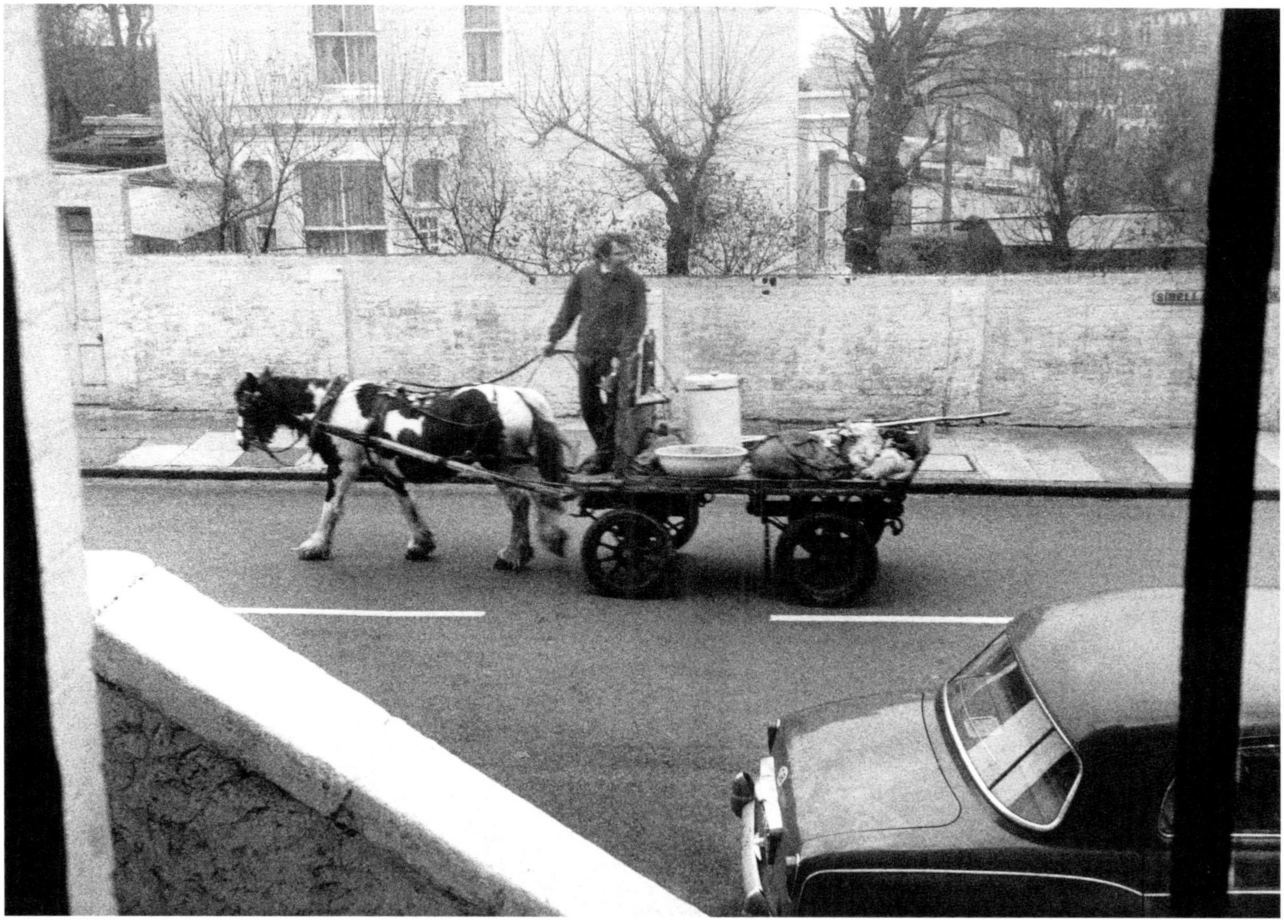

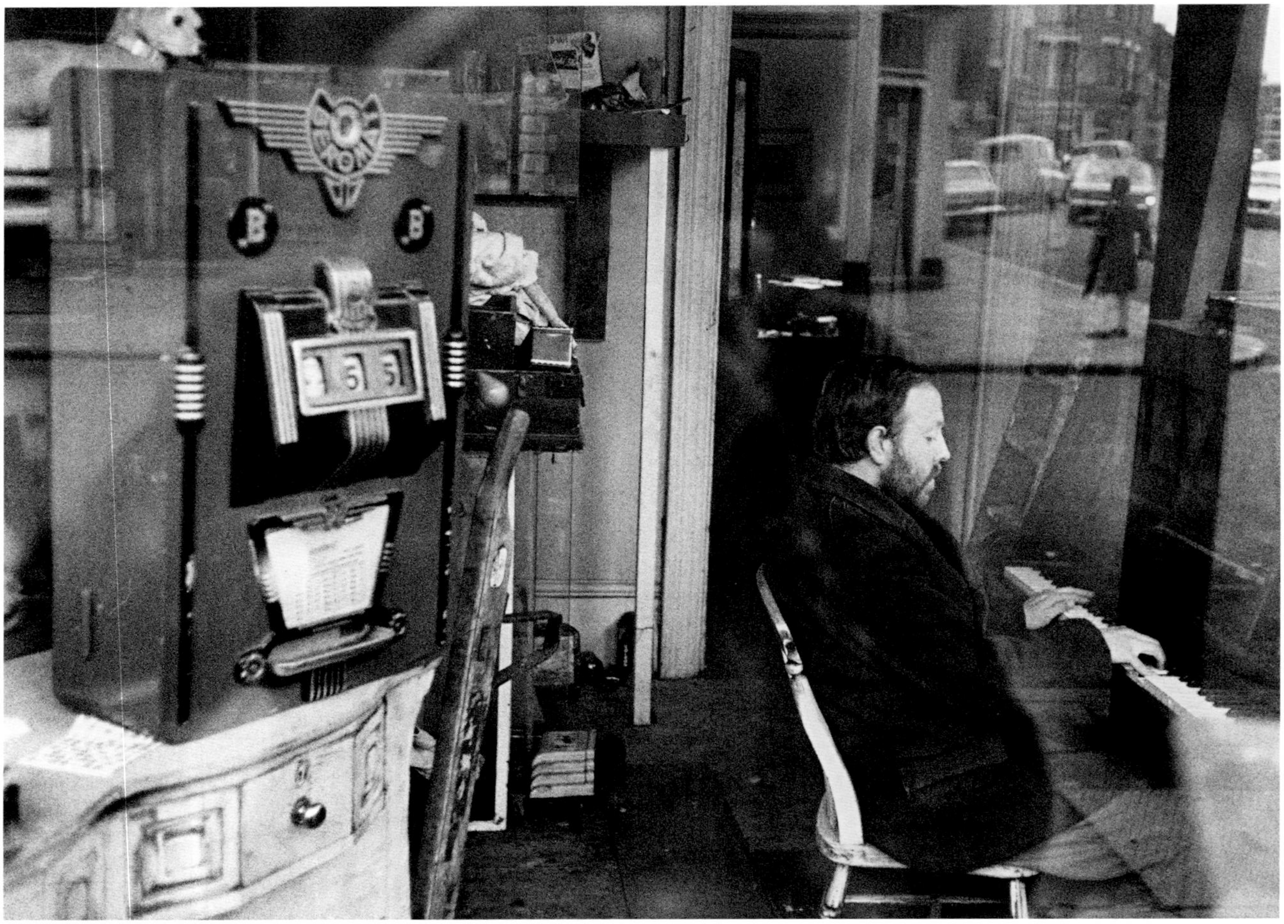

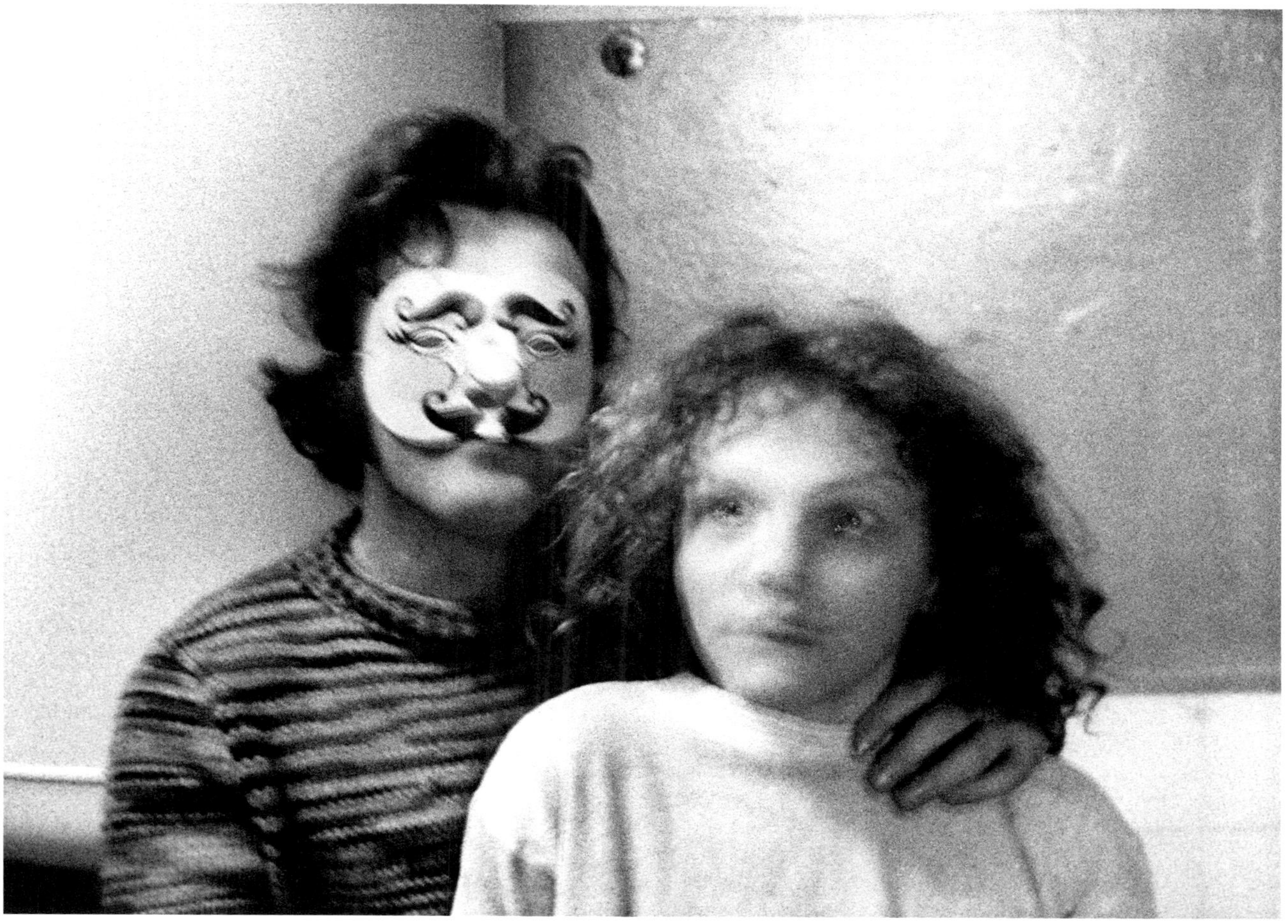

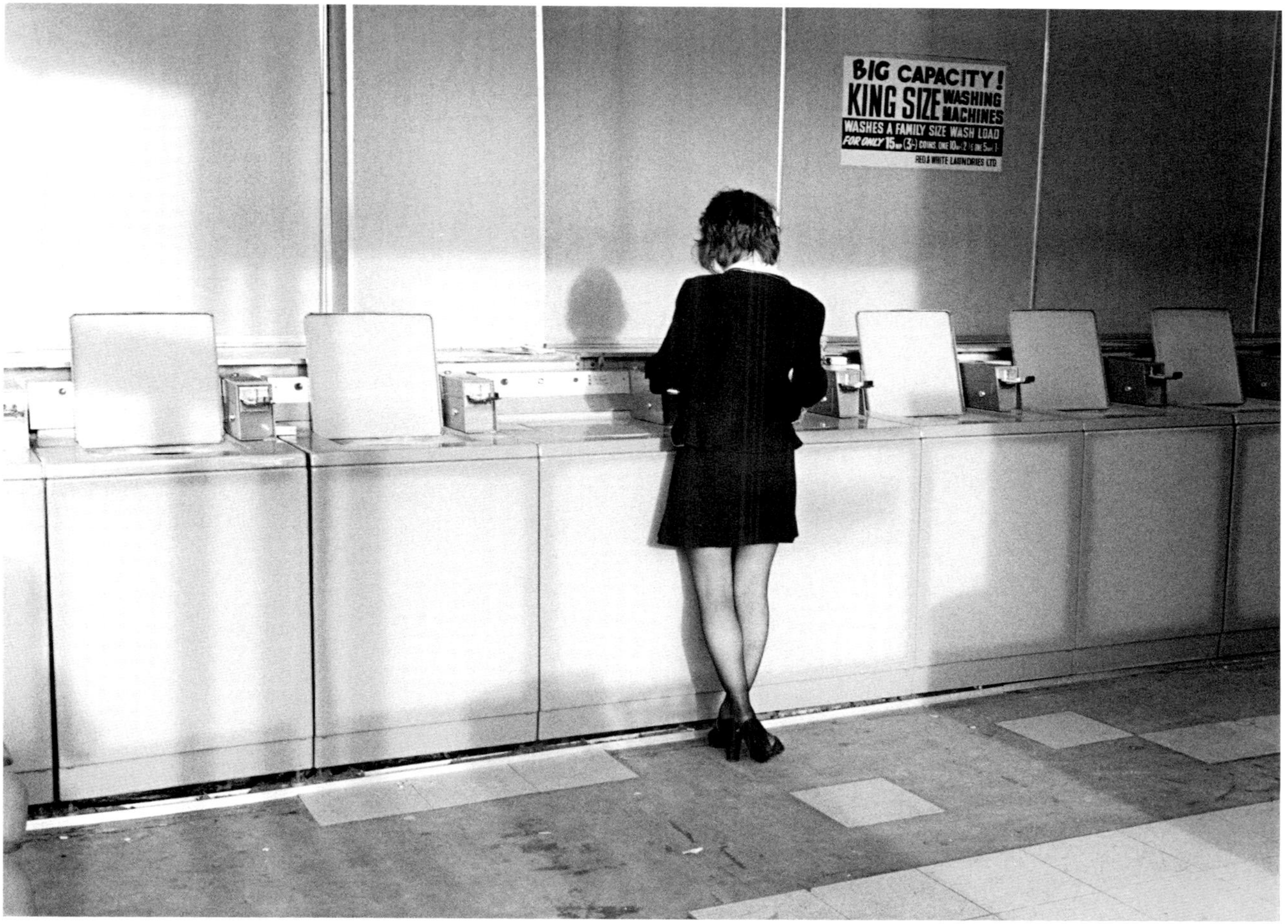
BIG CAPACITY!
KING SIZE WASHING MACHINES
WASHES A FAMILY SIZE WASH LOAD
RED & WHITE LAUNDRIES LTD

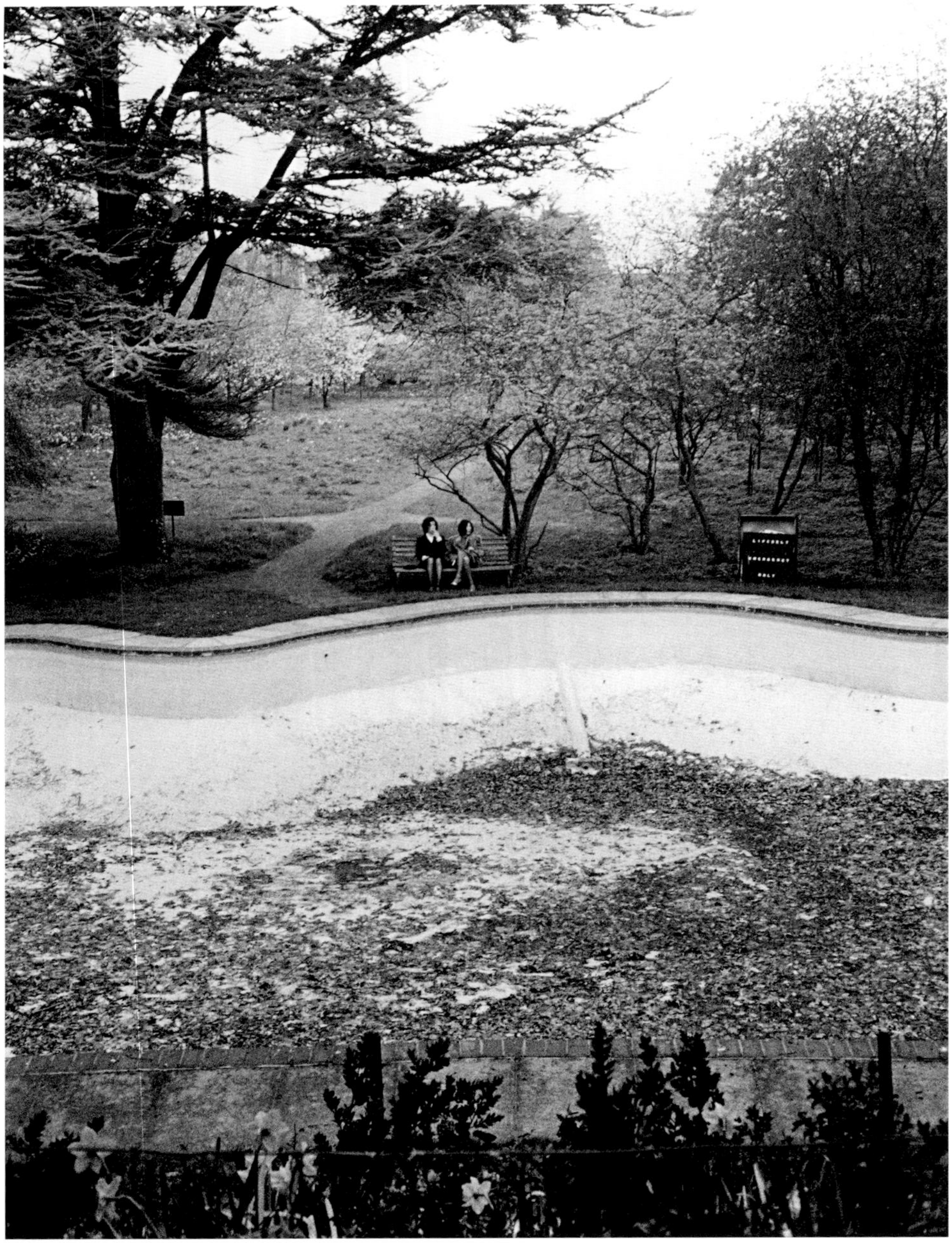

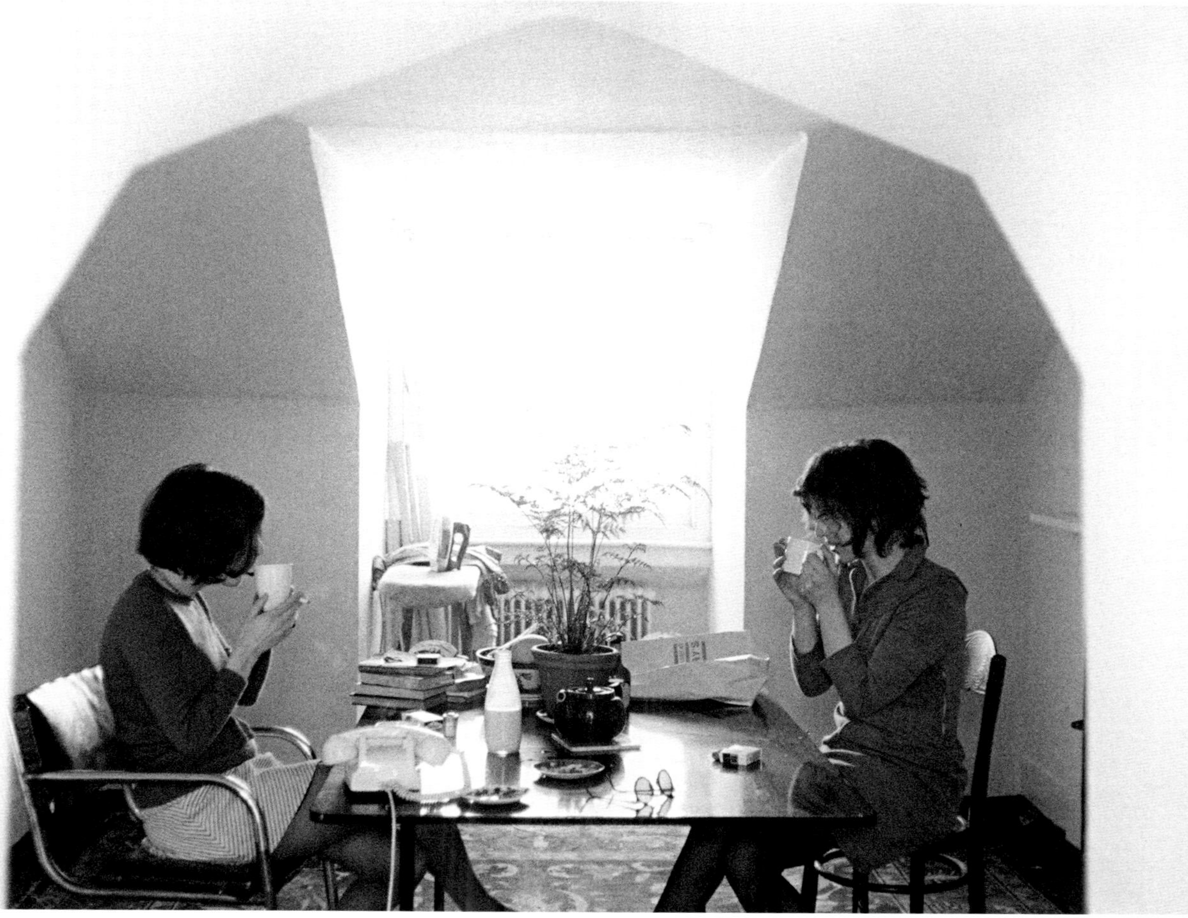

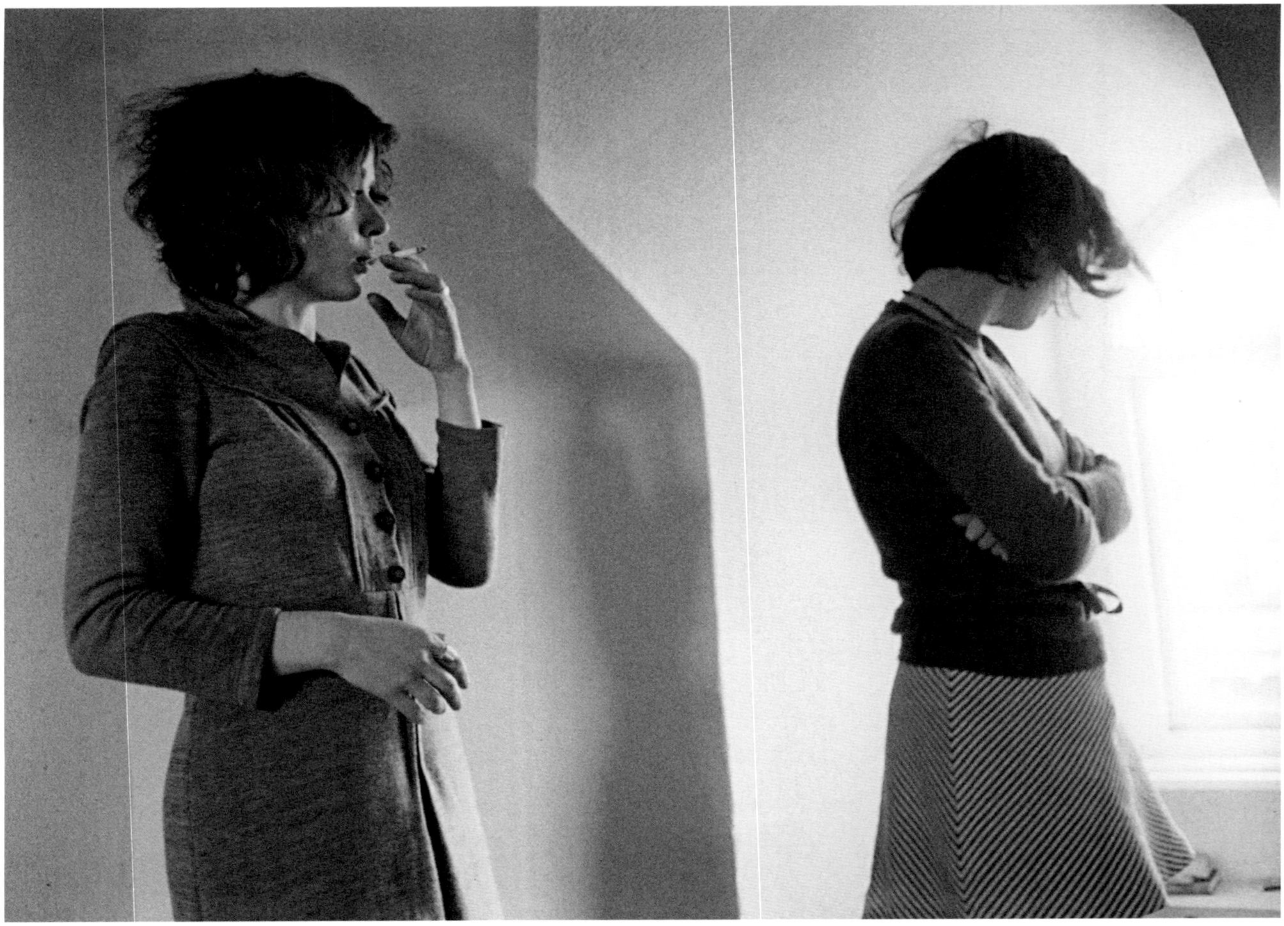

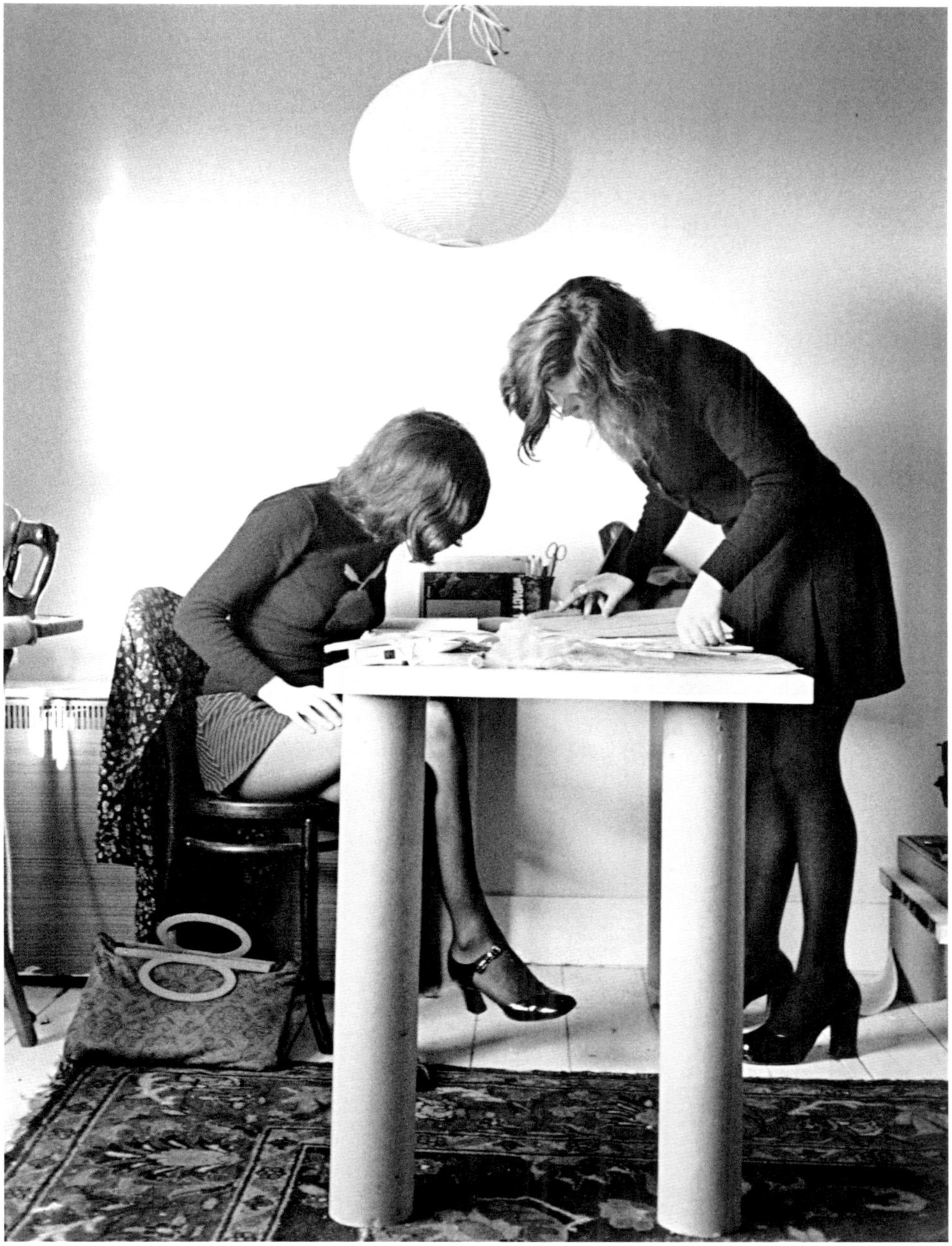

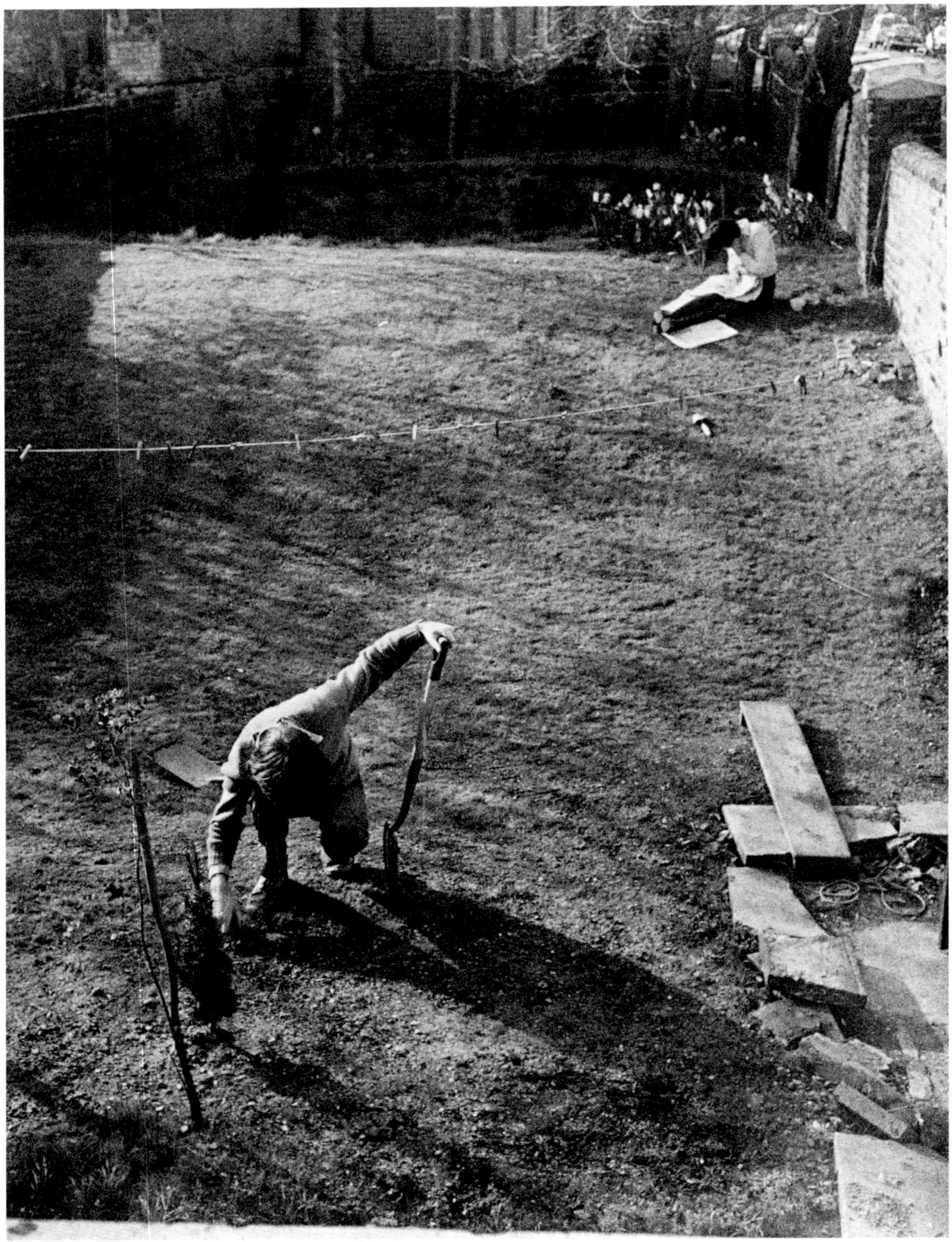

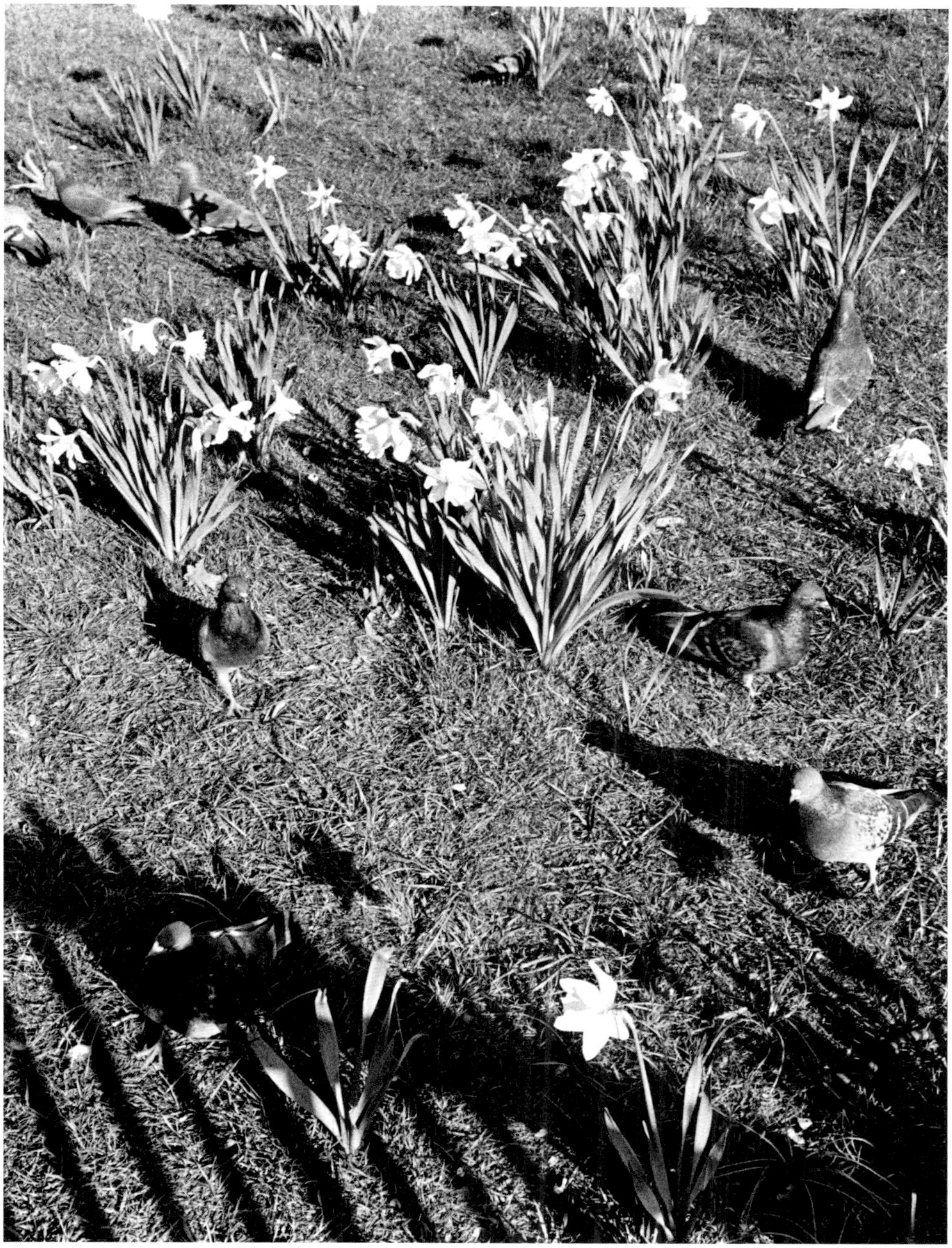

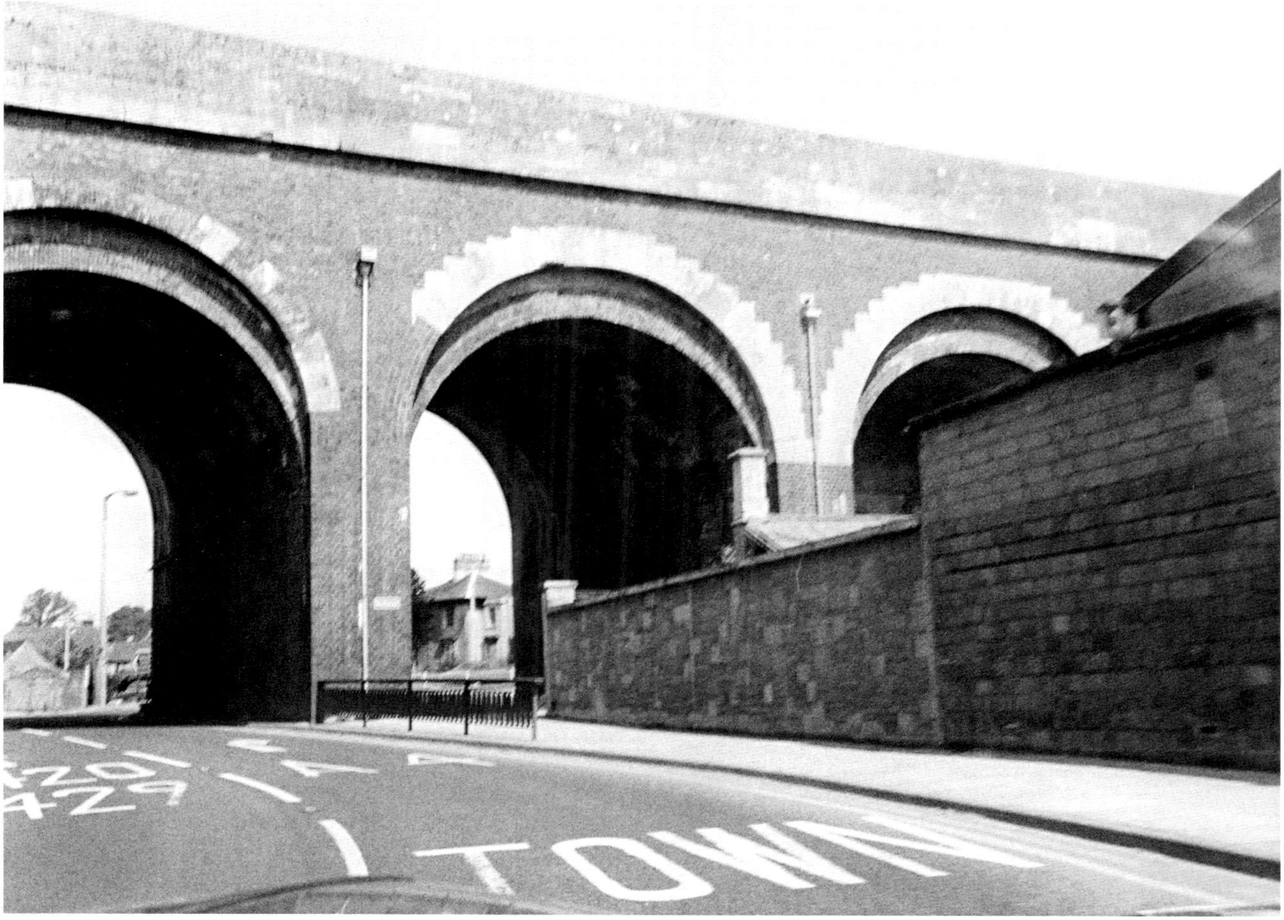
TOWN

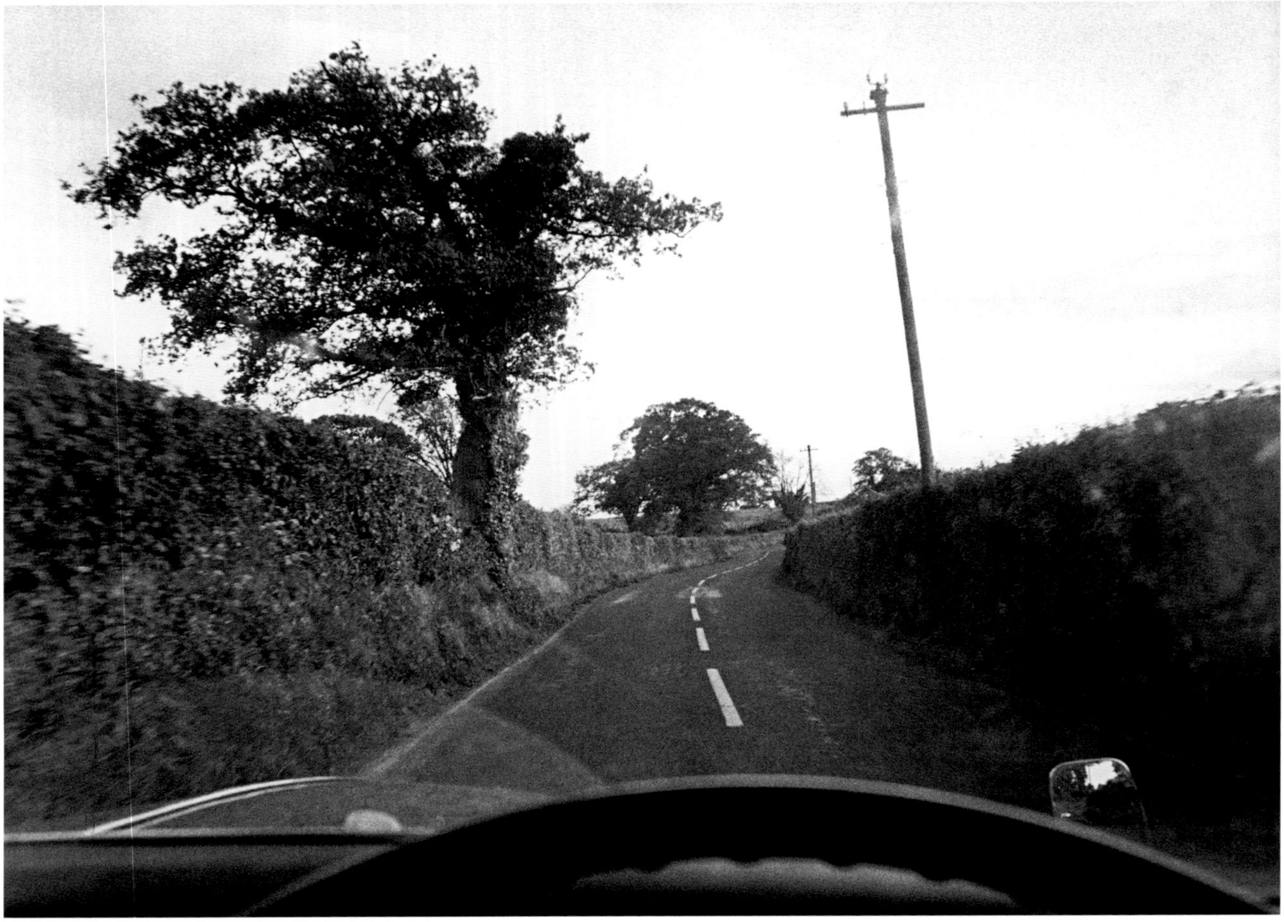

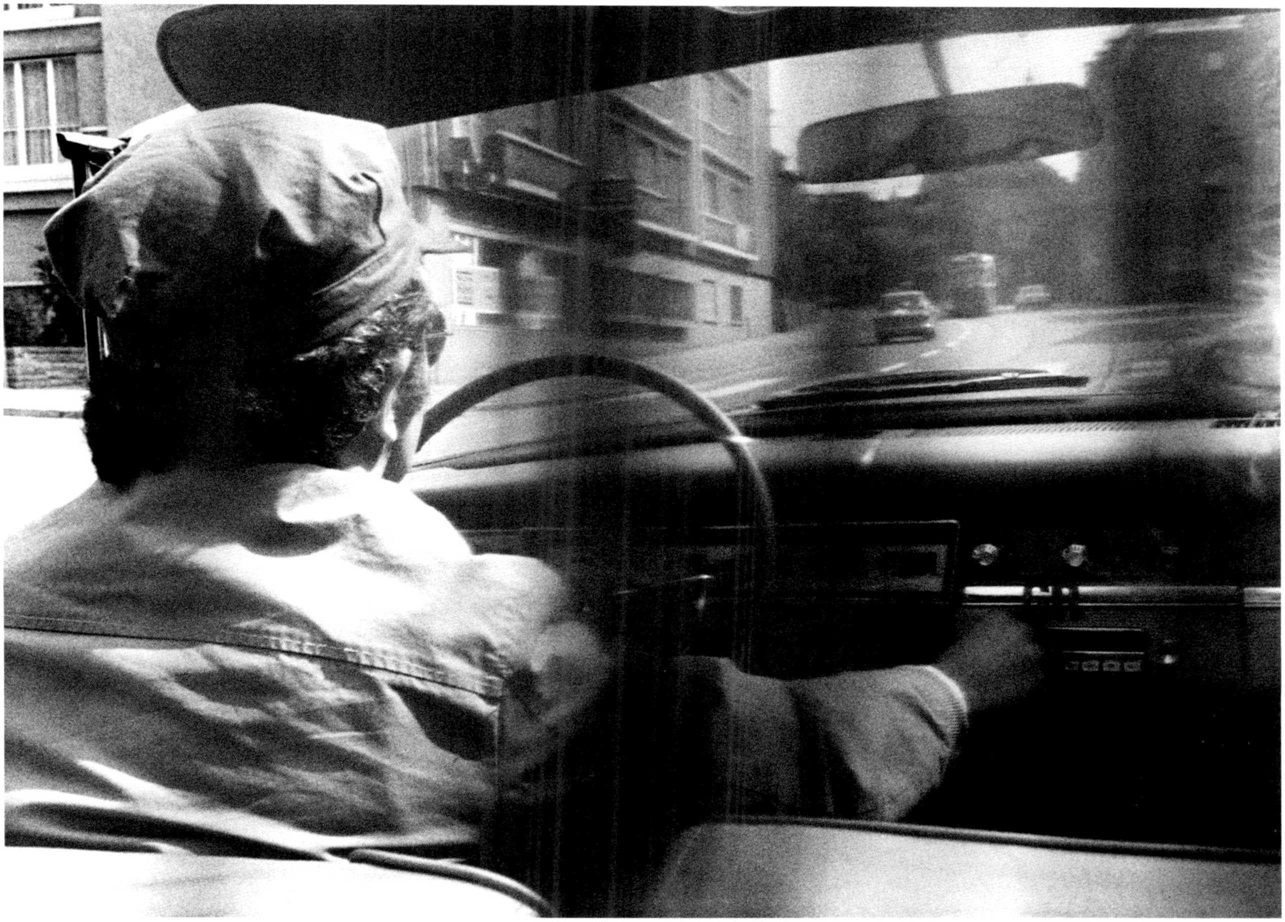

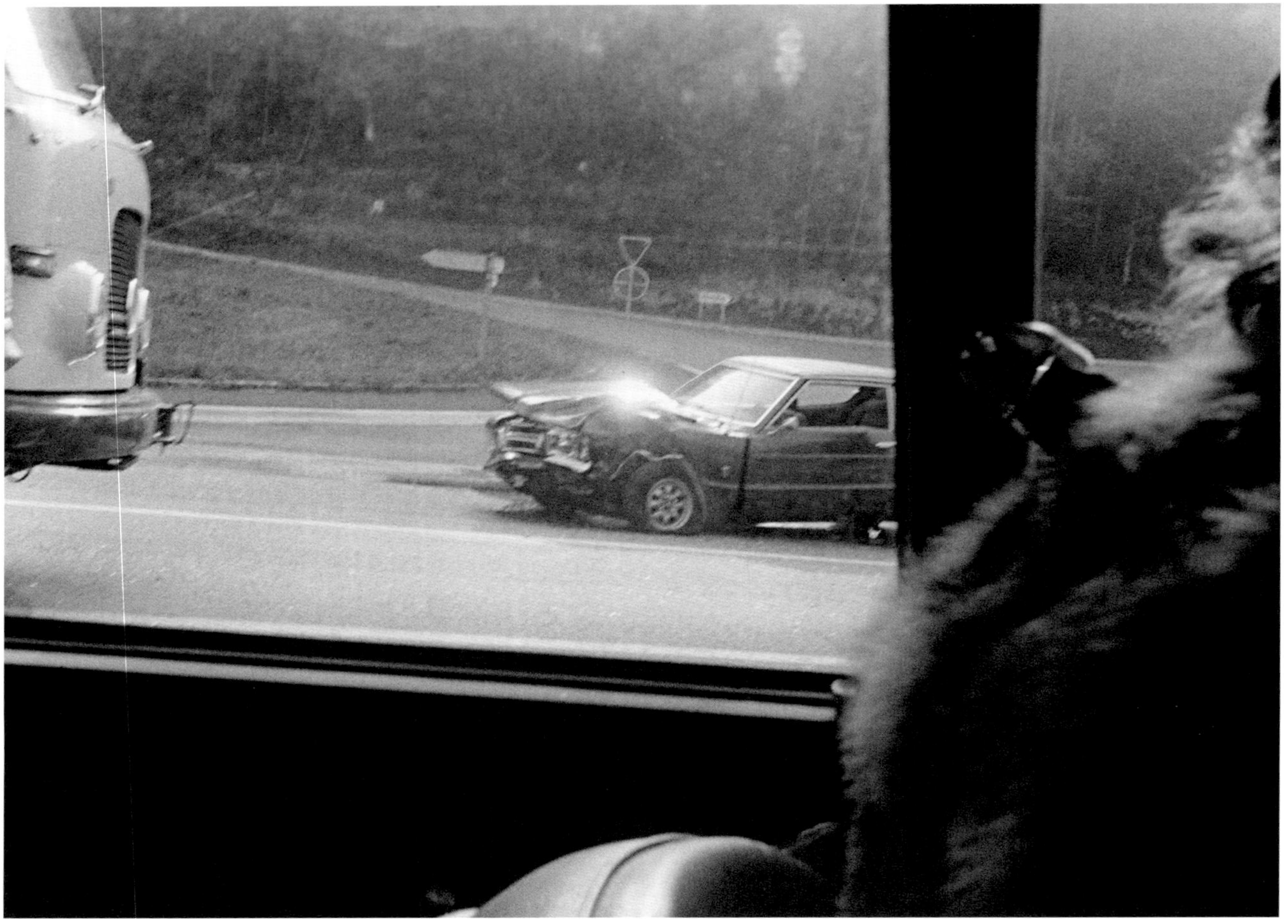

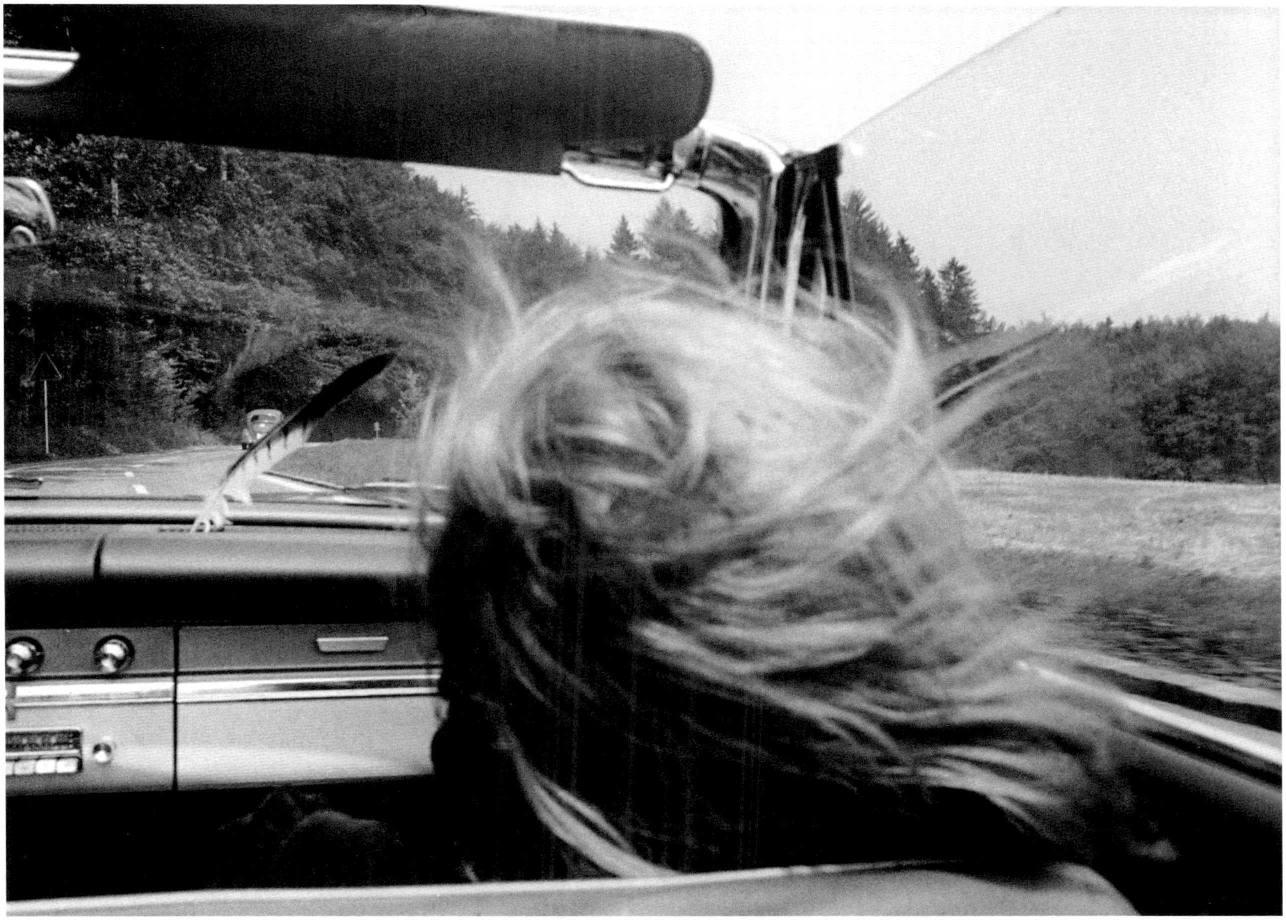

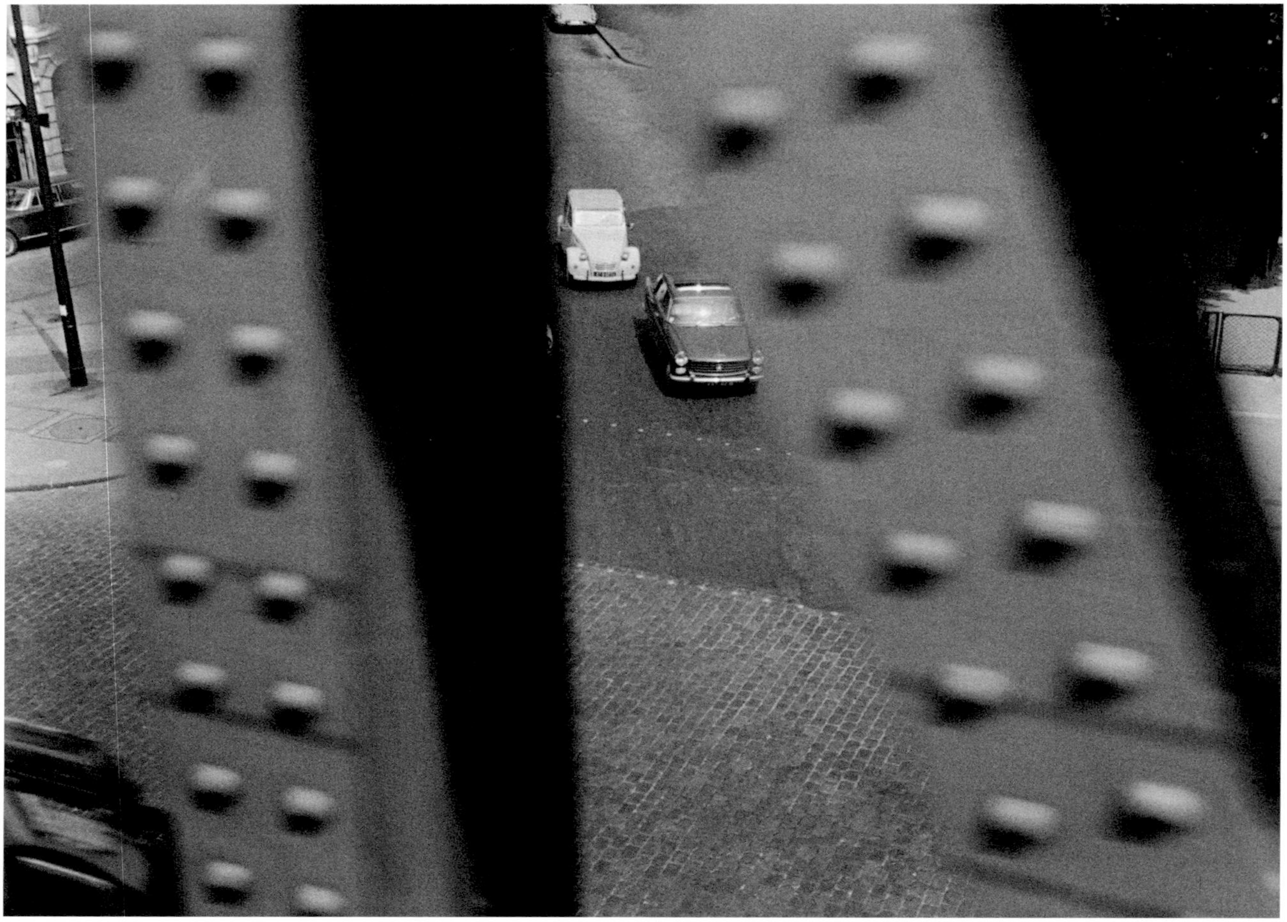

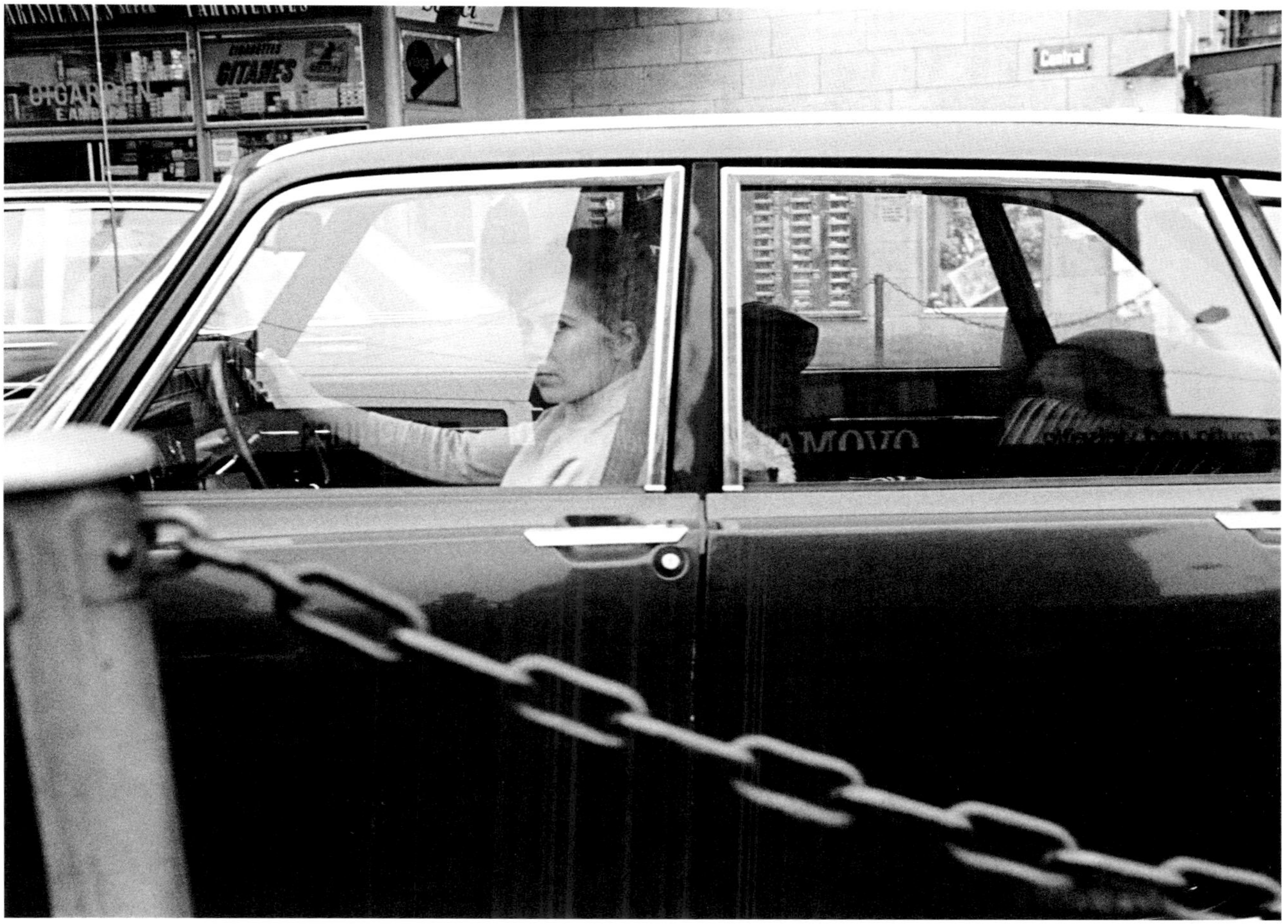
GITANES

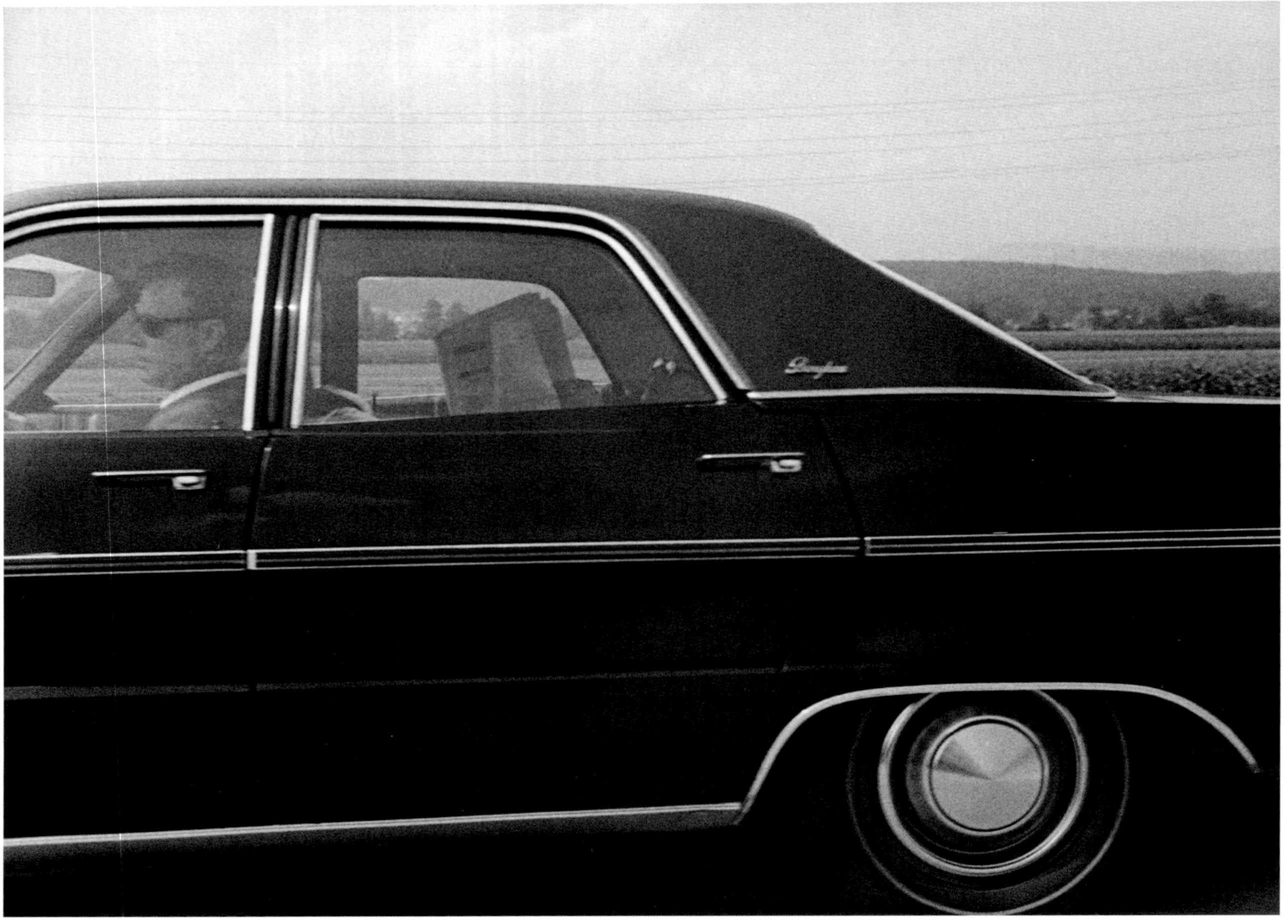

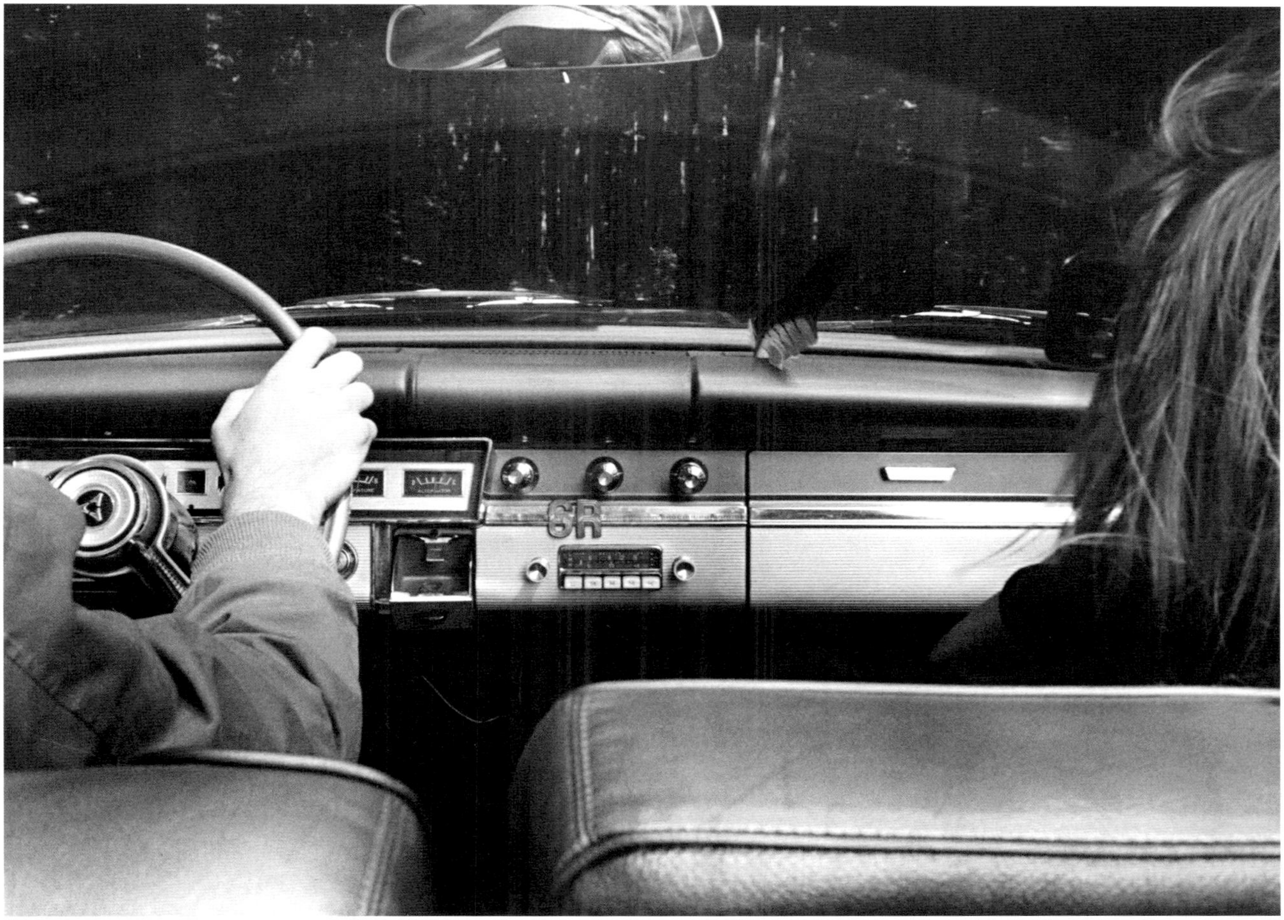

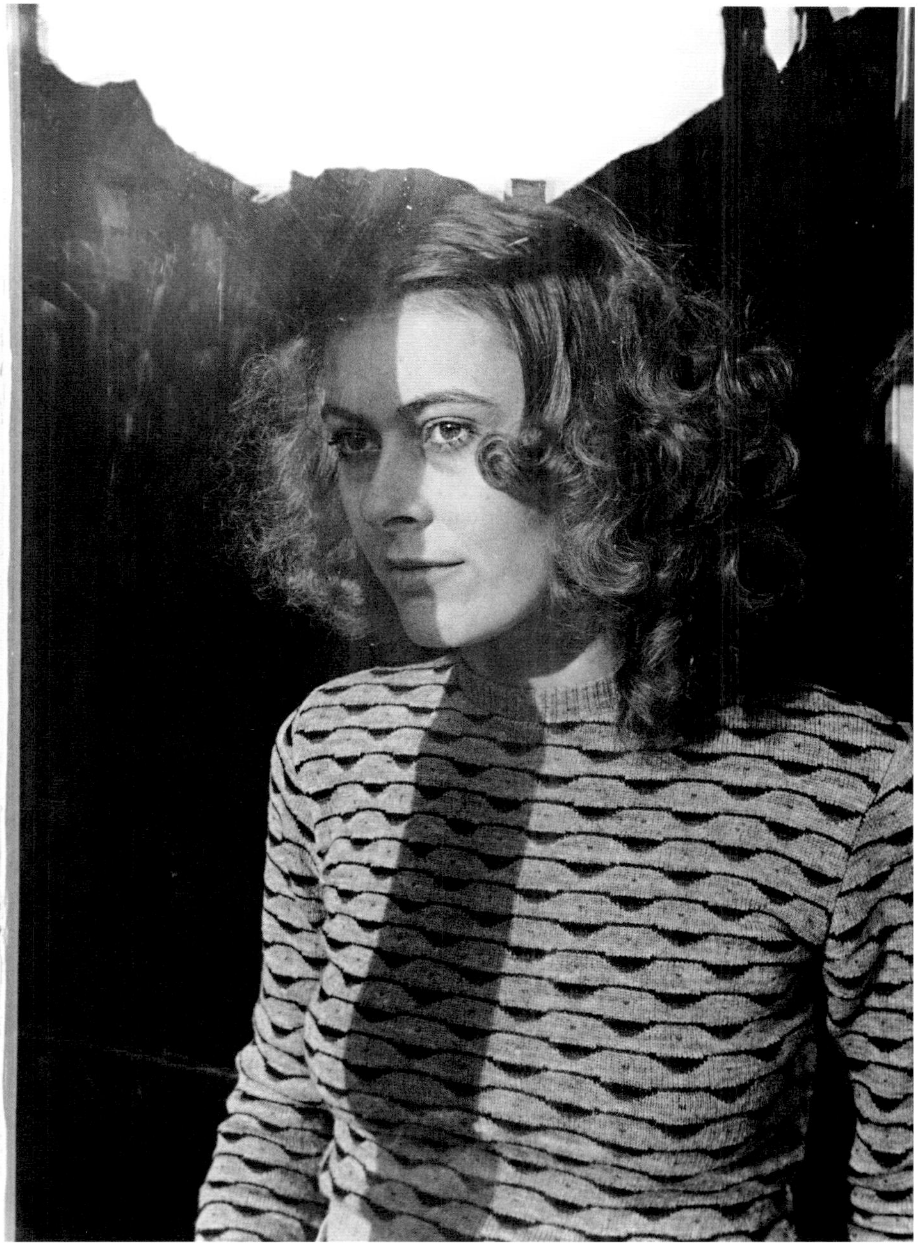

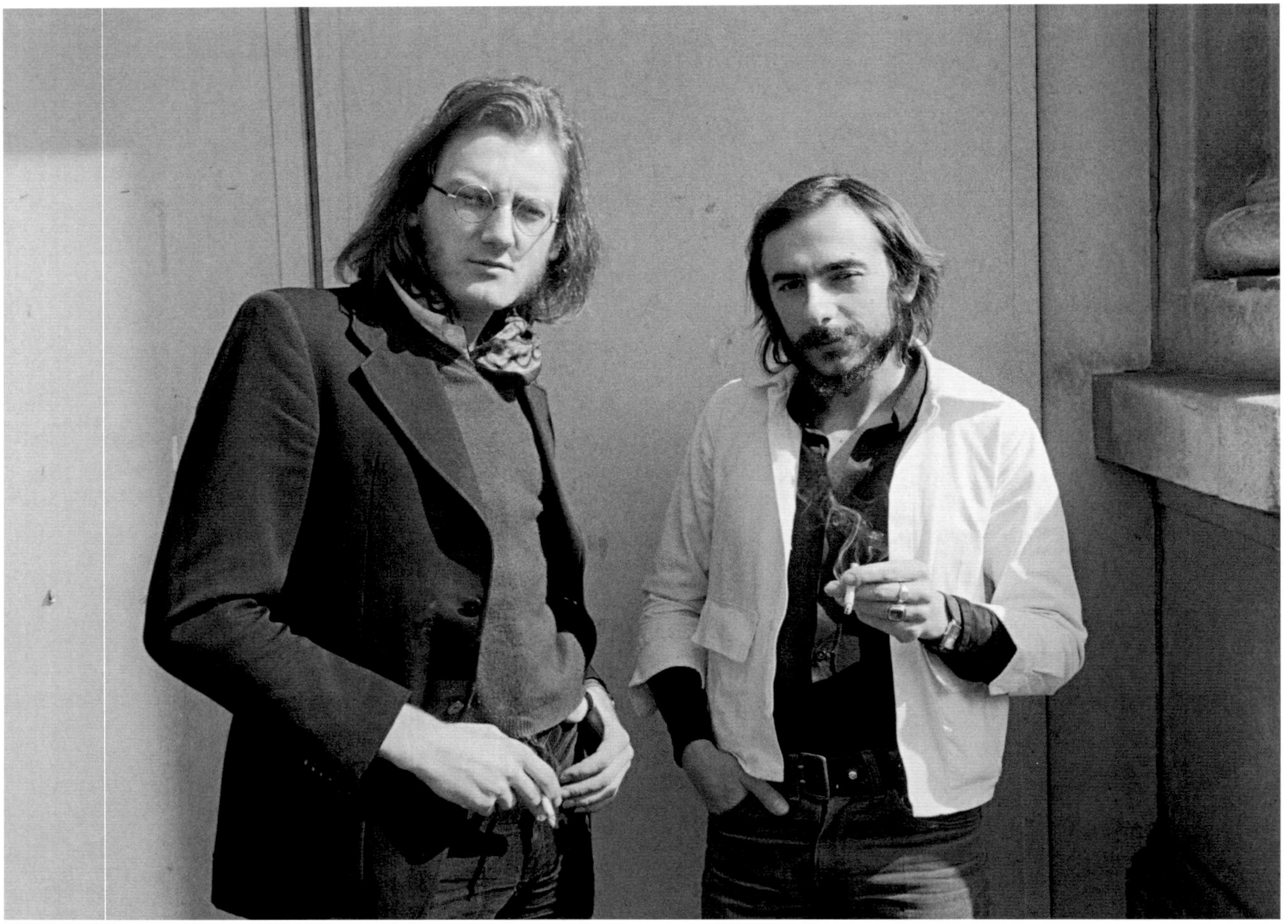

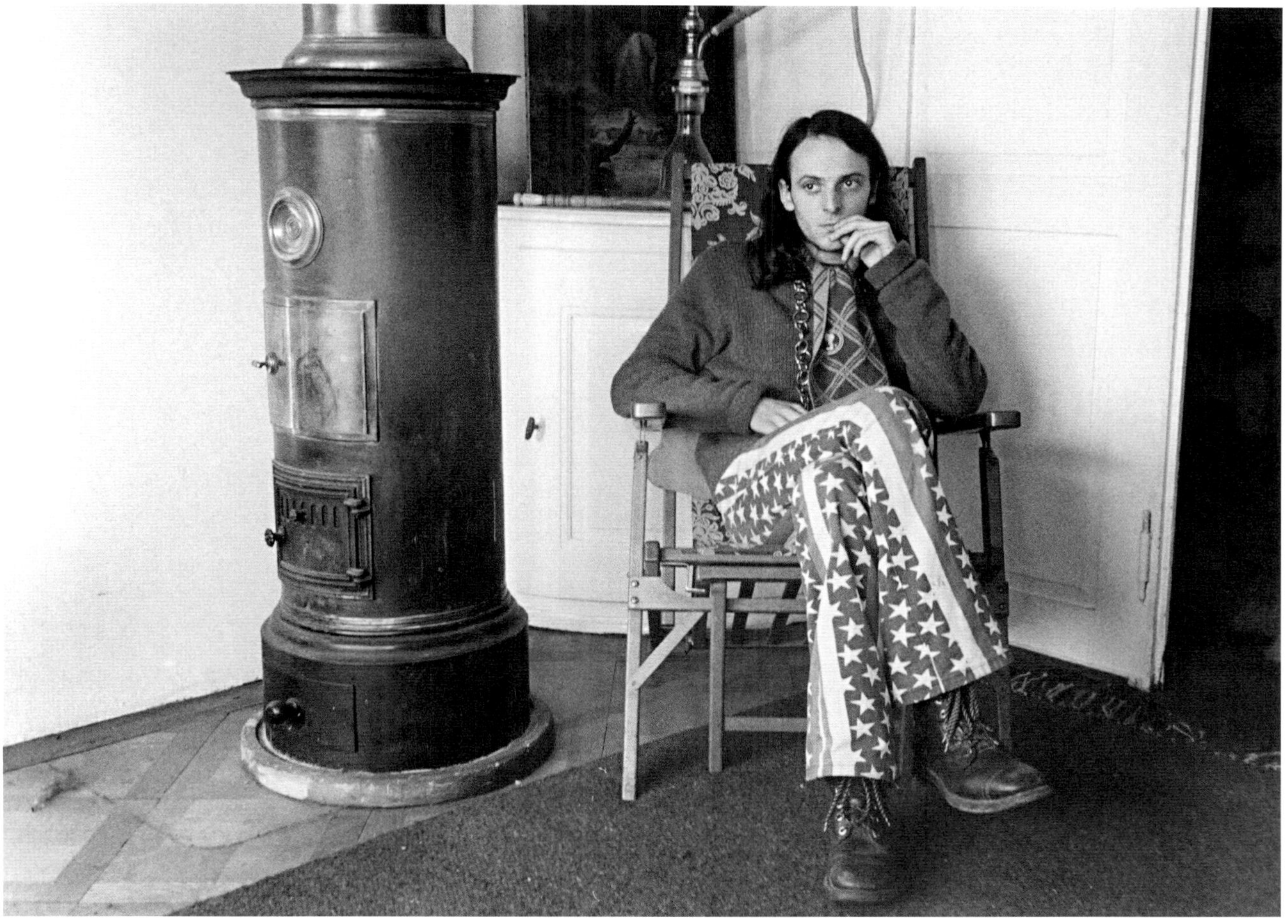

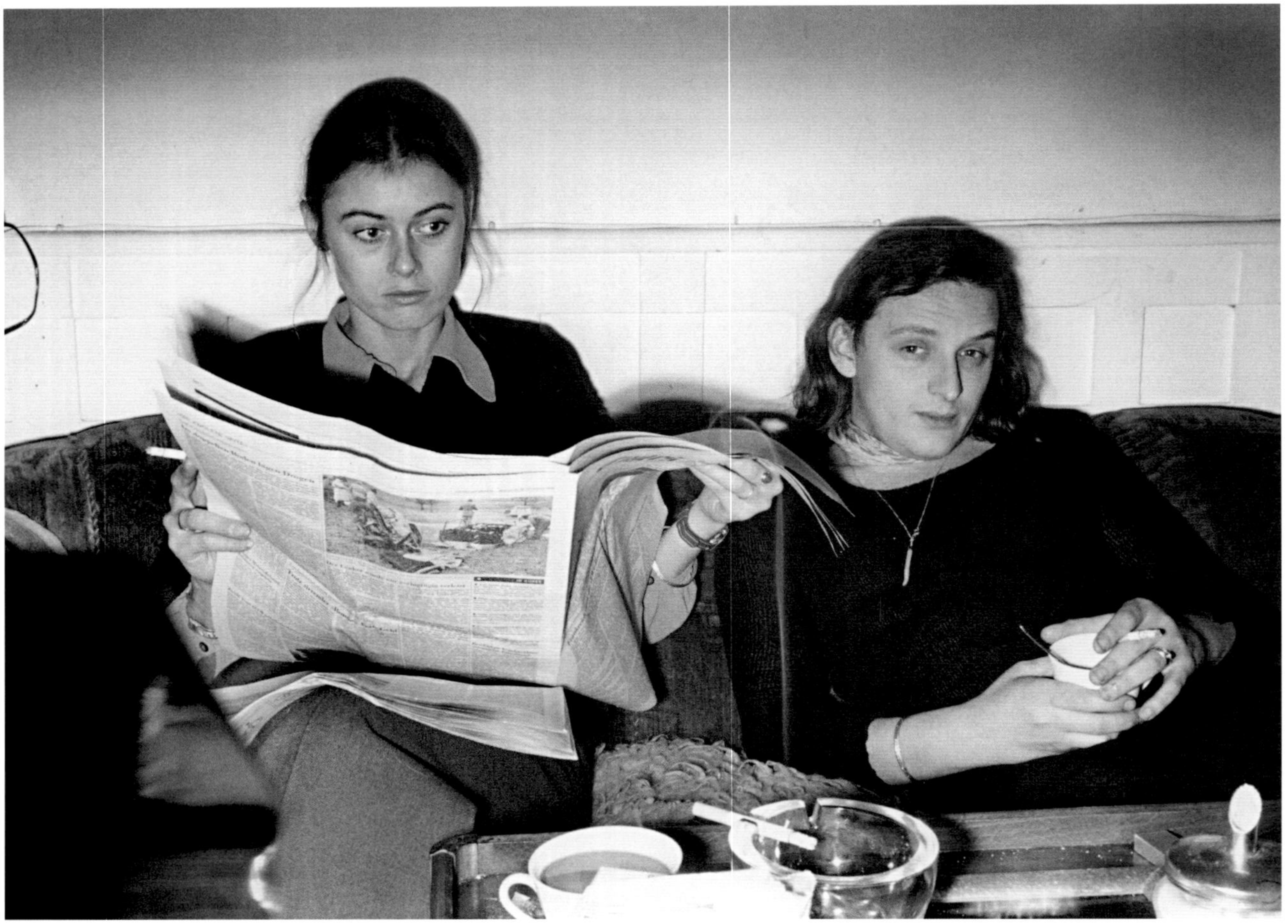

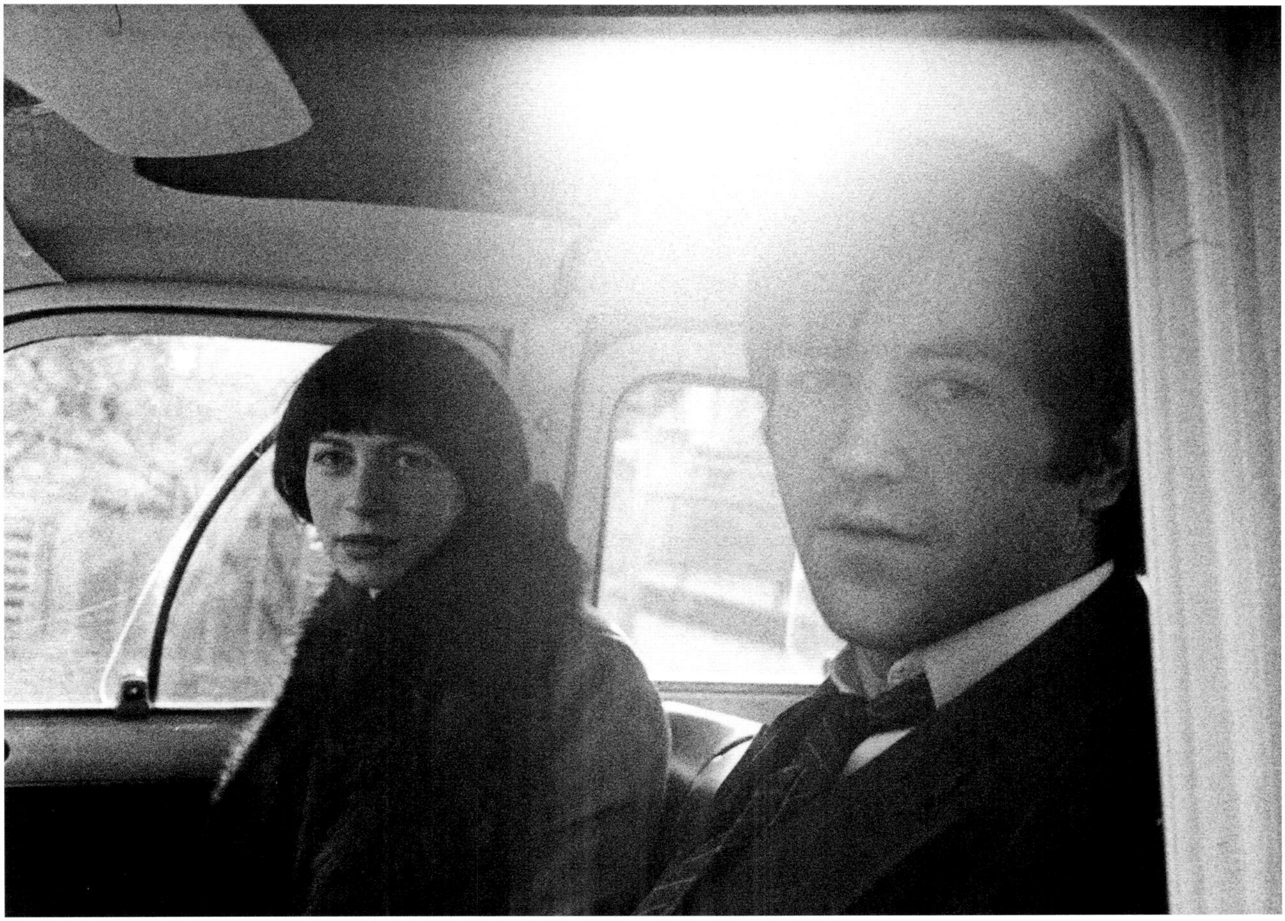

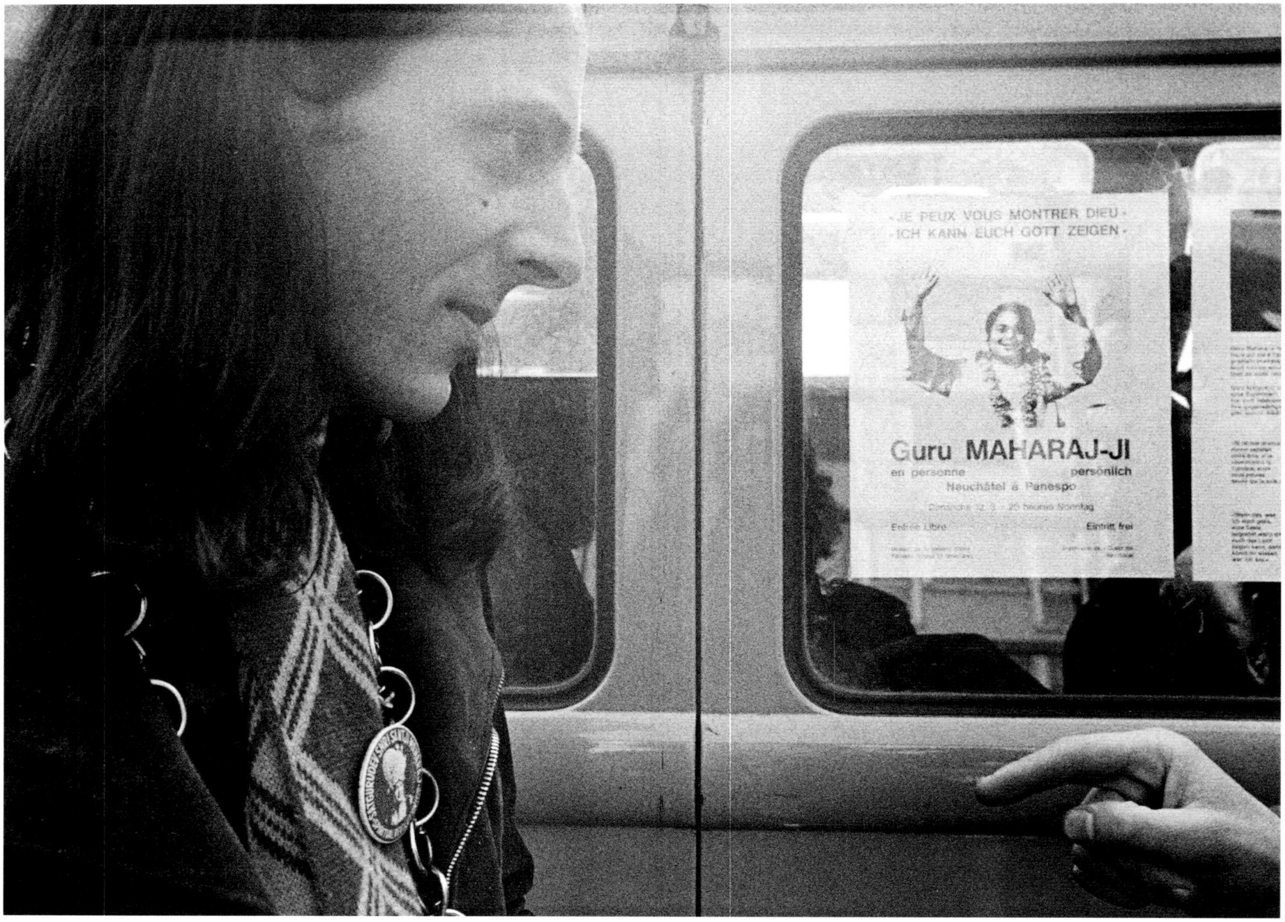
«JE PEUX VOUS MONTRER DIEU»
«ICH KANN EUCH GOTT ZEIGEN»
Guru MAHARAJ-JI
en personne
persönlich
Neuchâtel à Panespo
Entrée Libre
Eintritt frei

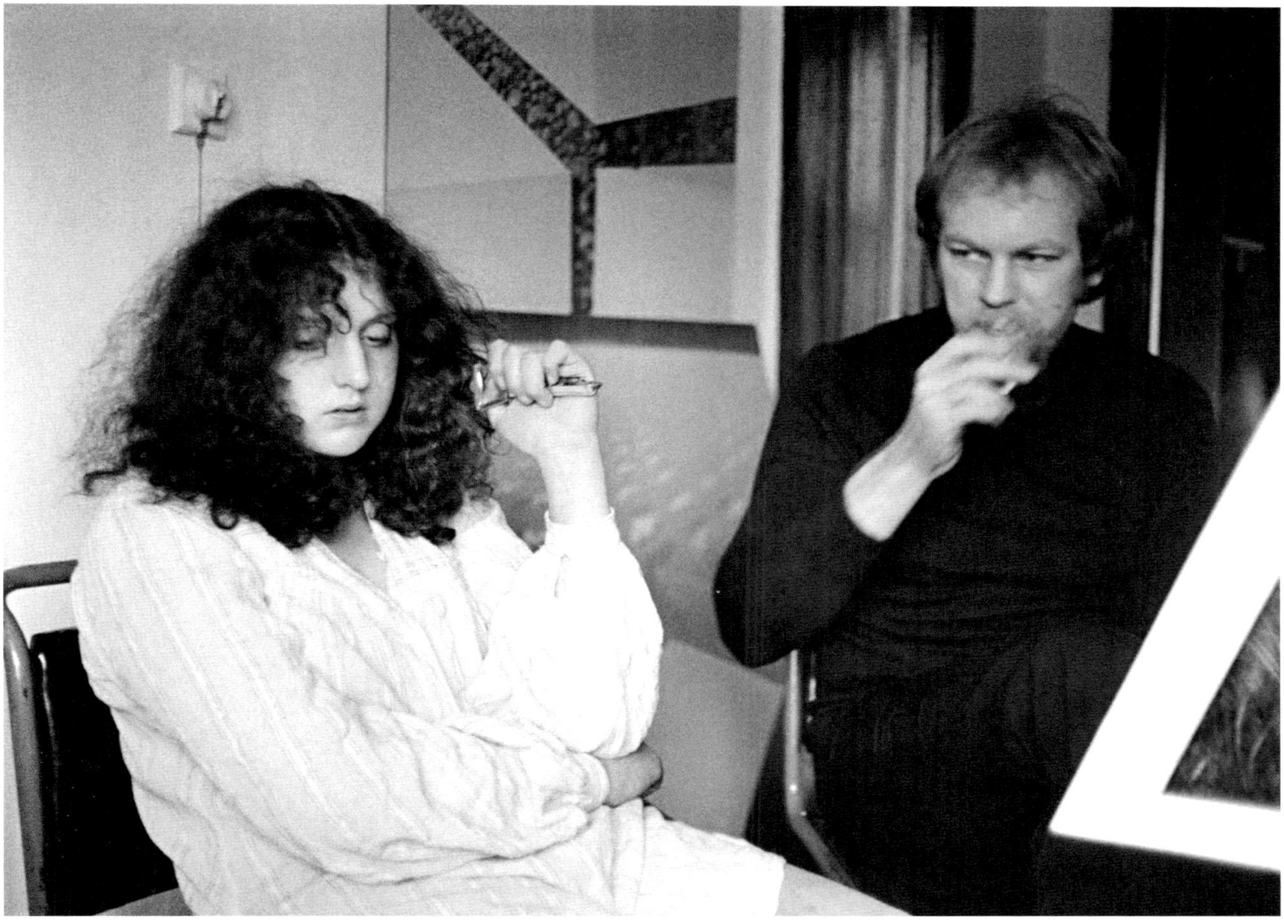

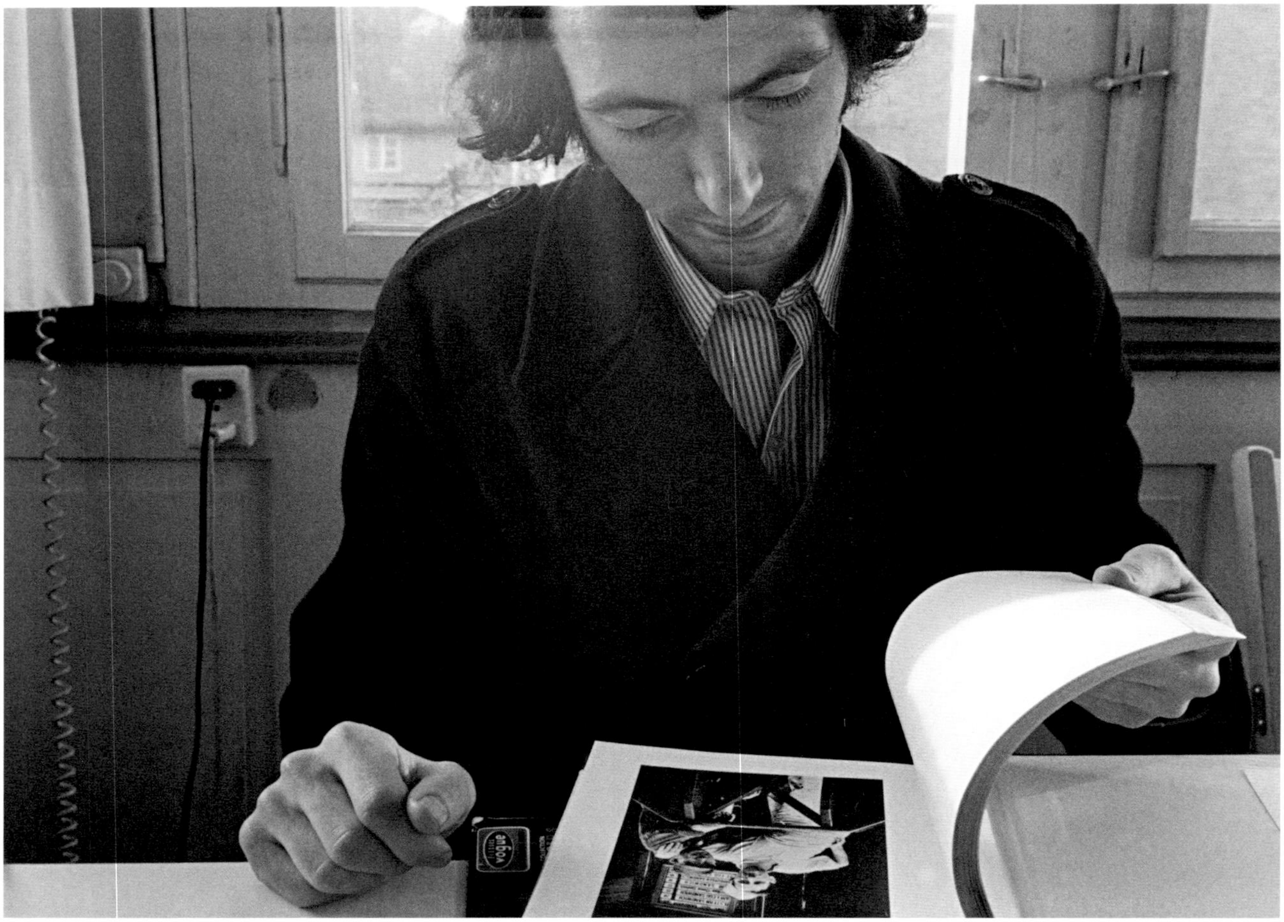

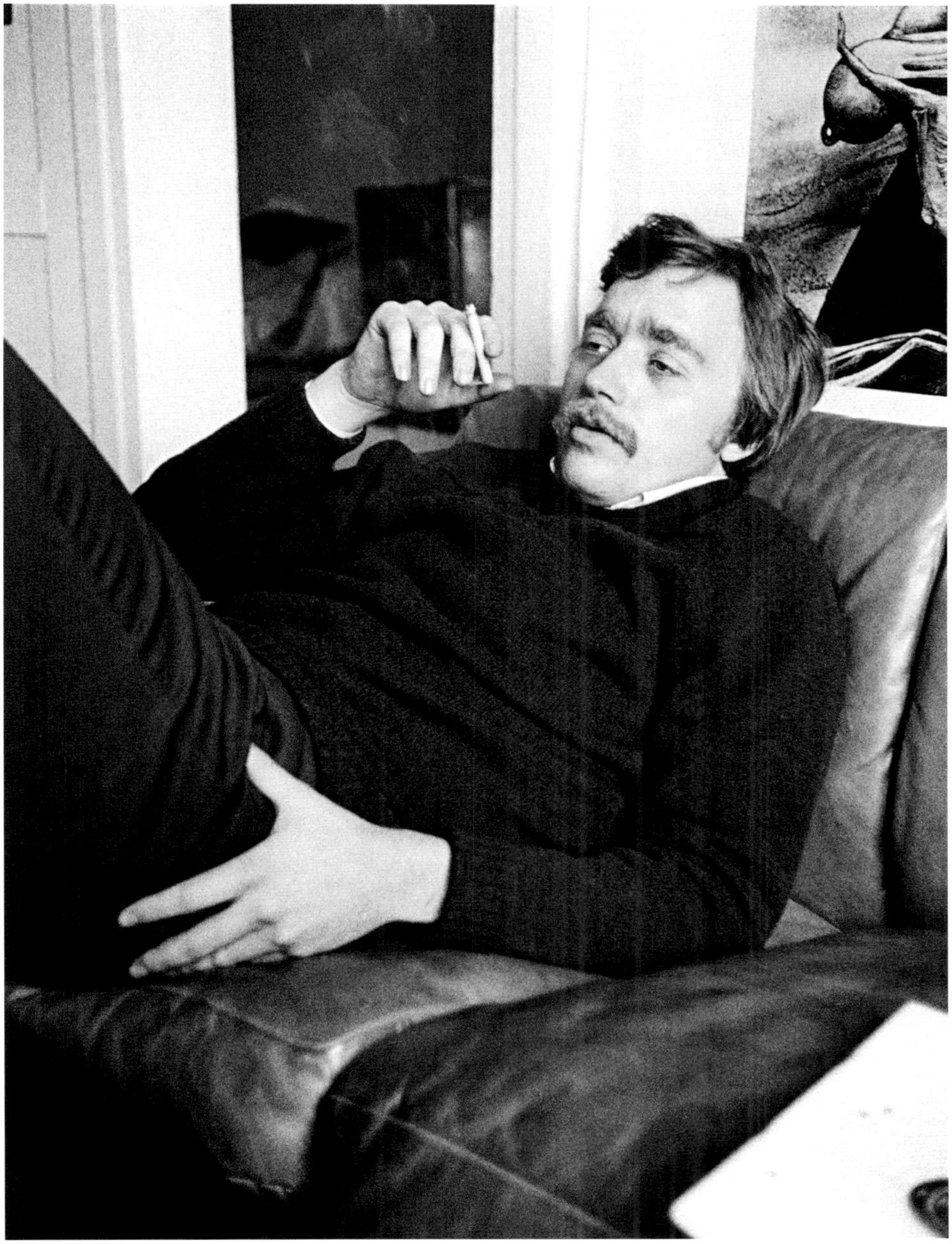

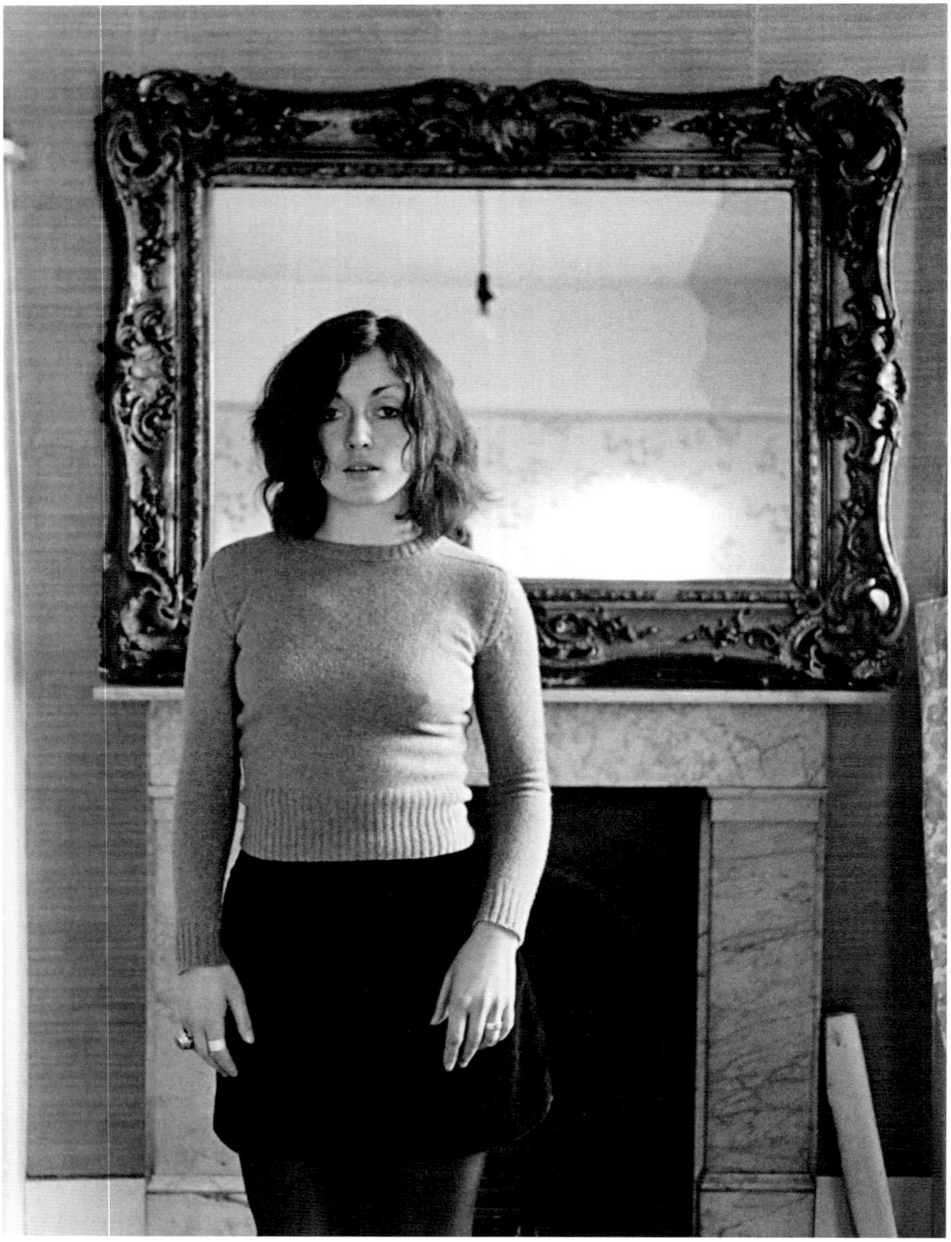

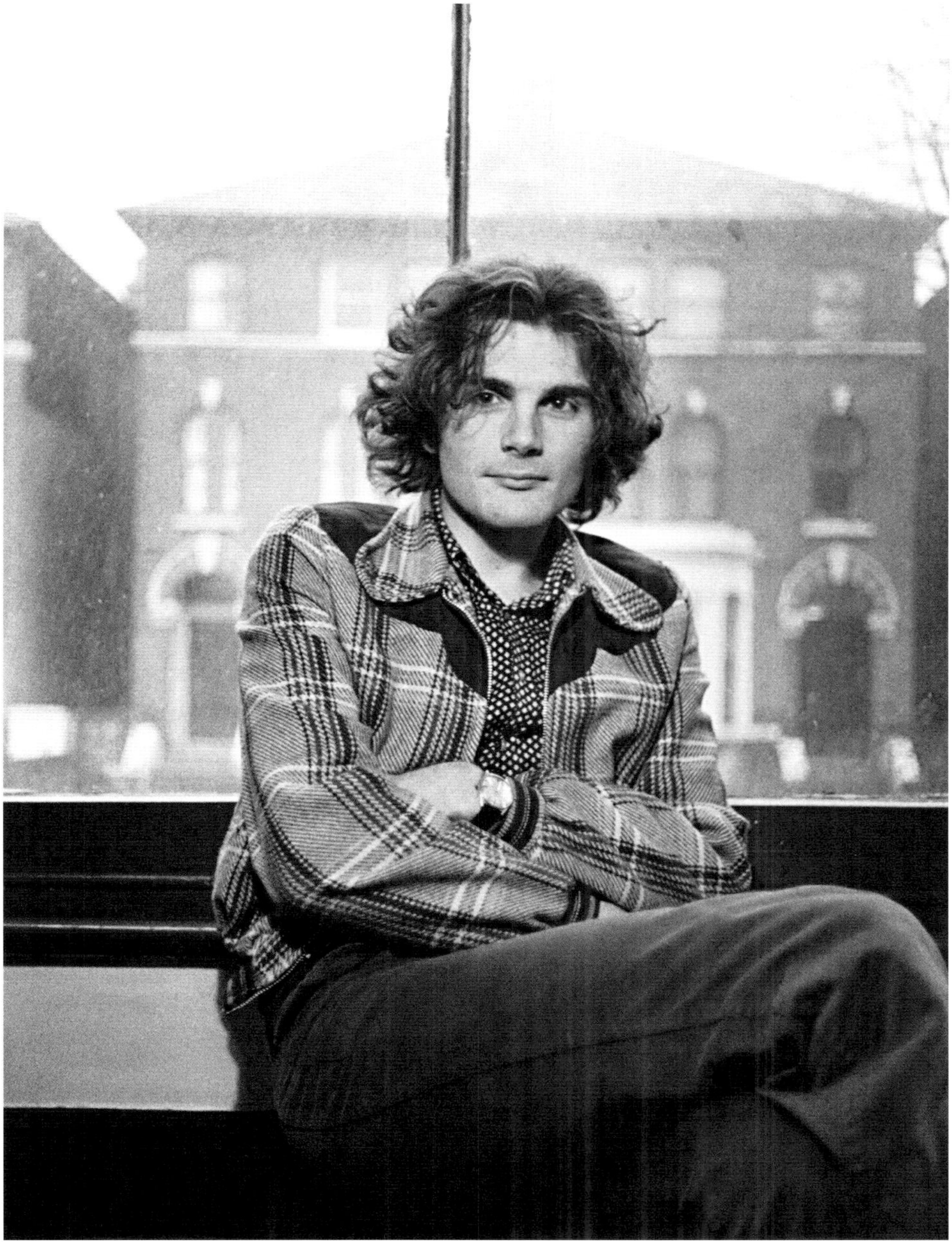

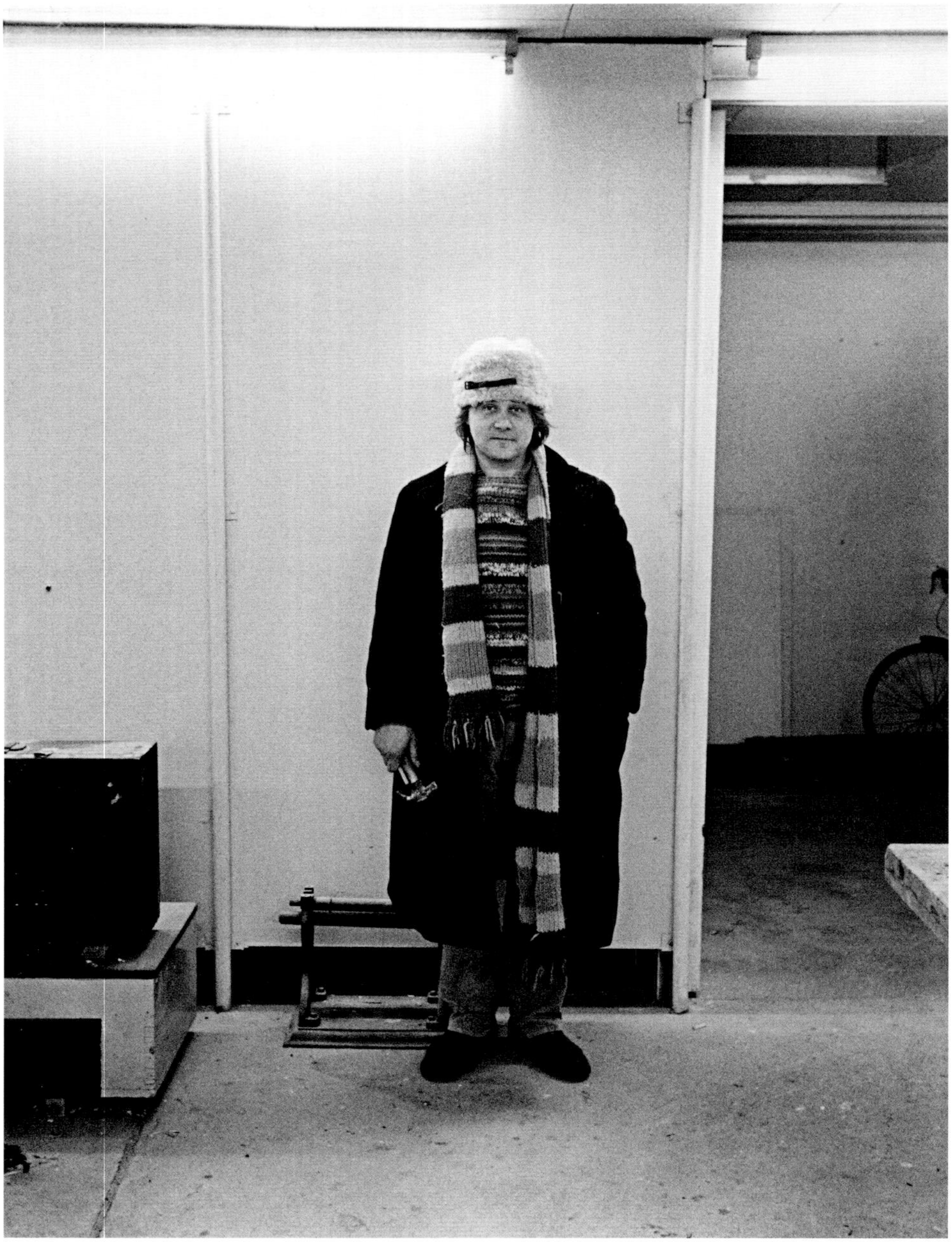

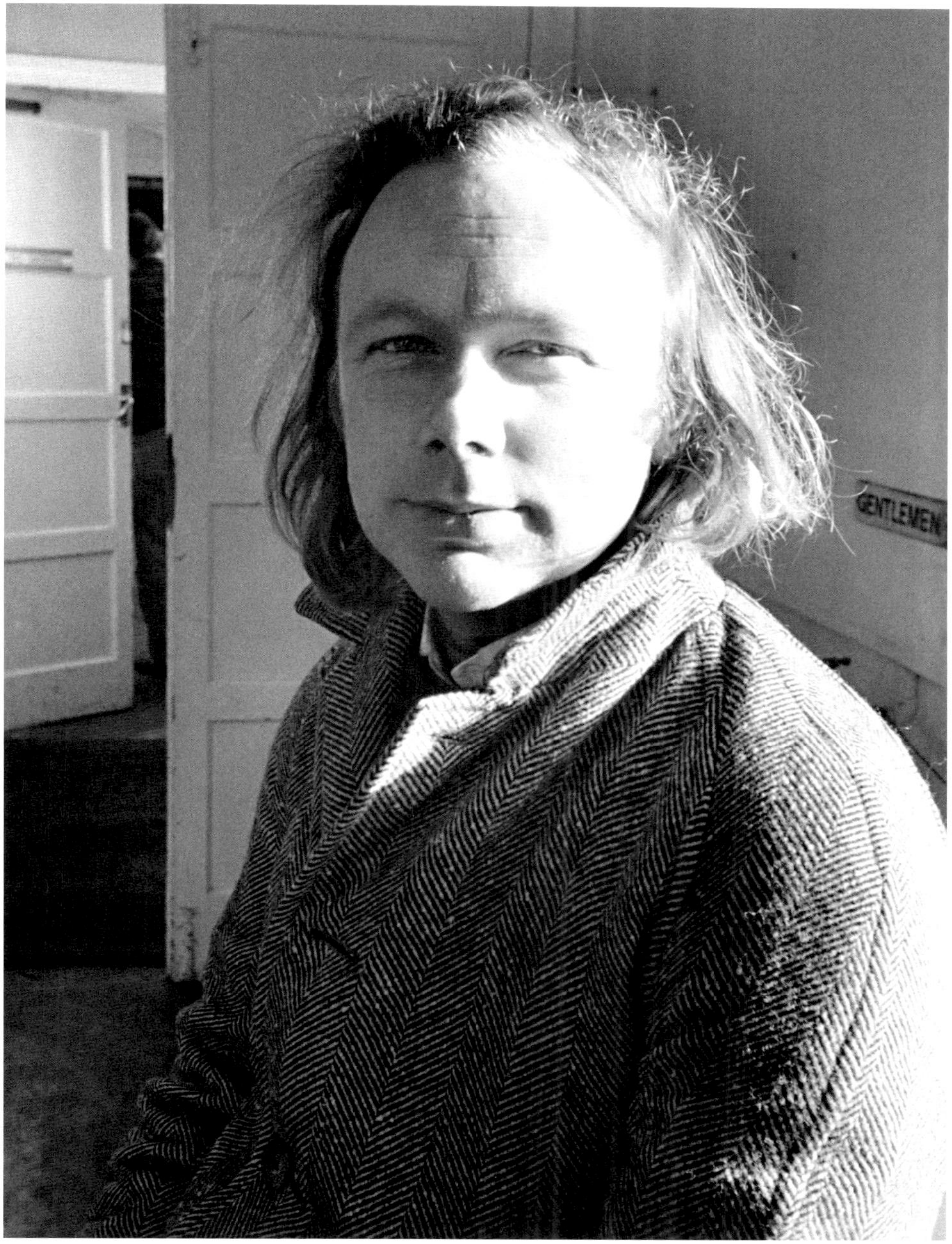
GENTLEMEN

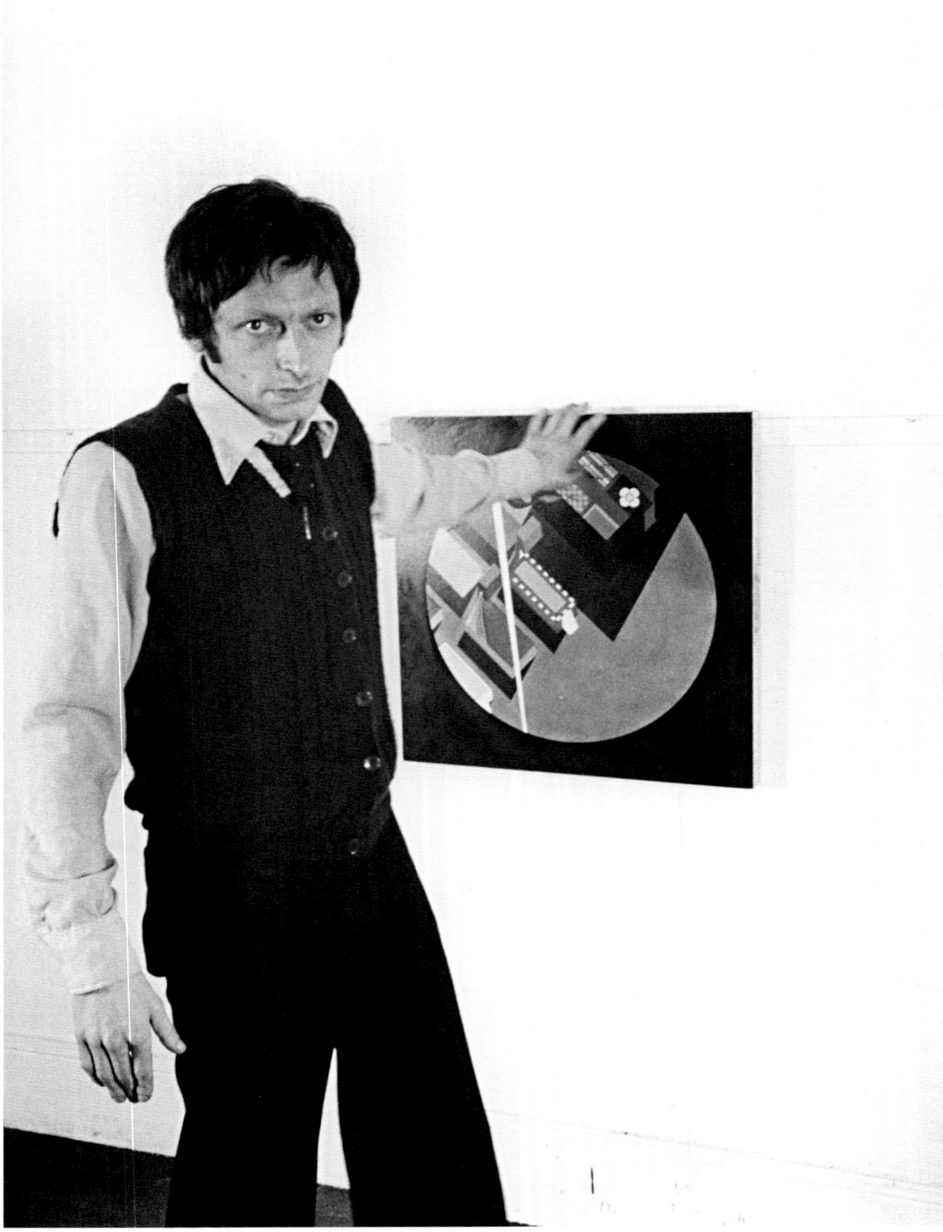

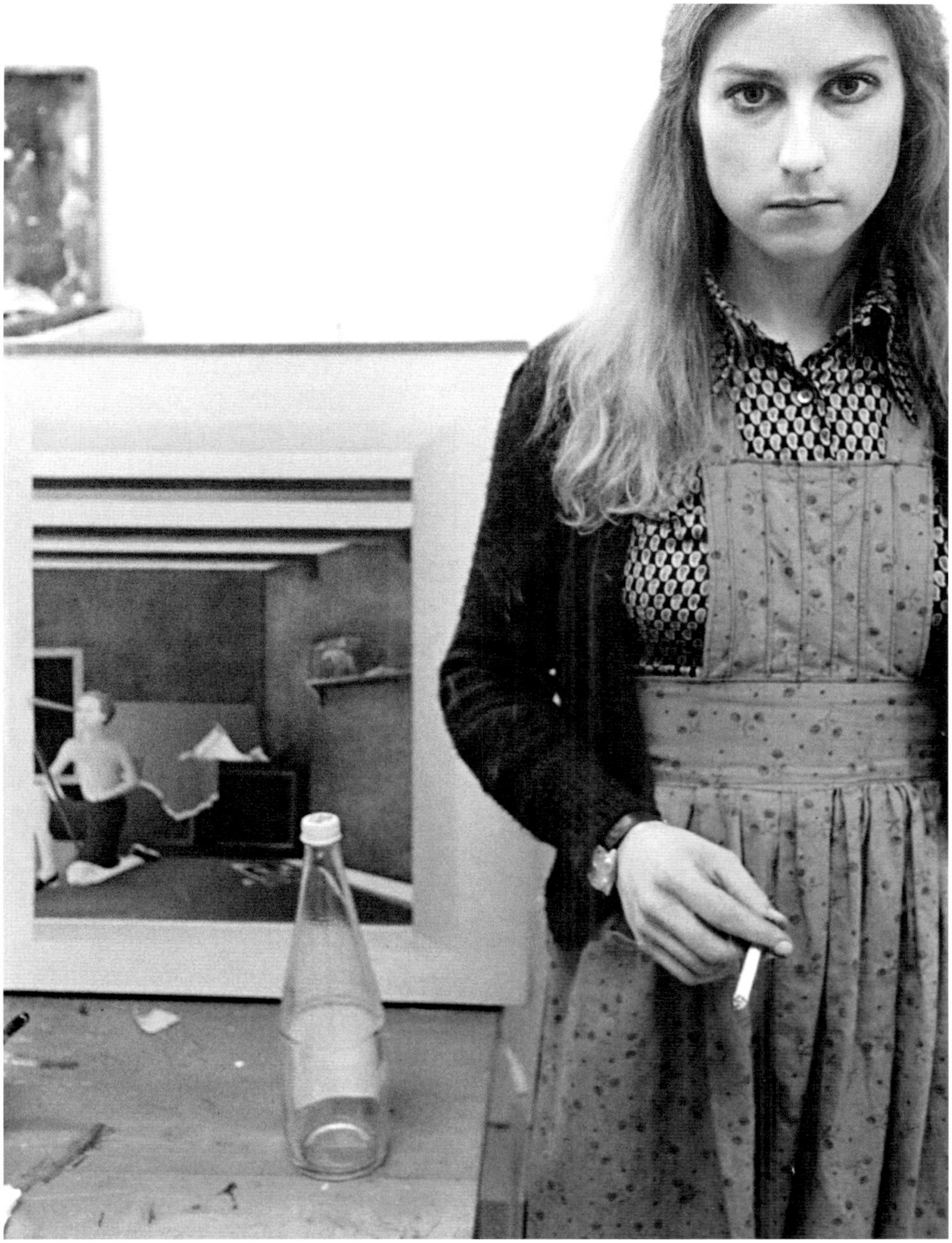

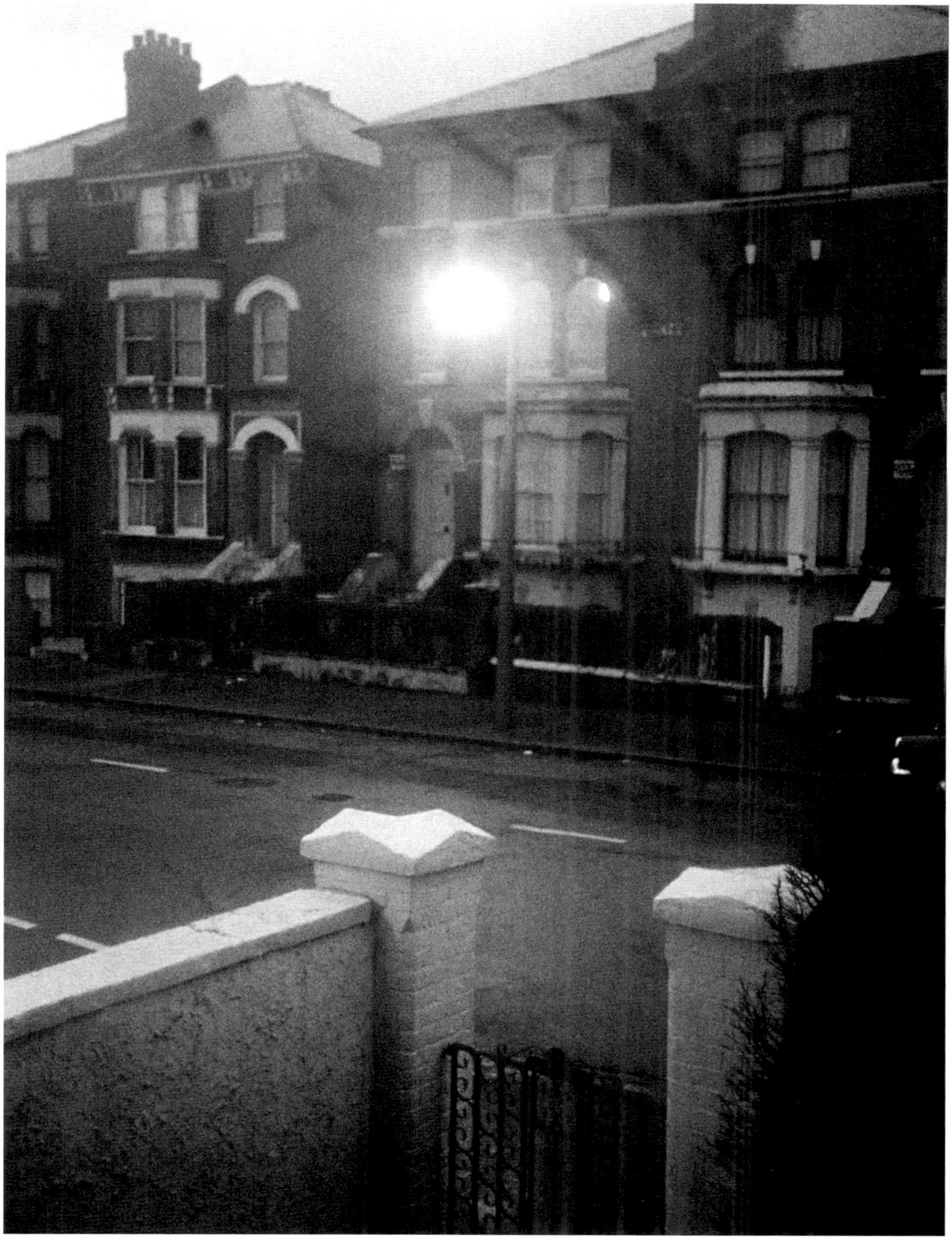

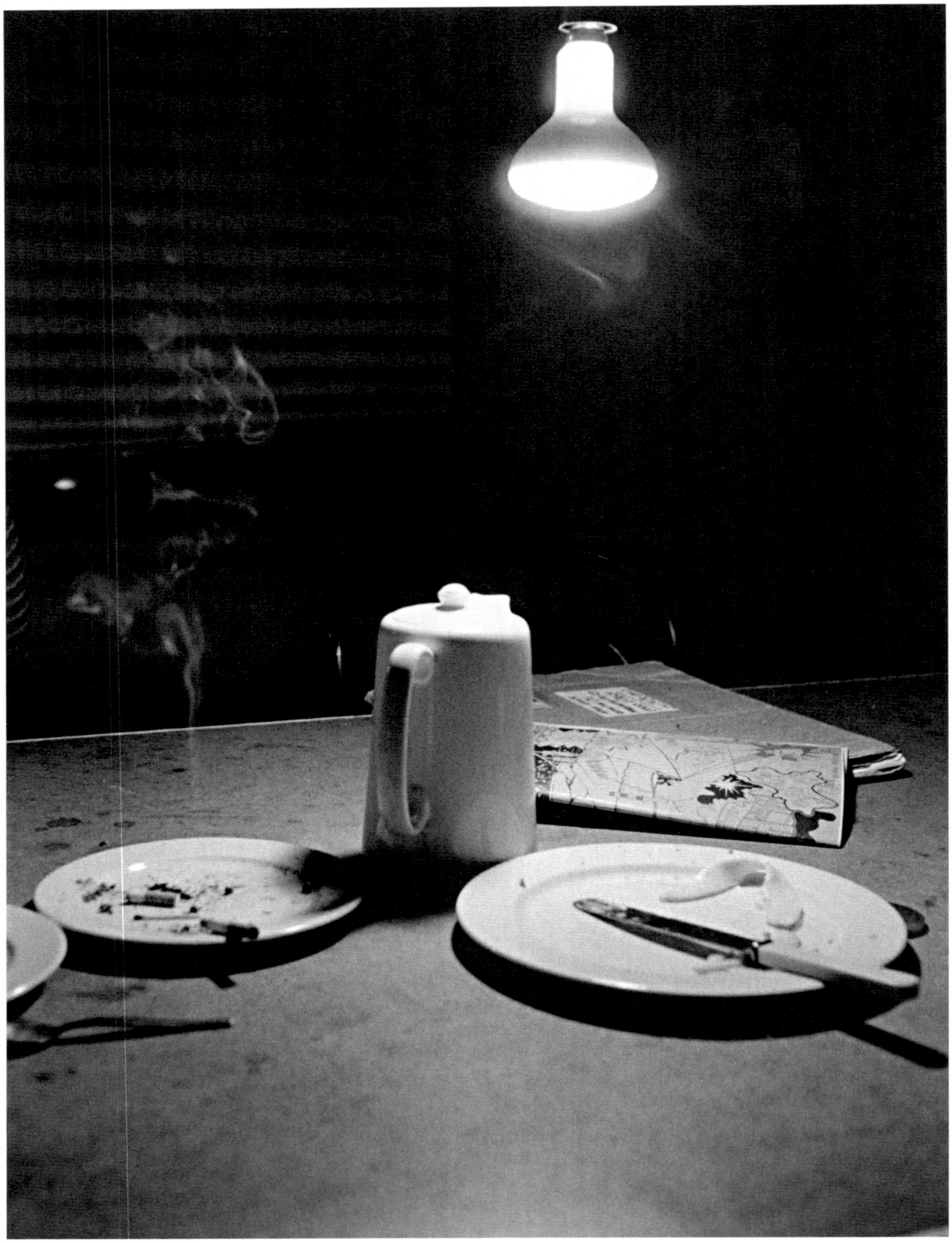

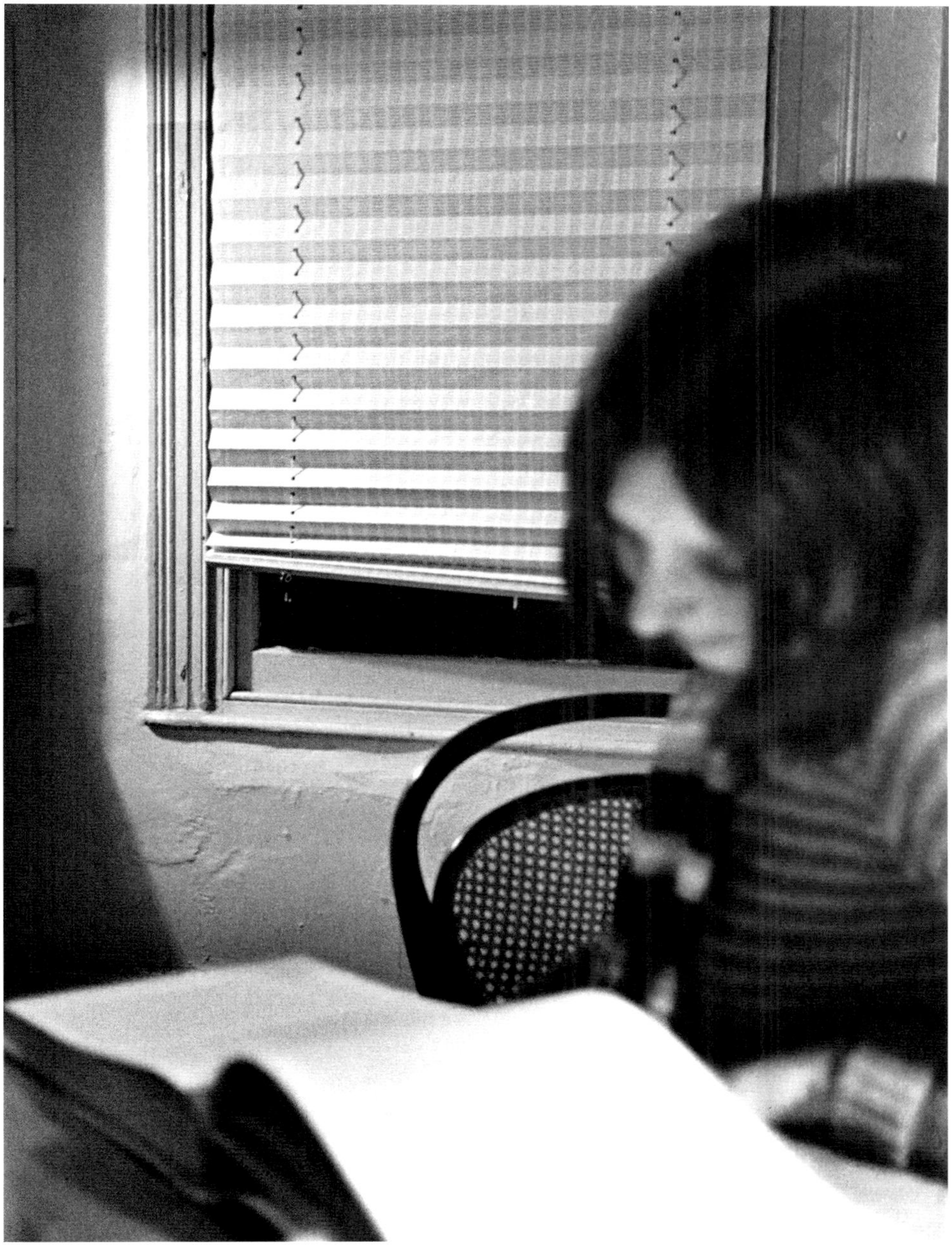

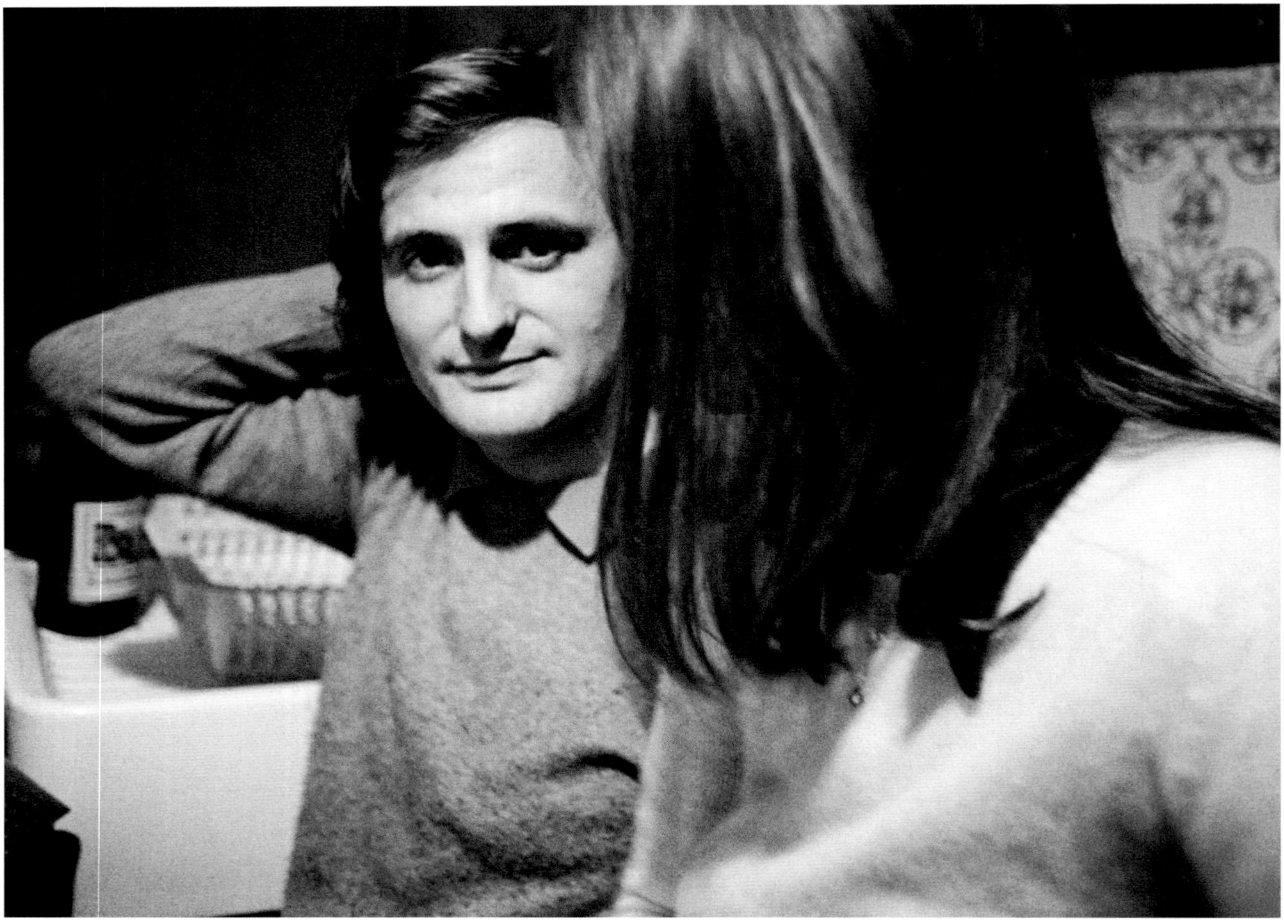

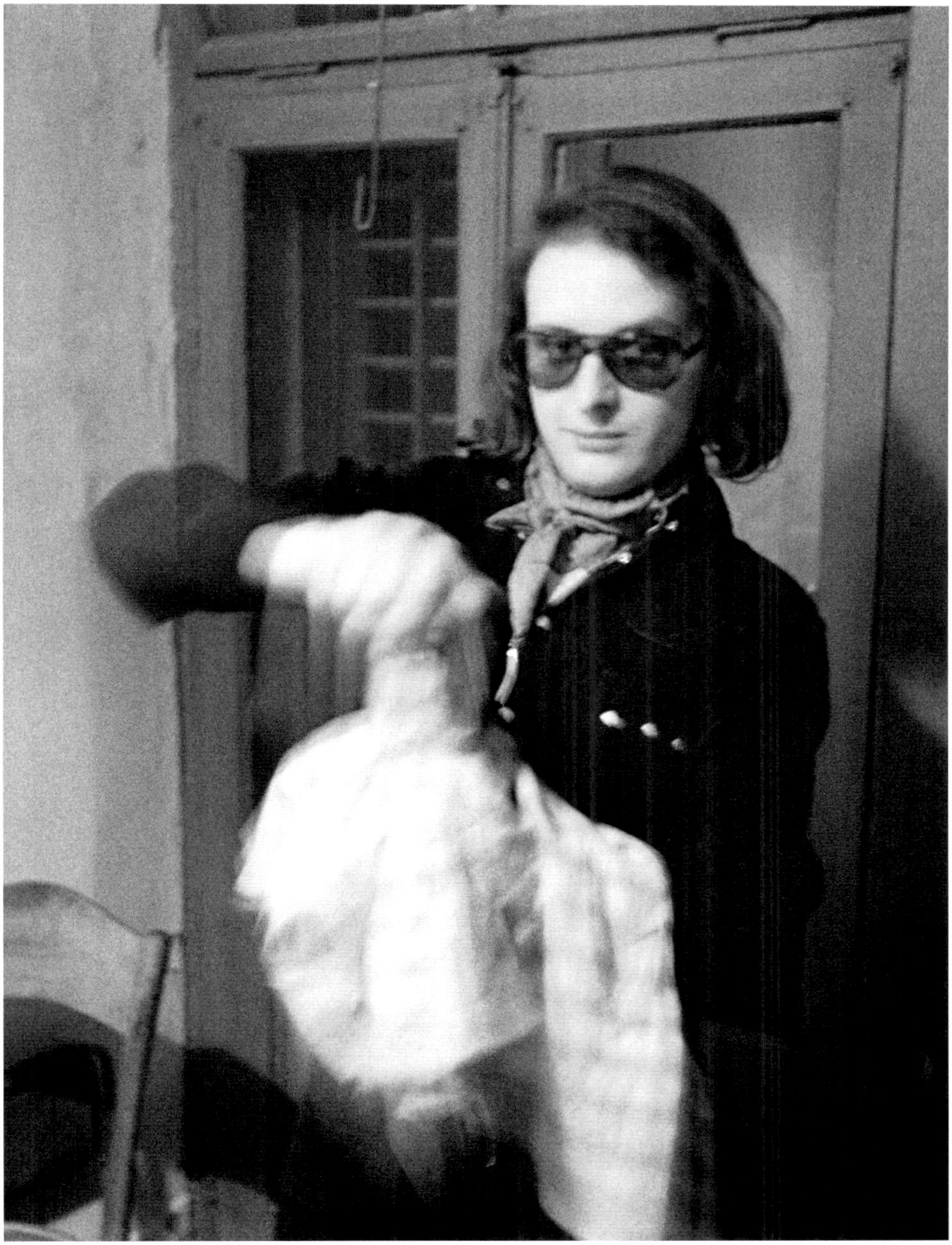

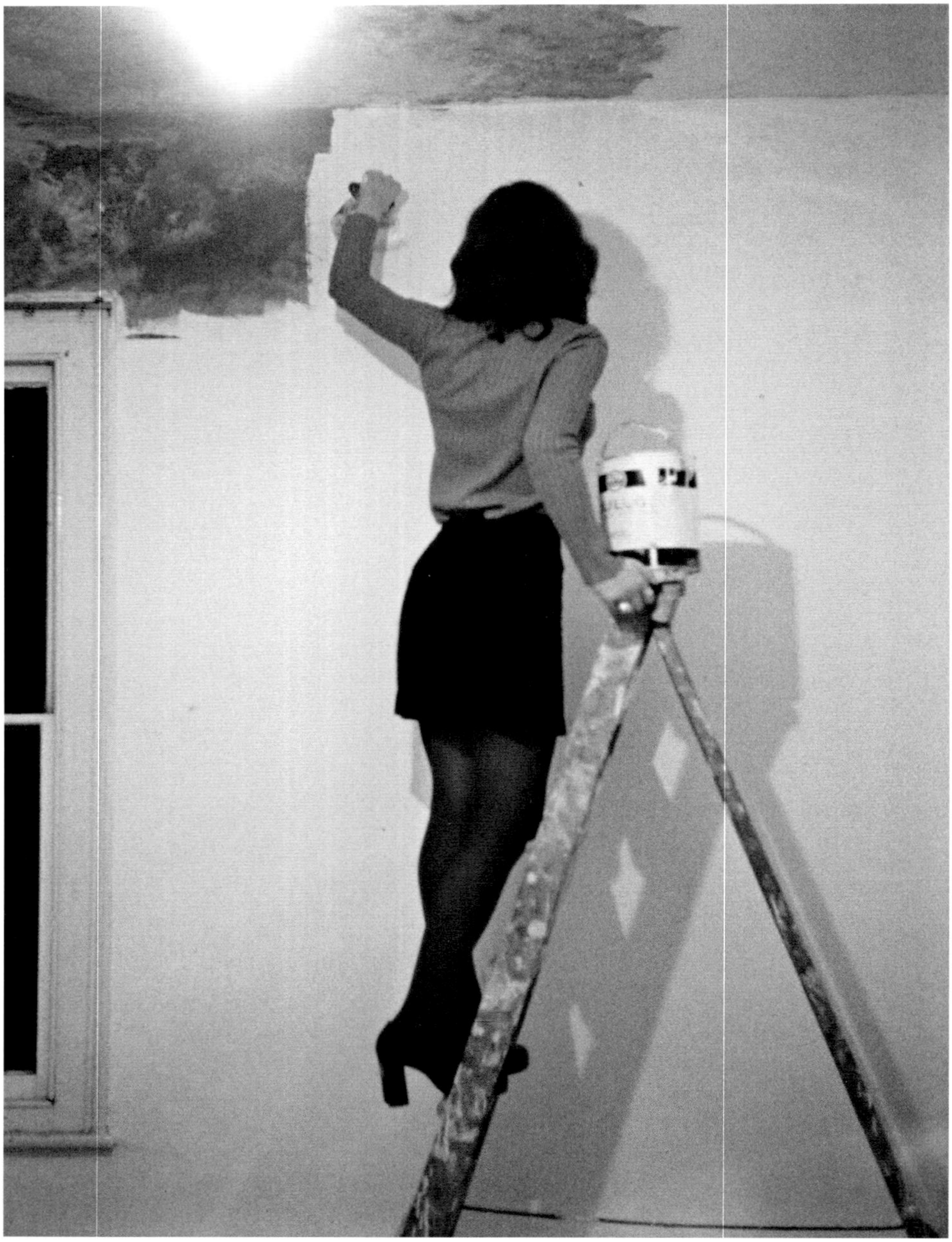

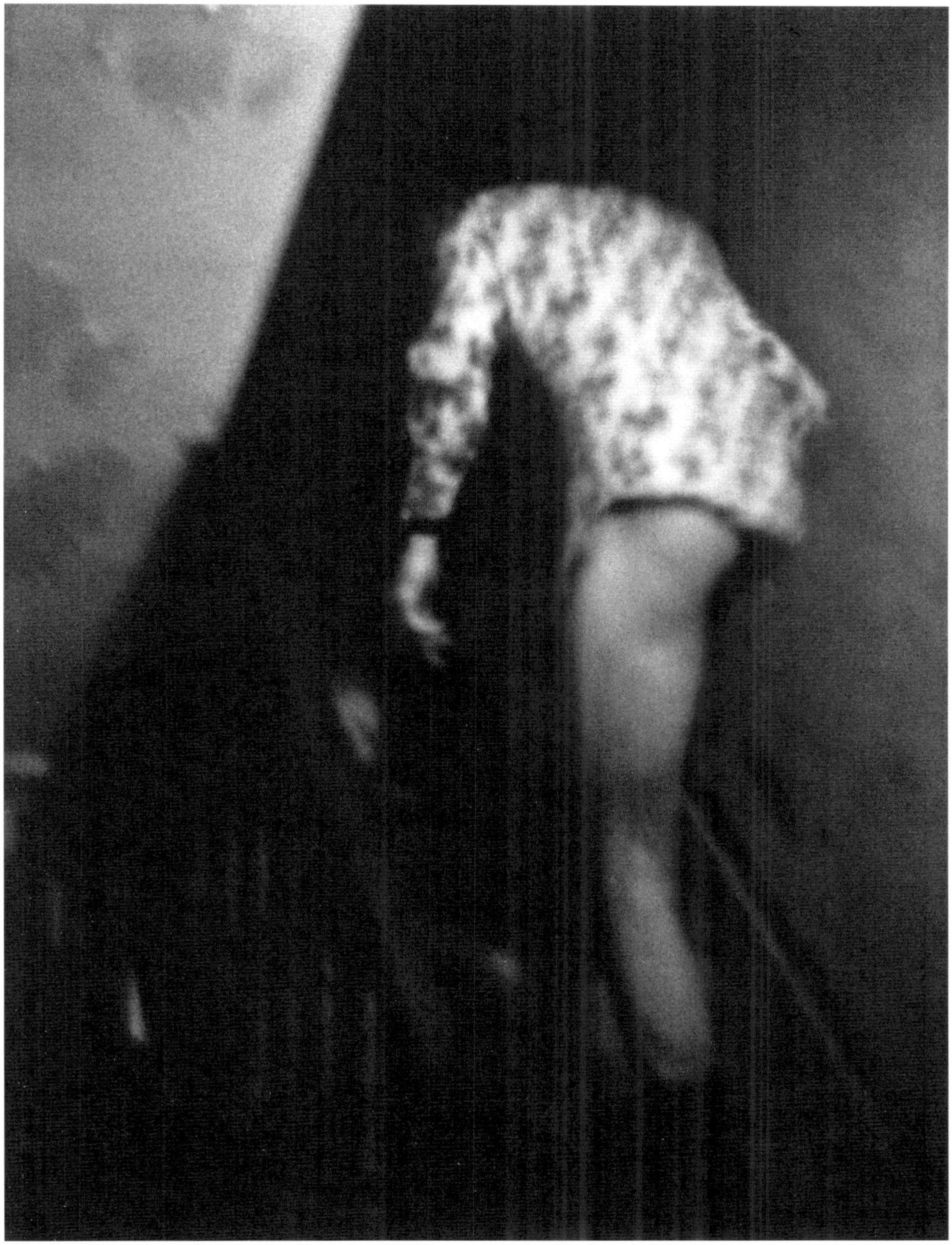

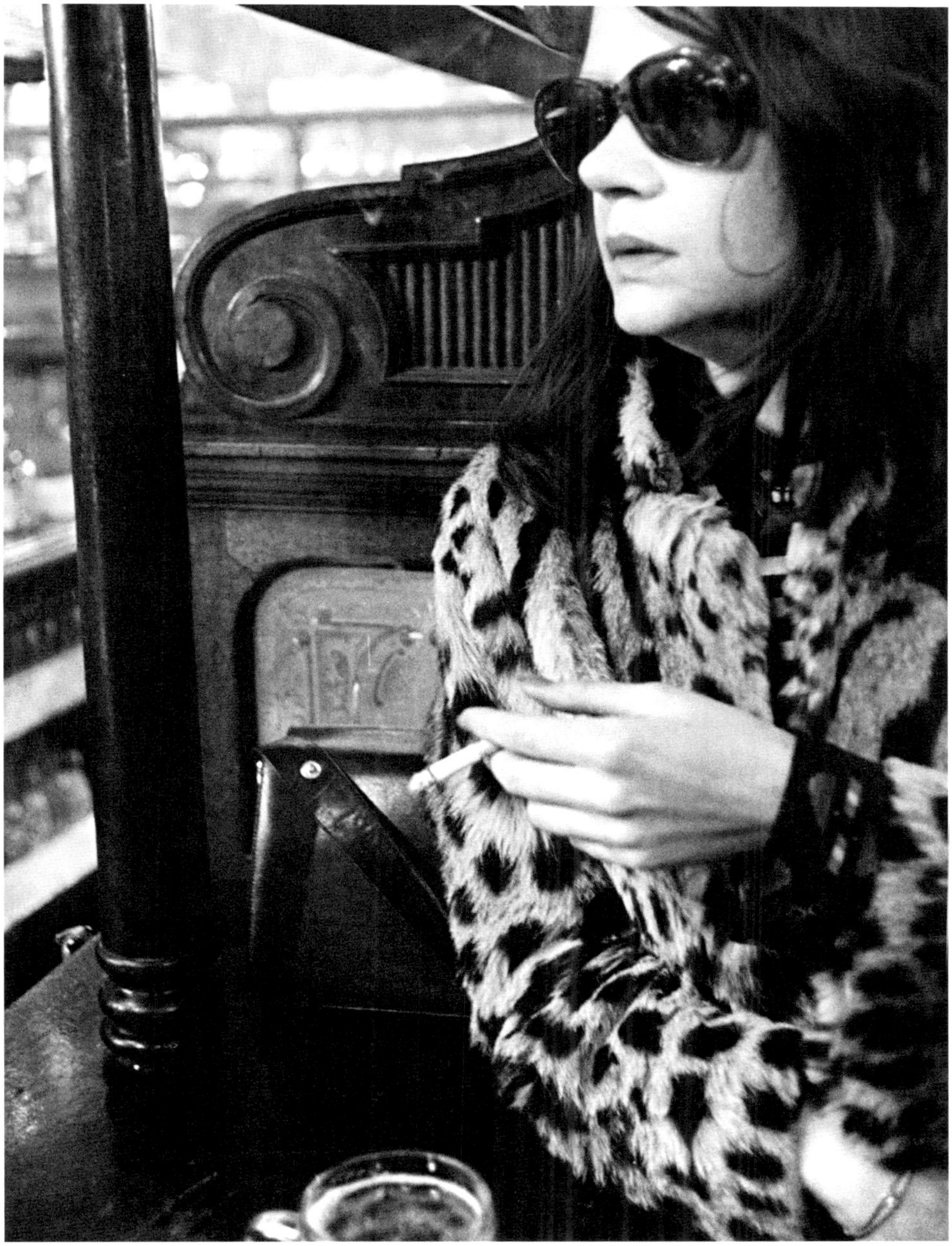

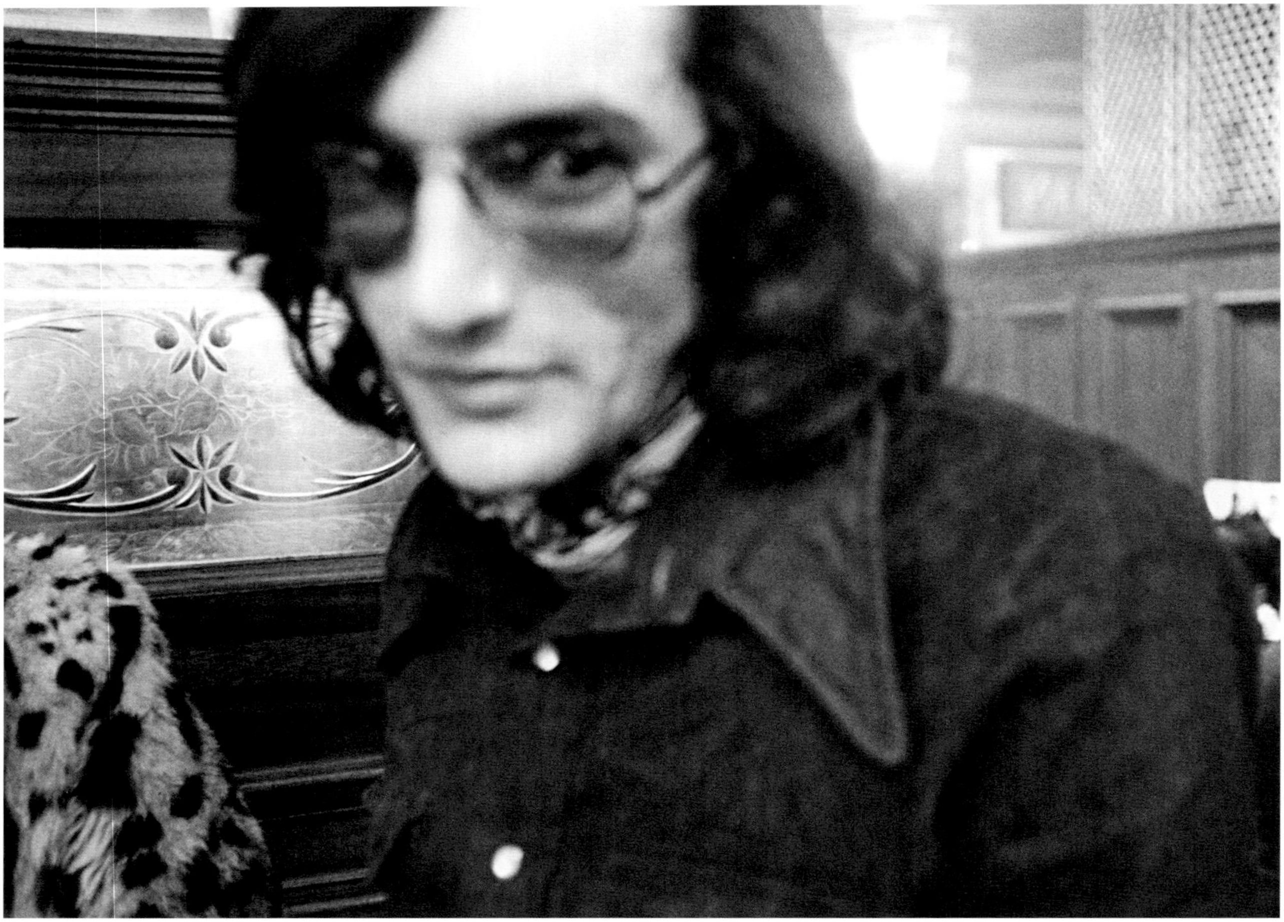

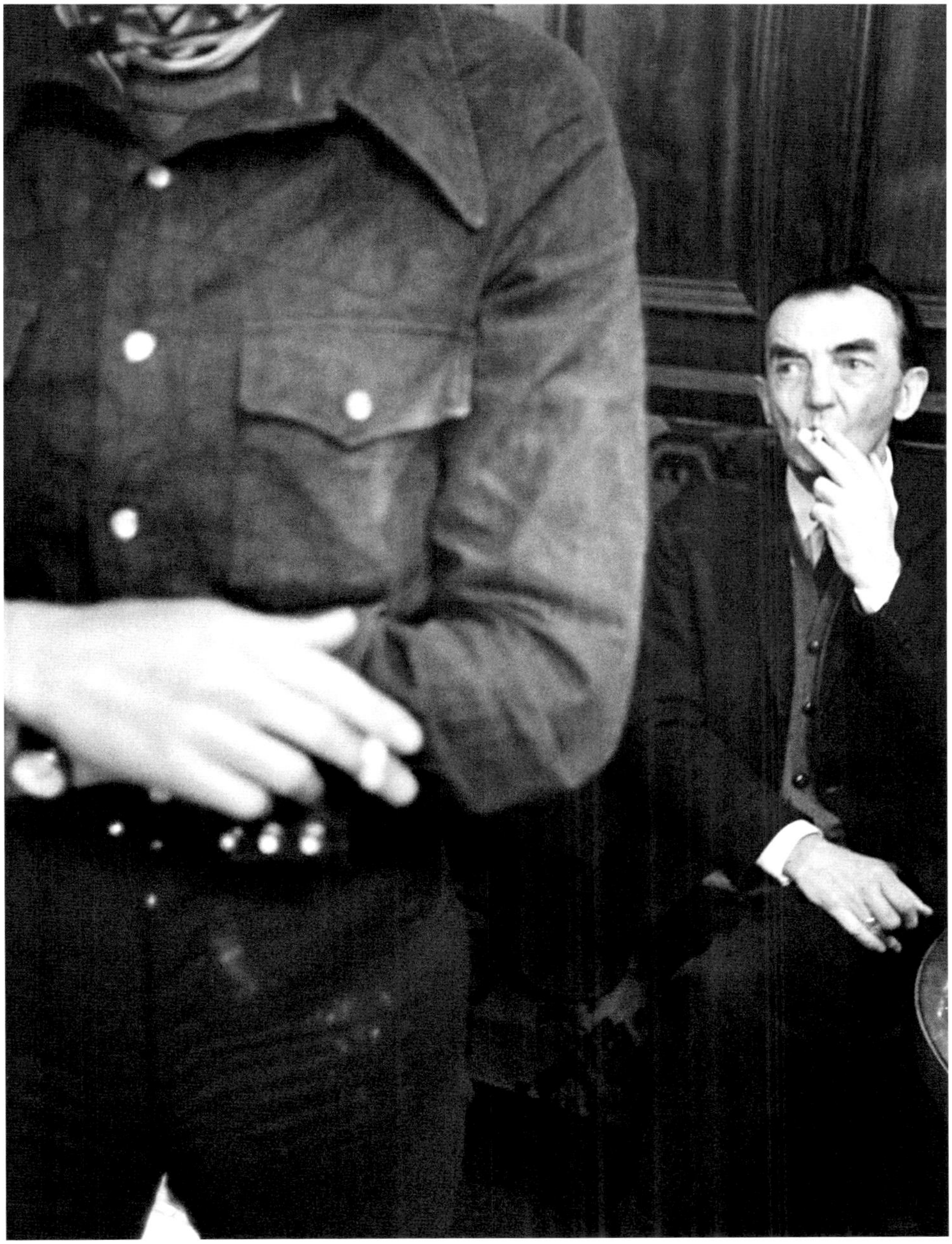

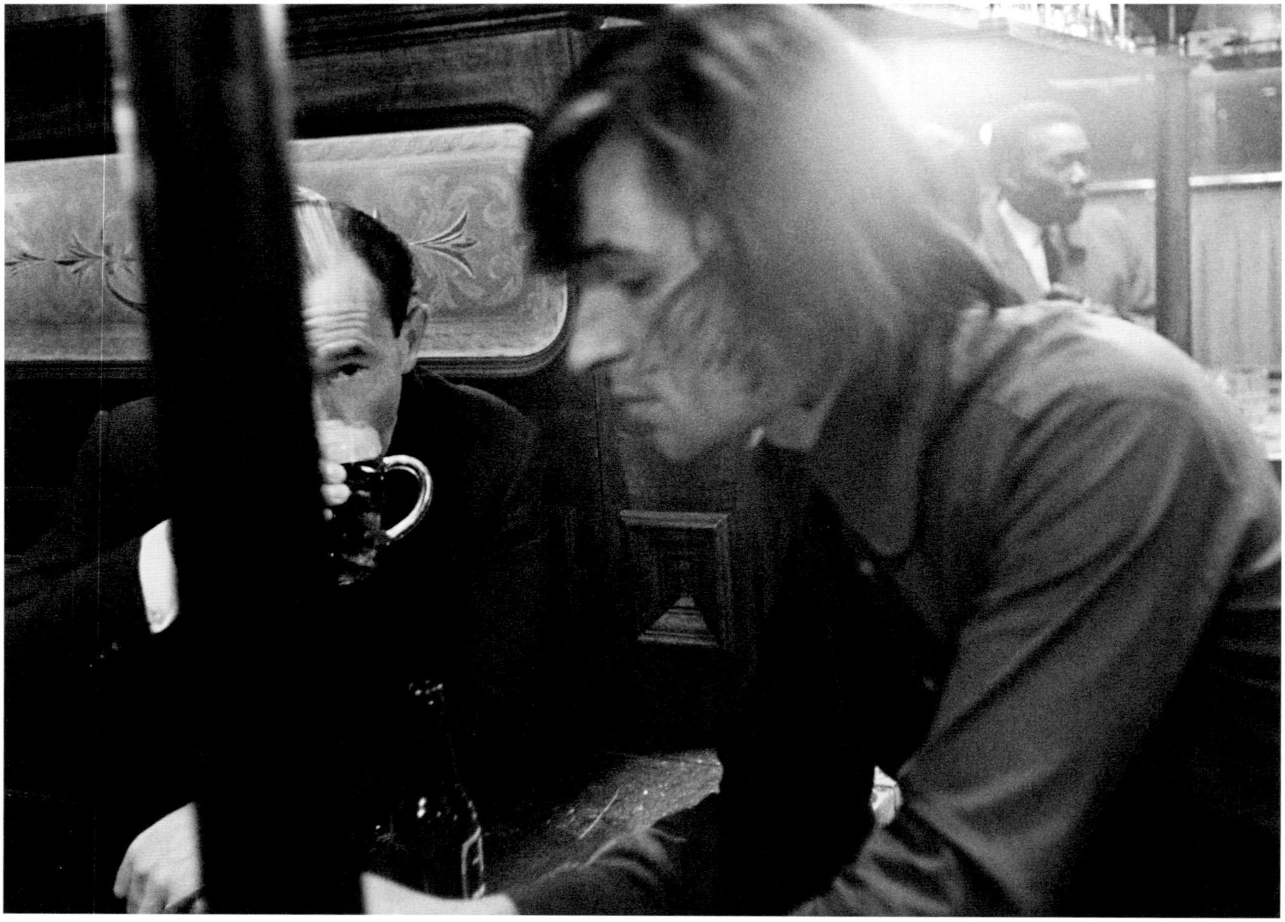

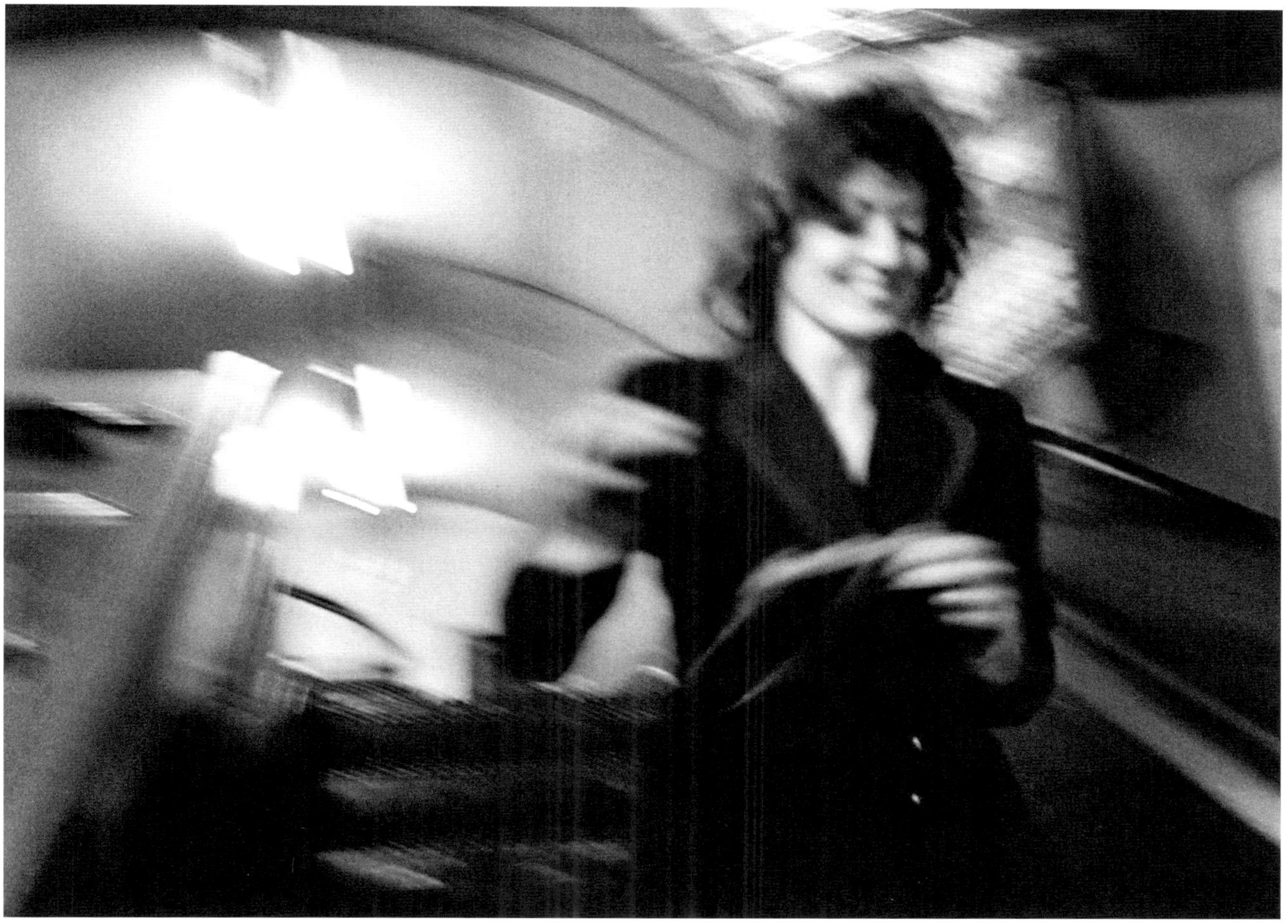

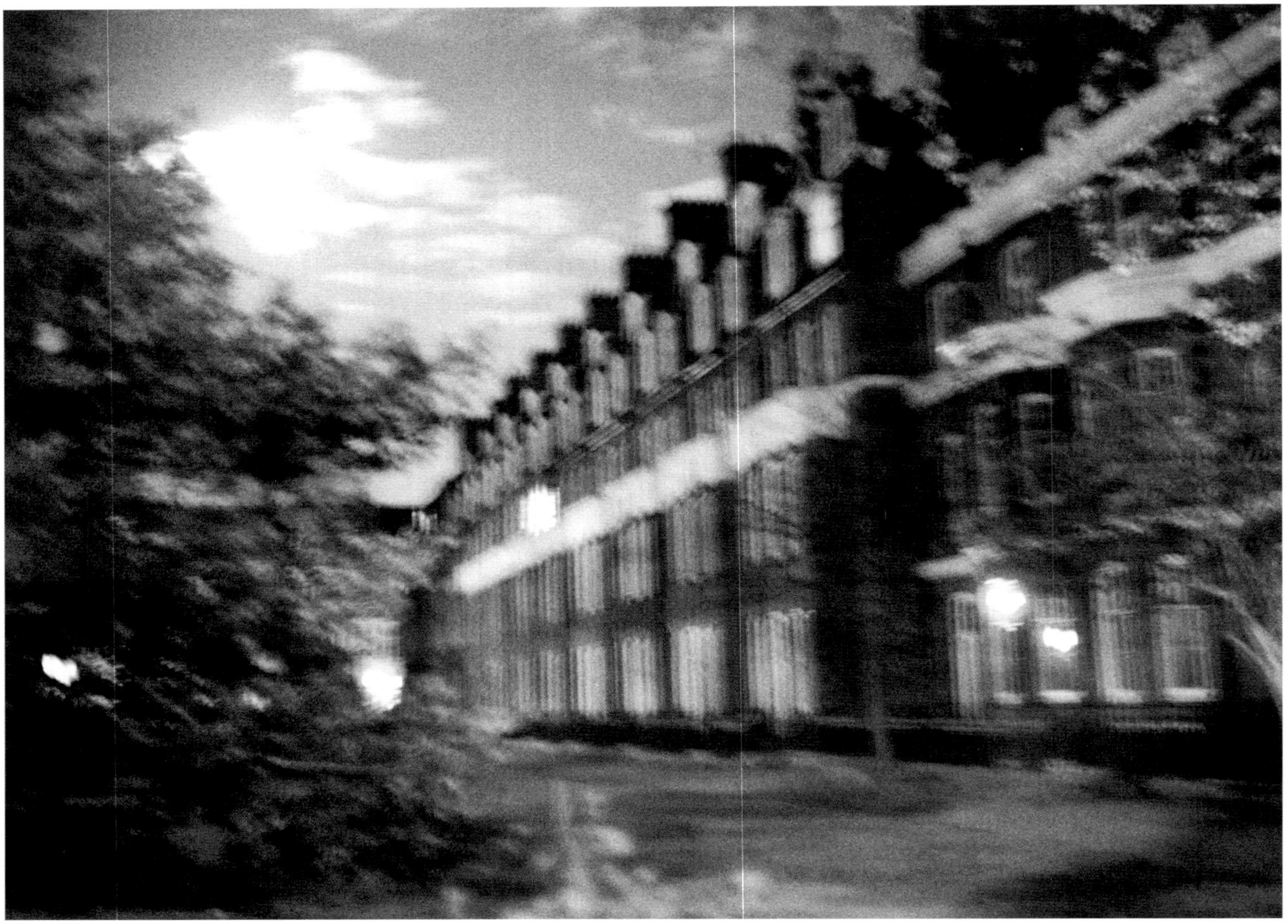

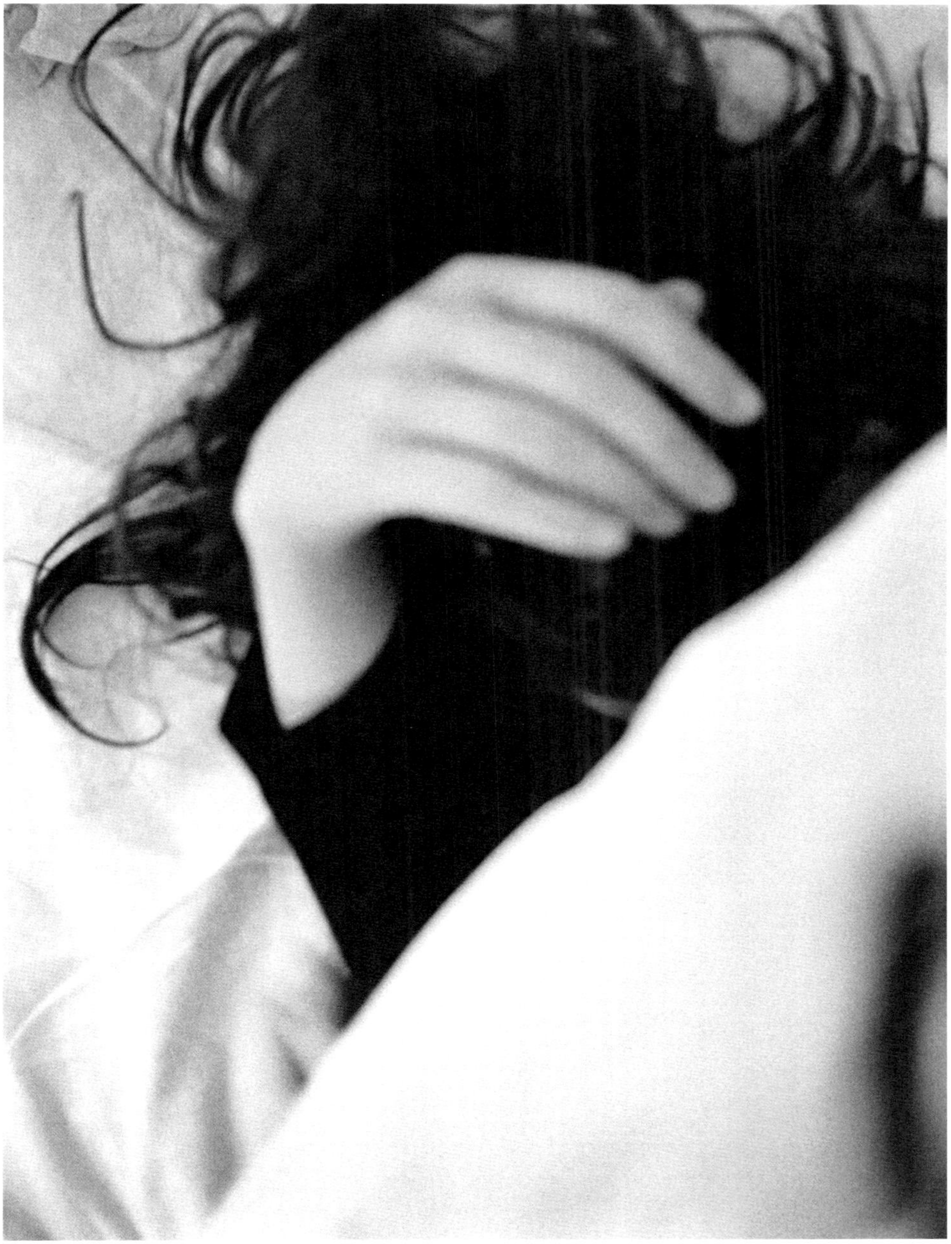

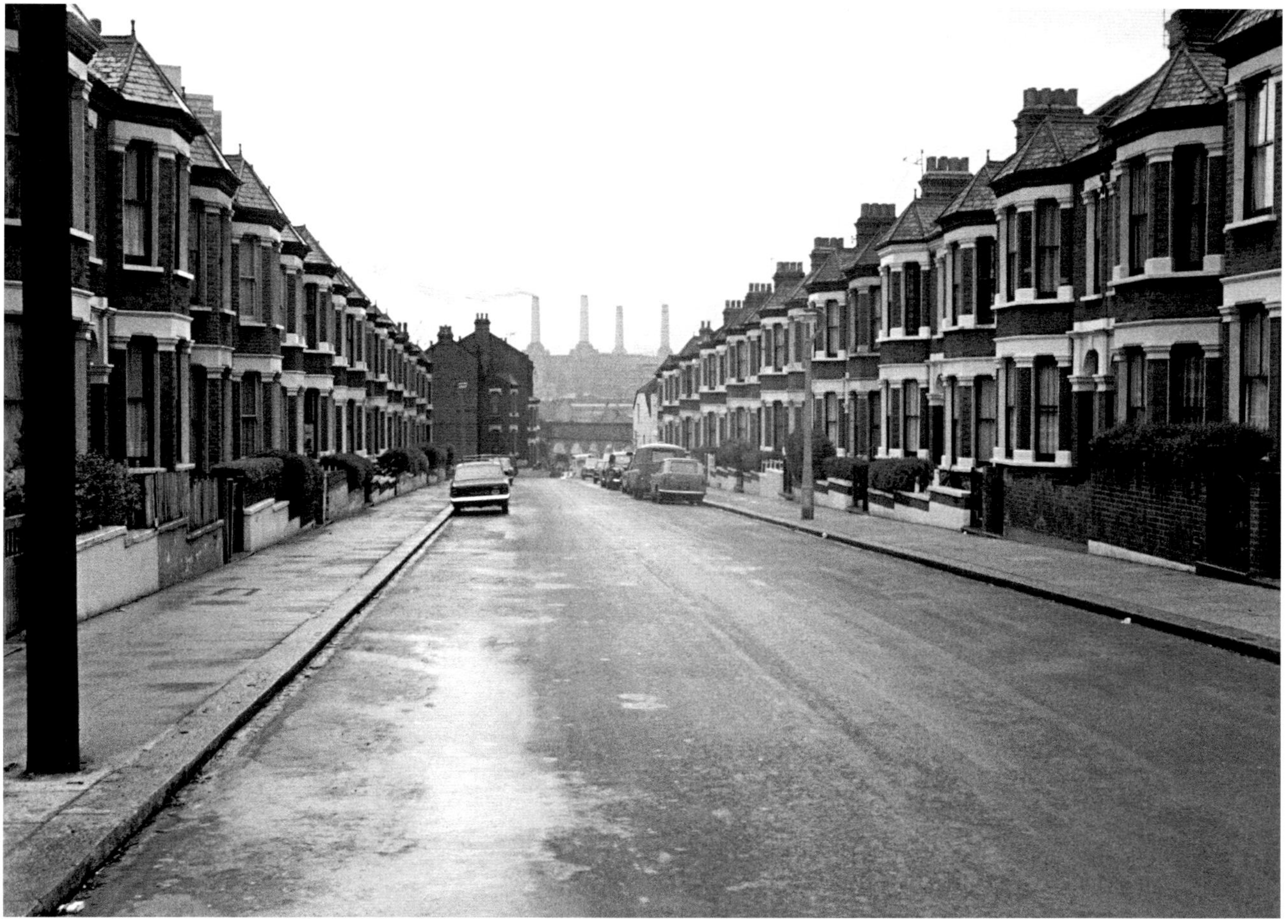

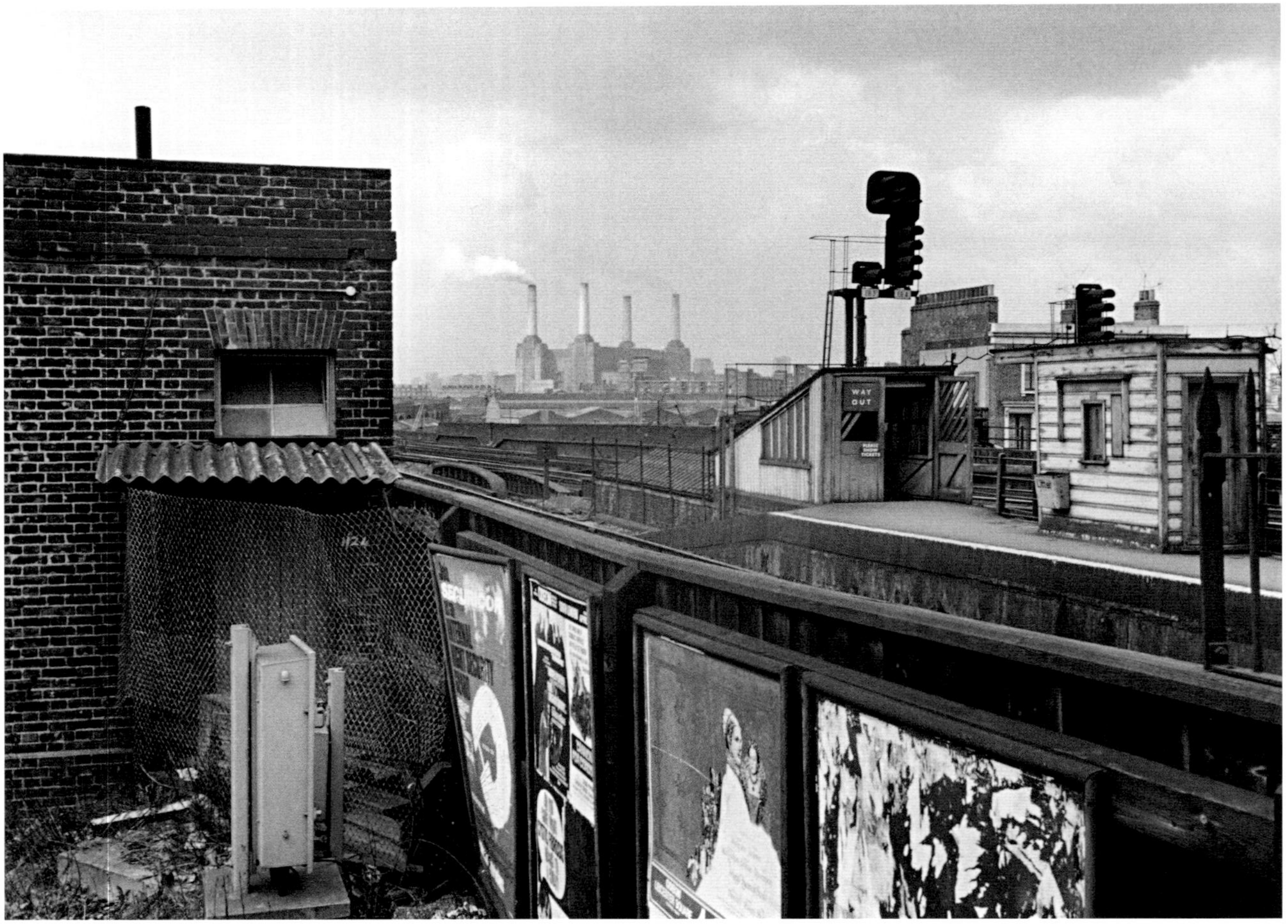
WAY
OUT

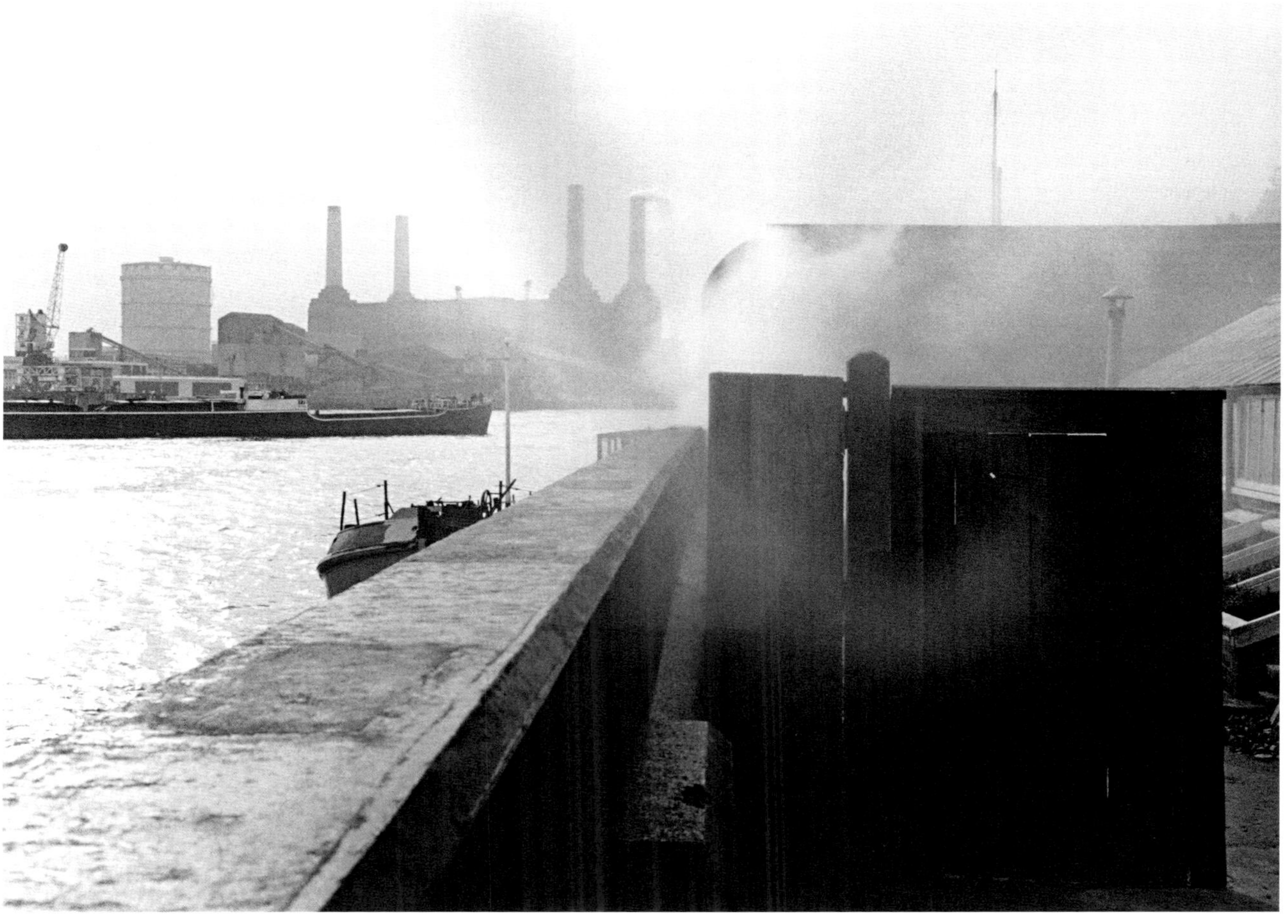

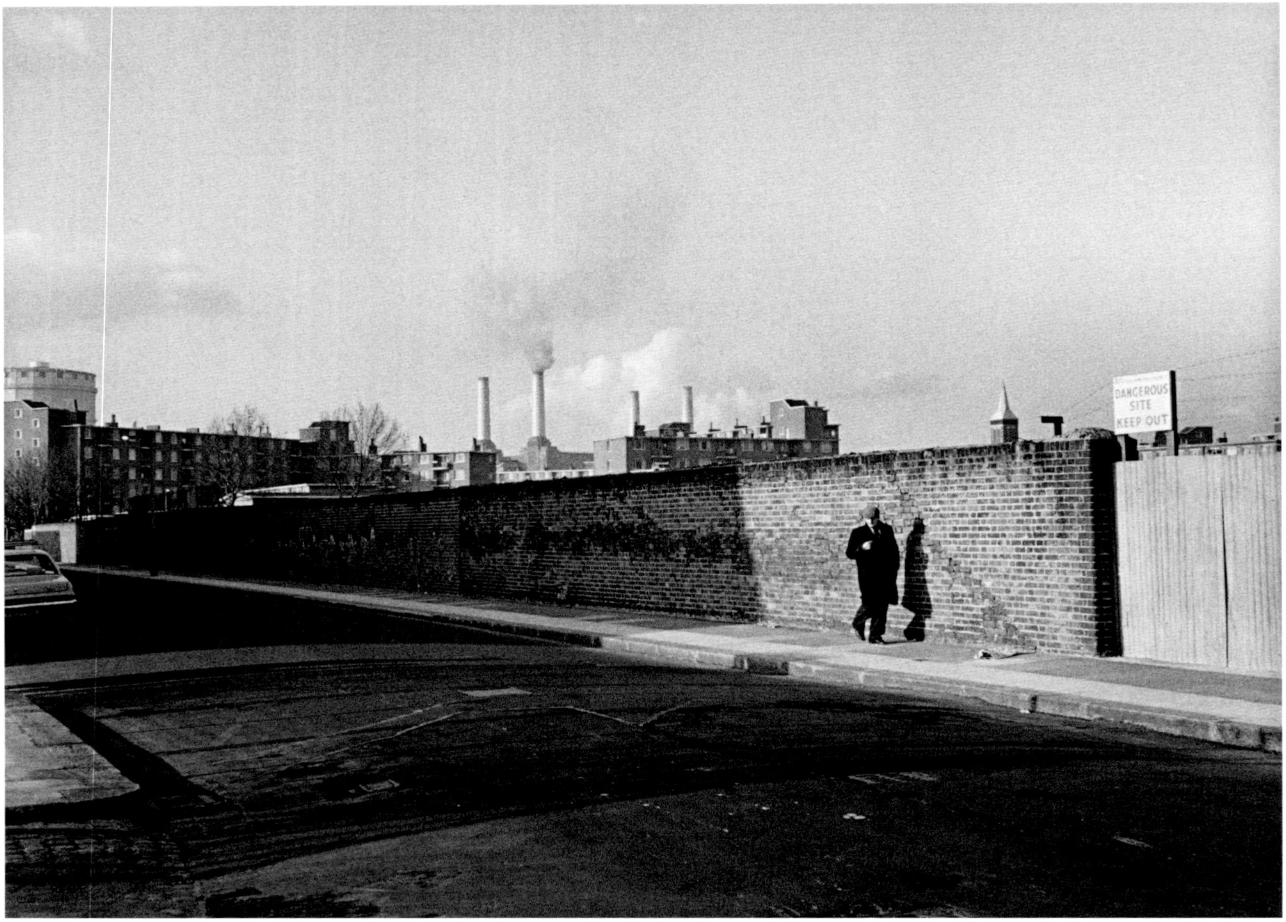
DANGEROUS
SITE
KEEP OUT

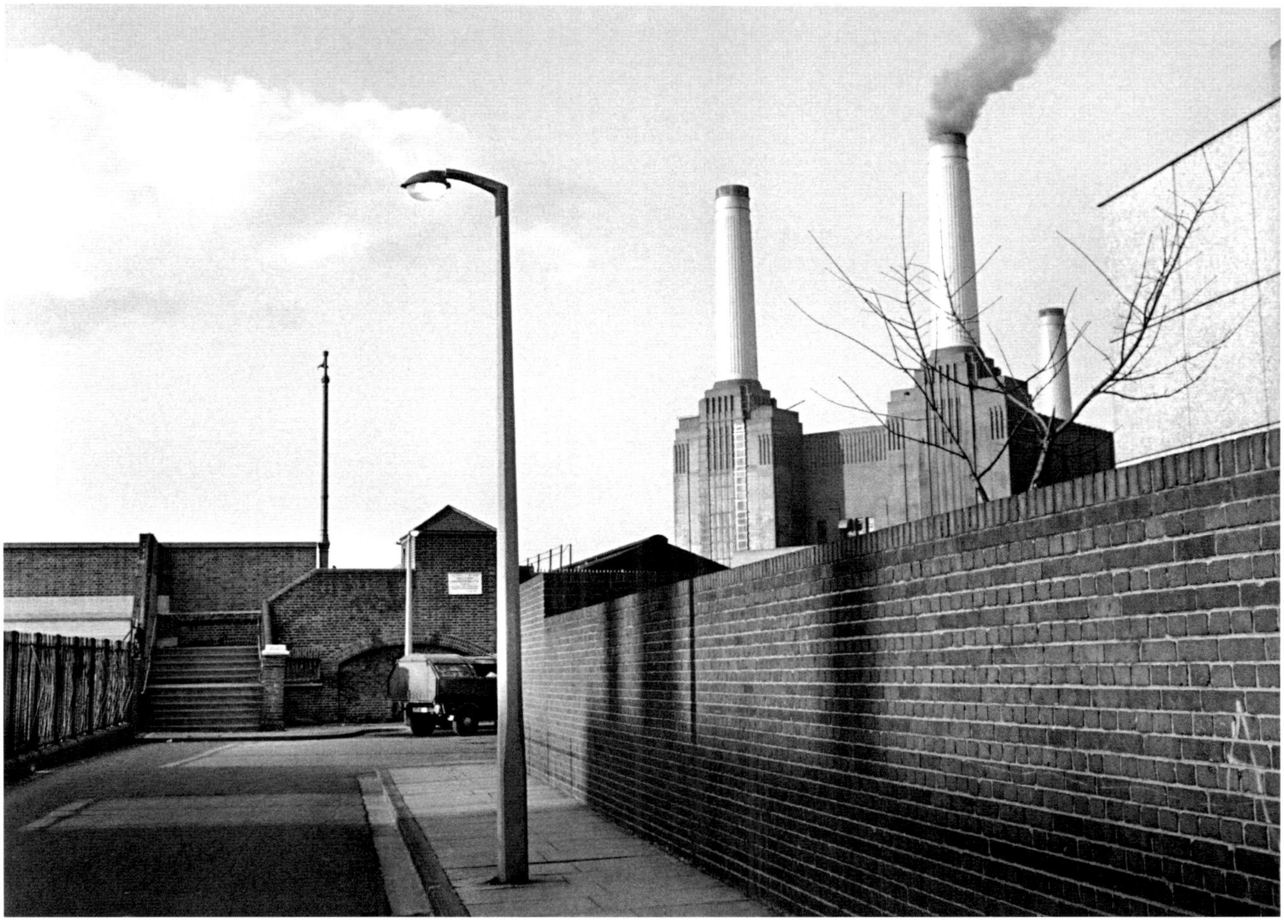

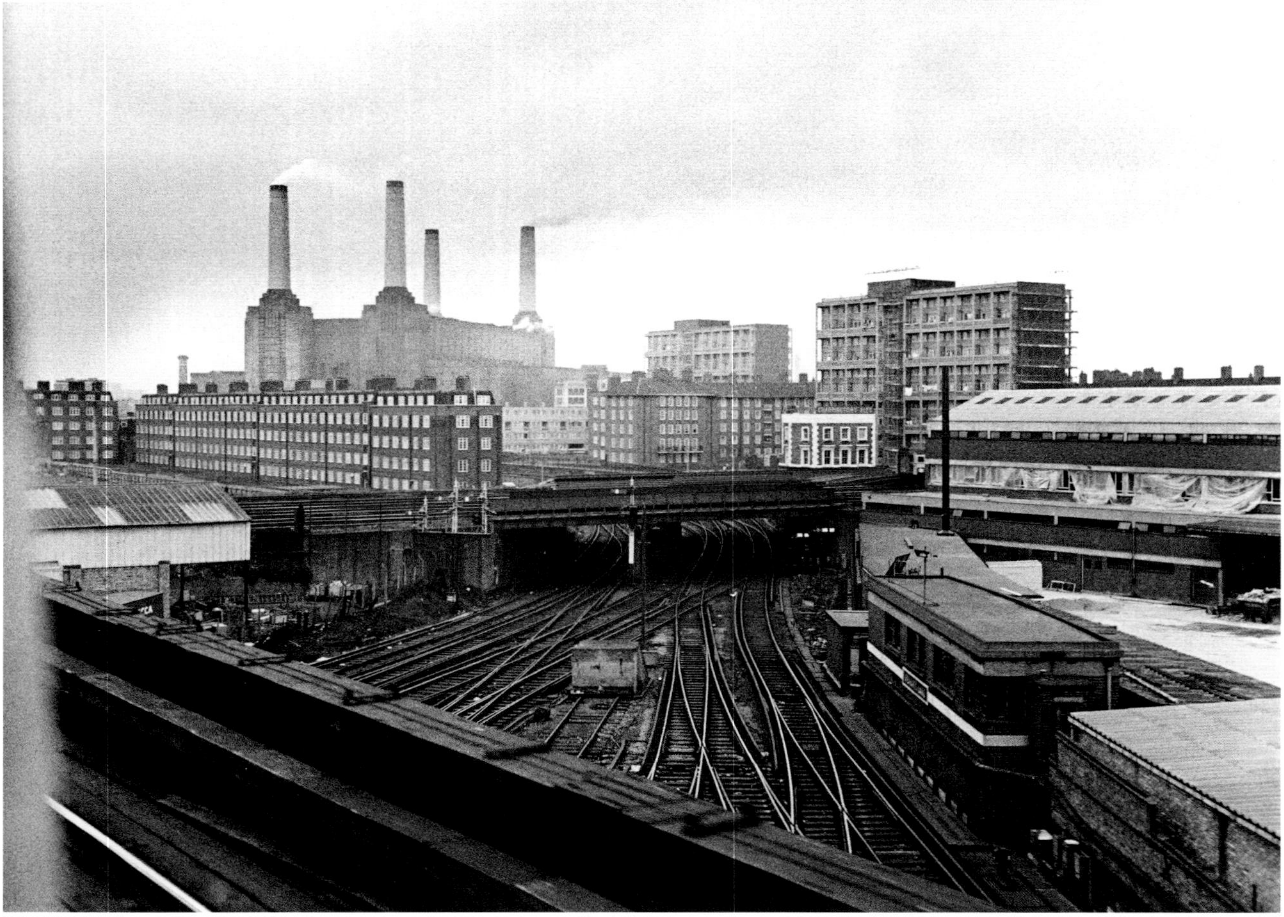

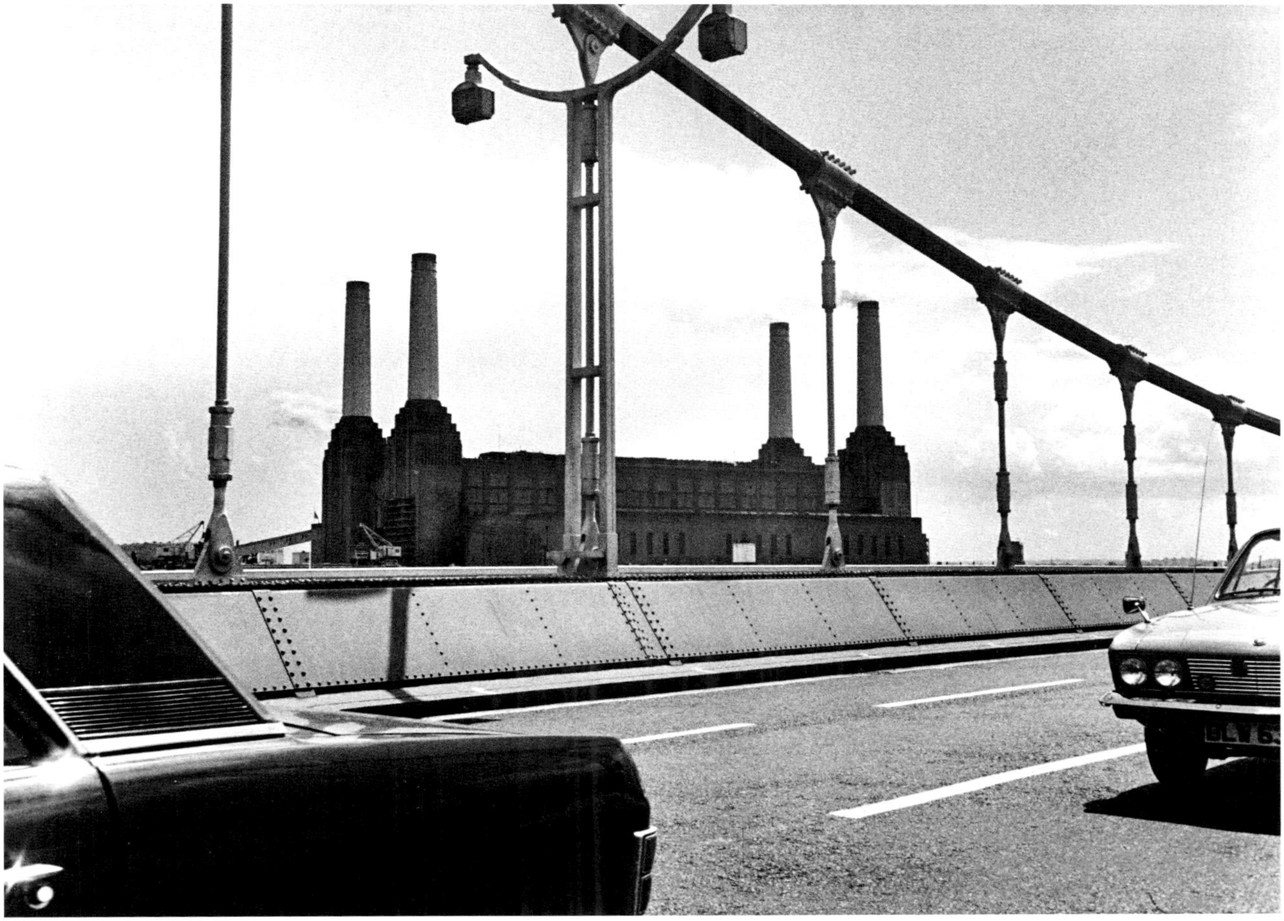

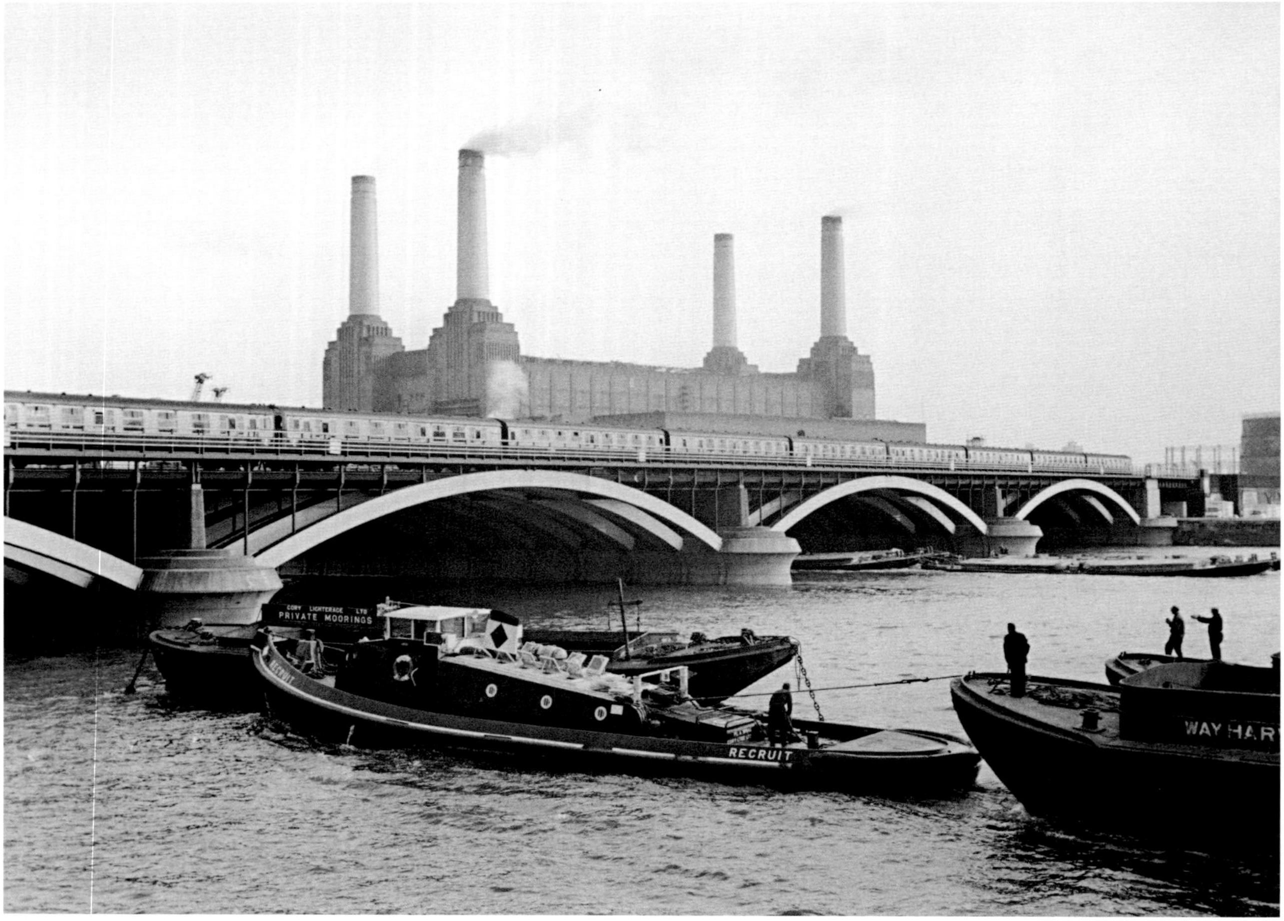
CORY LIGHTERAGE LTD
PRIVATE MOORINGS
RECRUIT

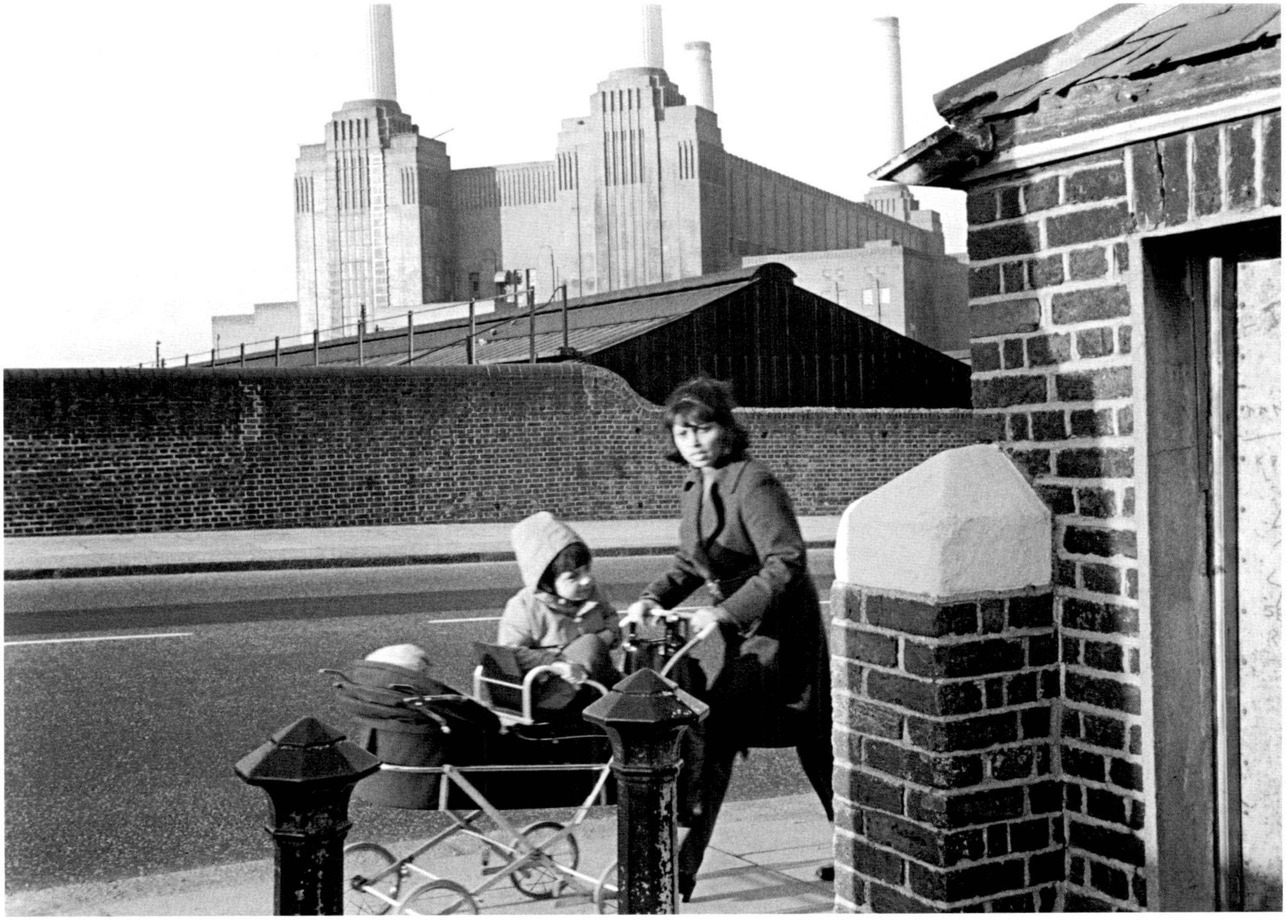

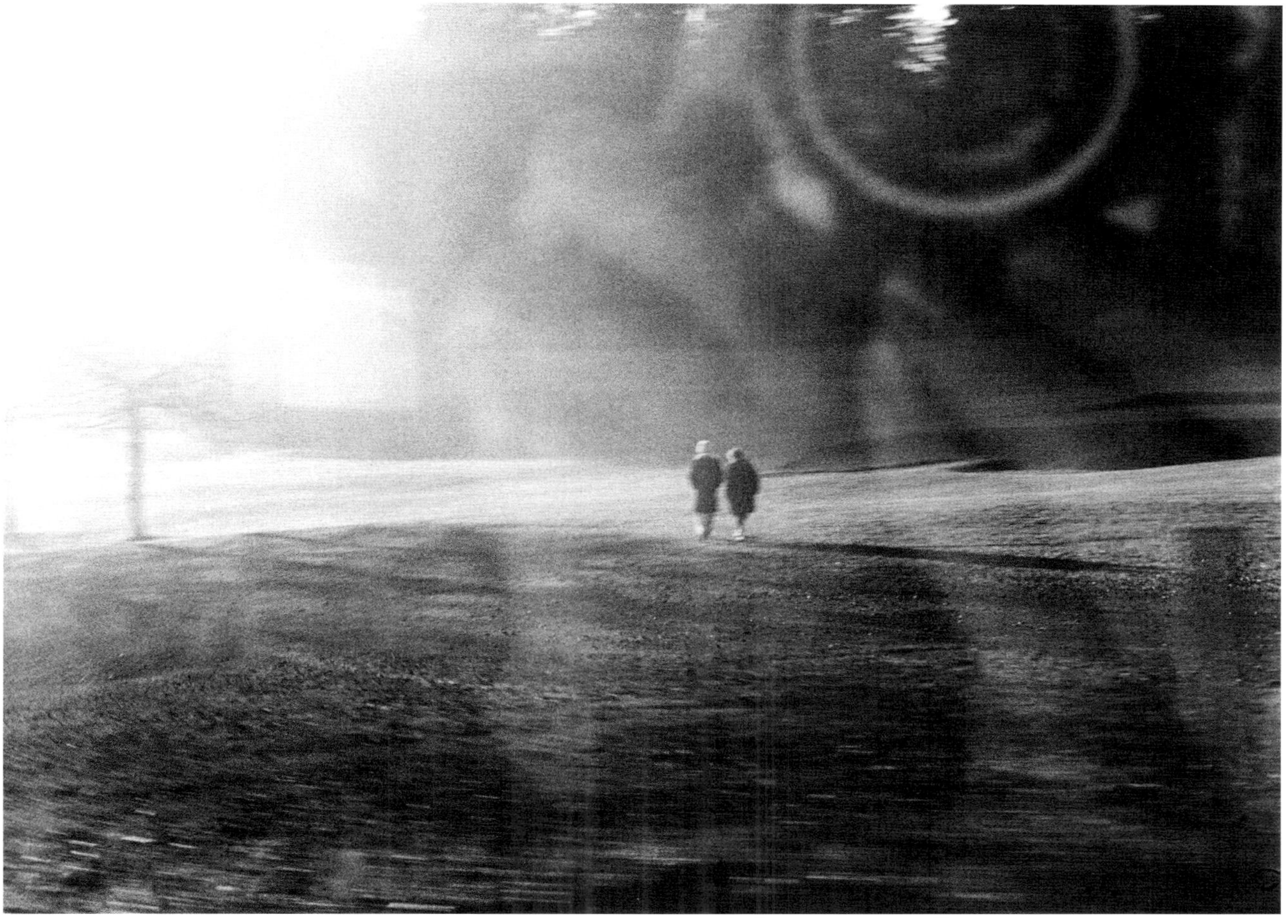

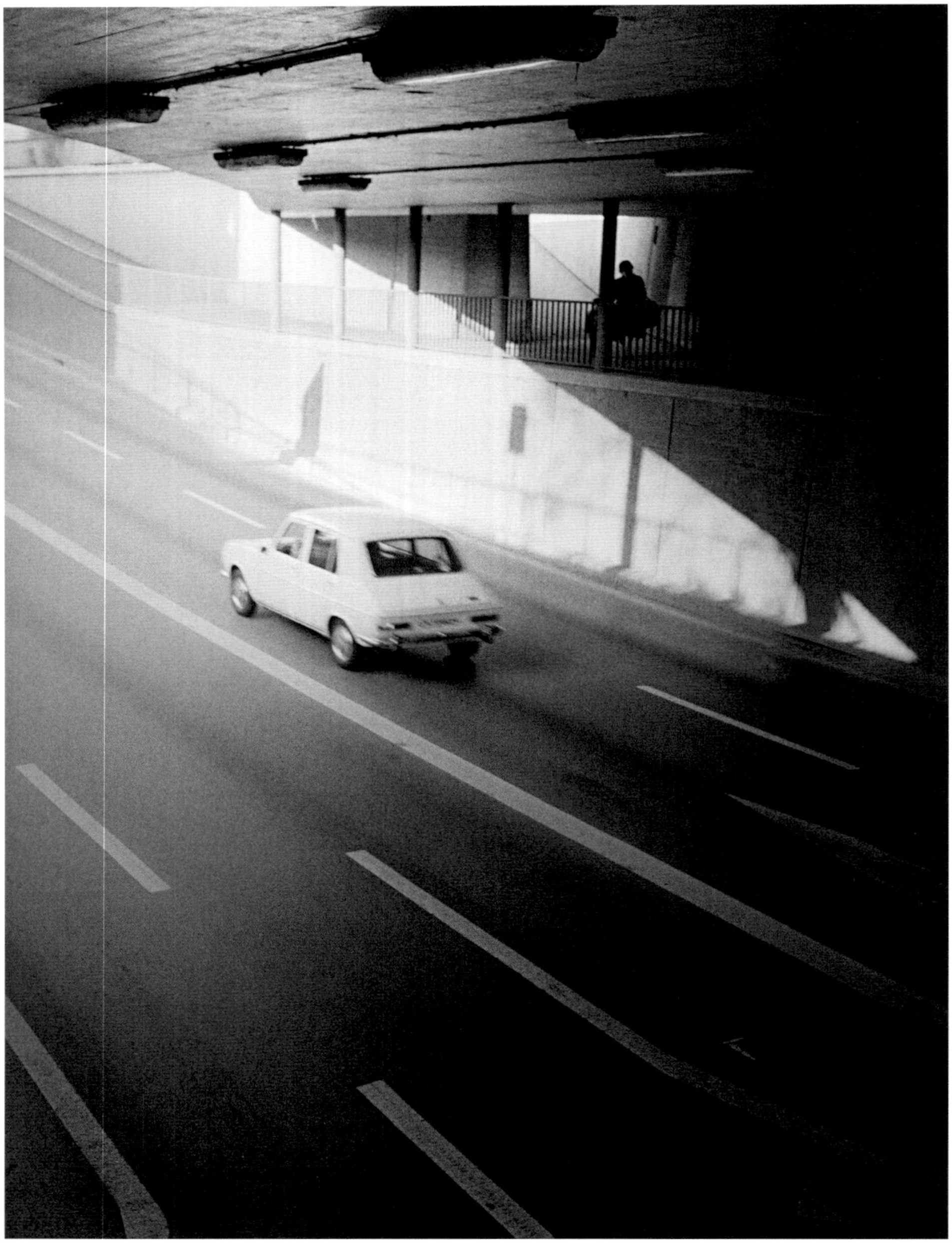

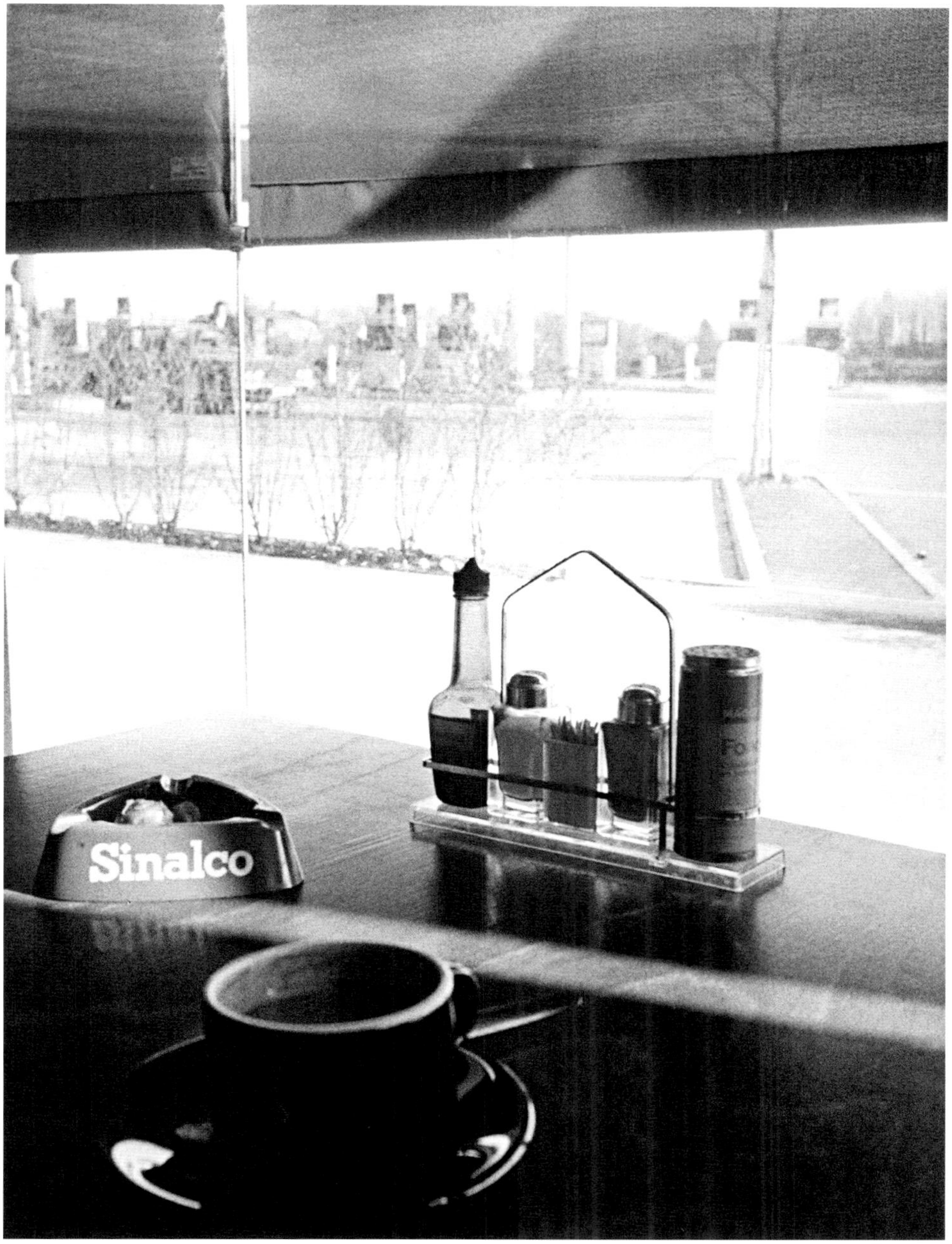
Sinalco

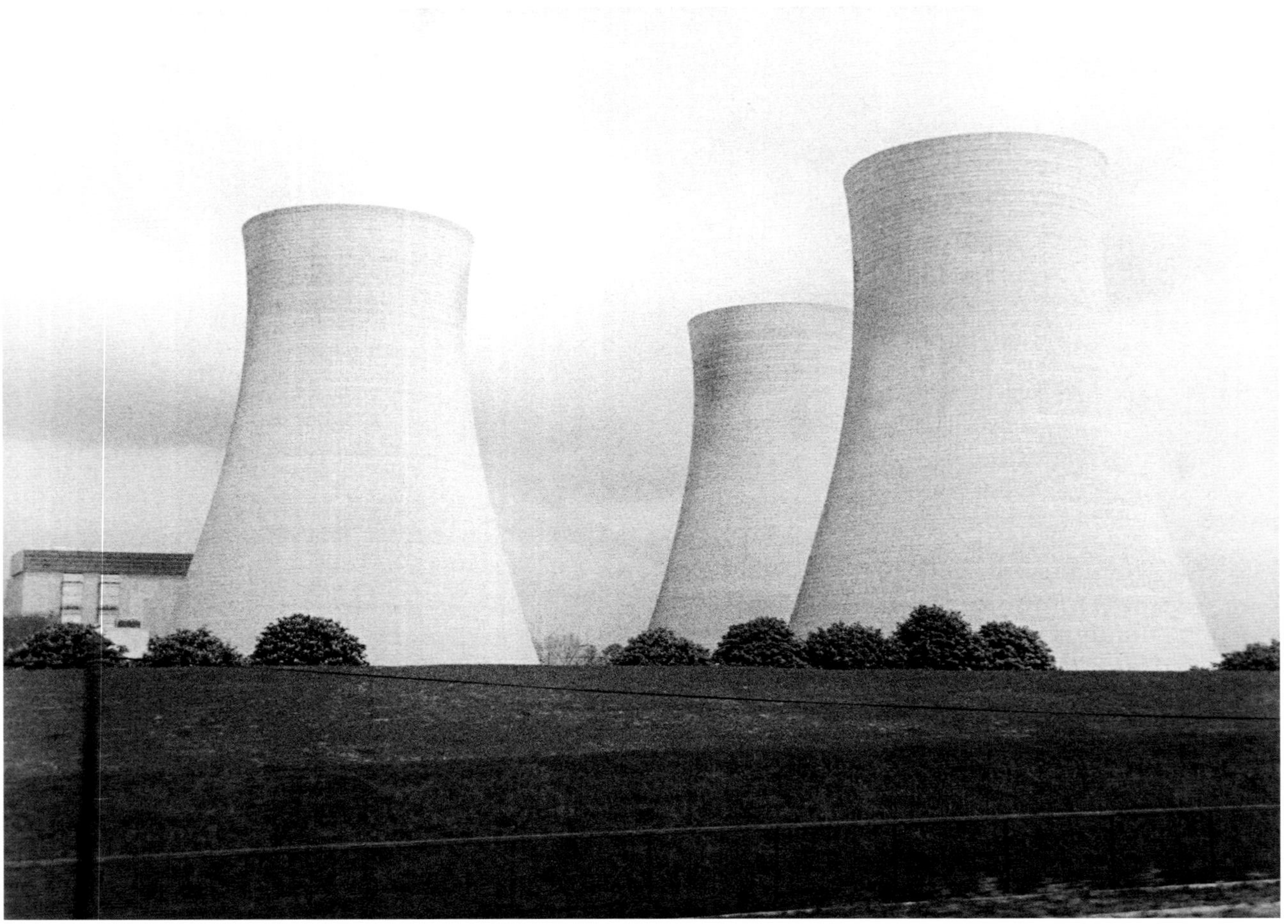

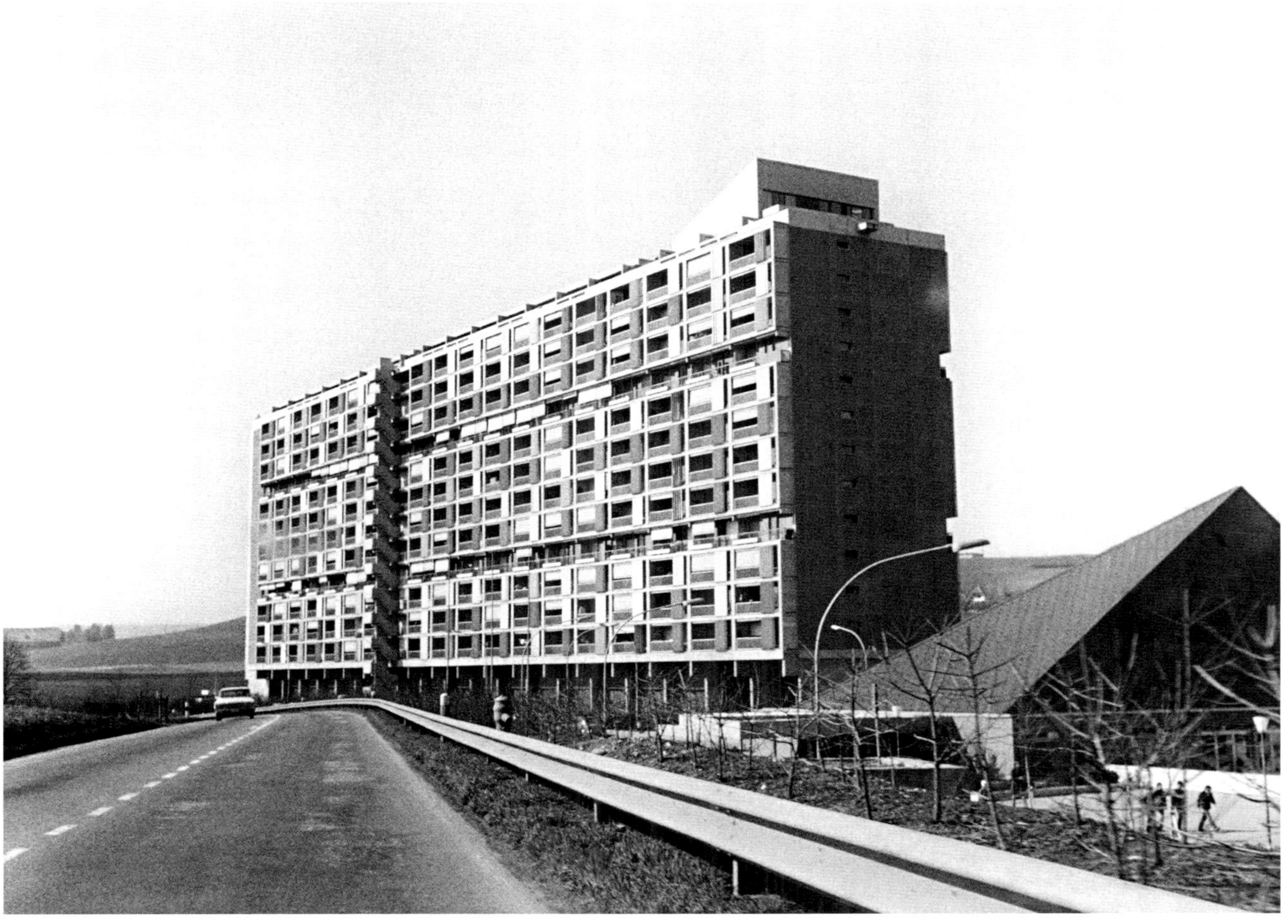

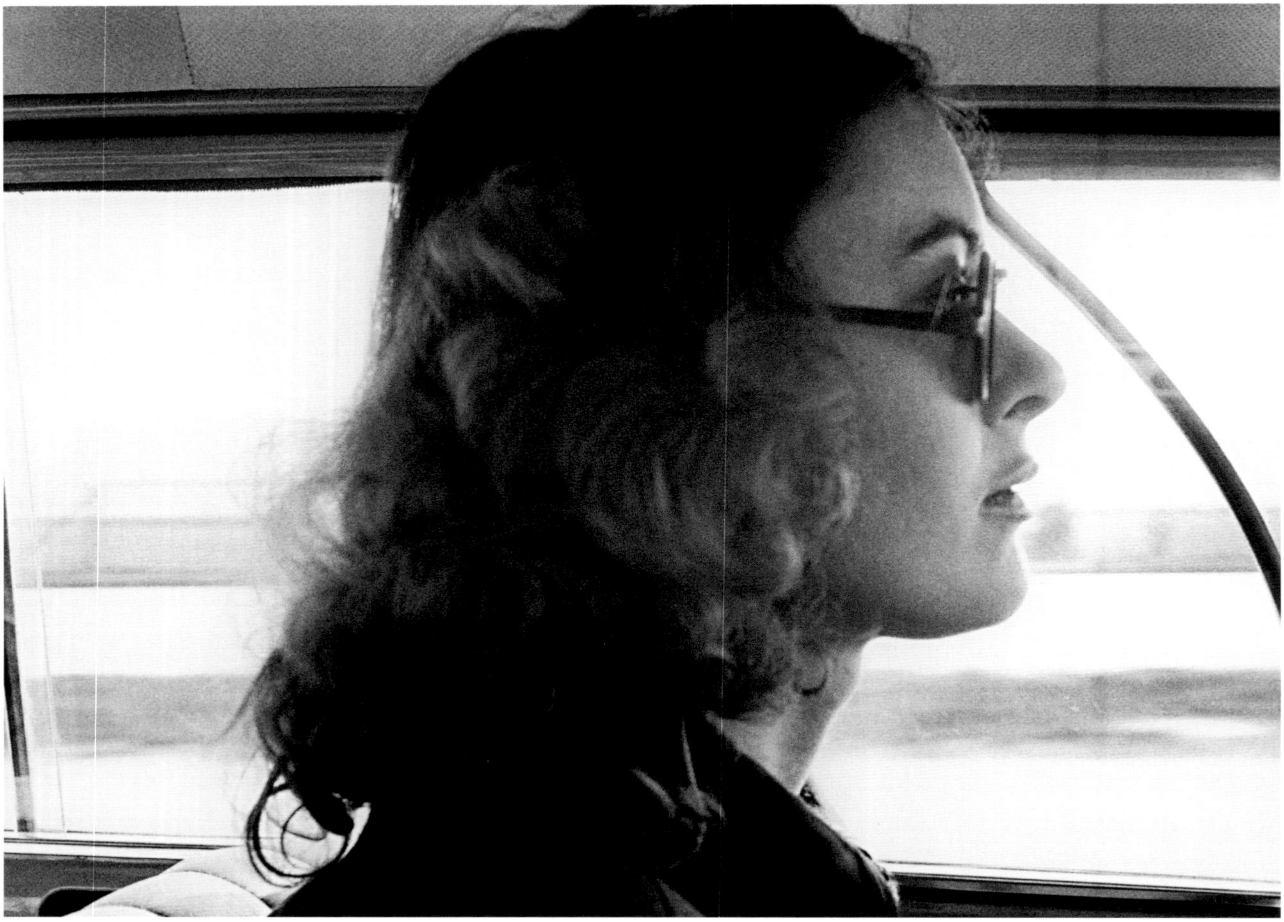

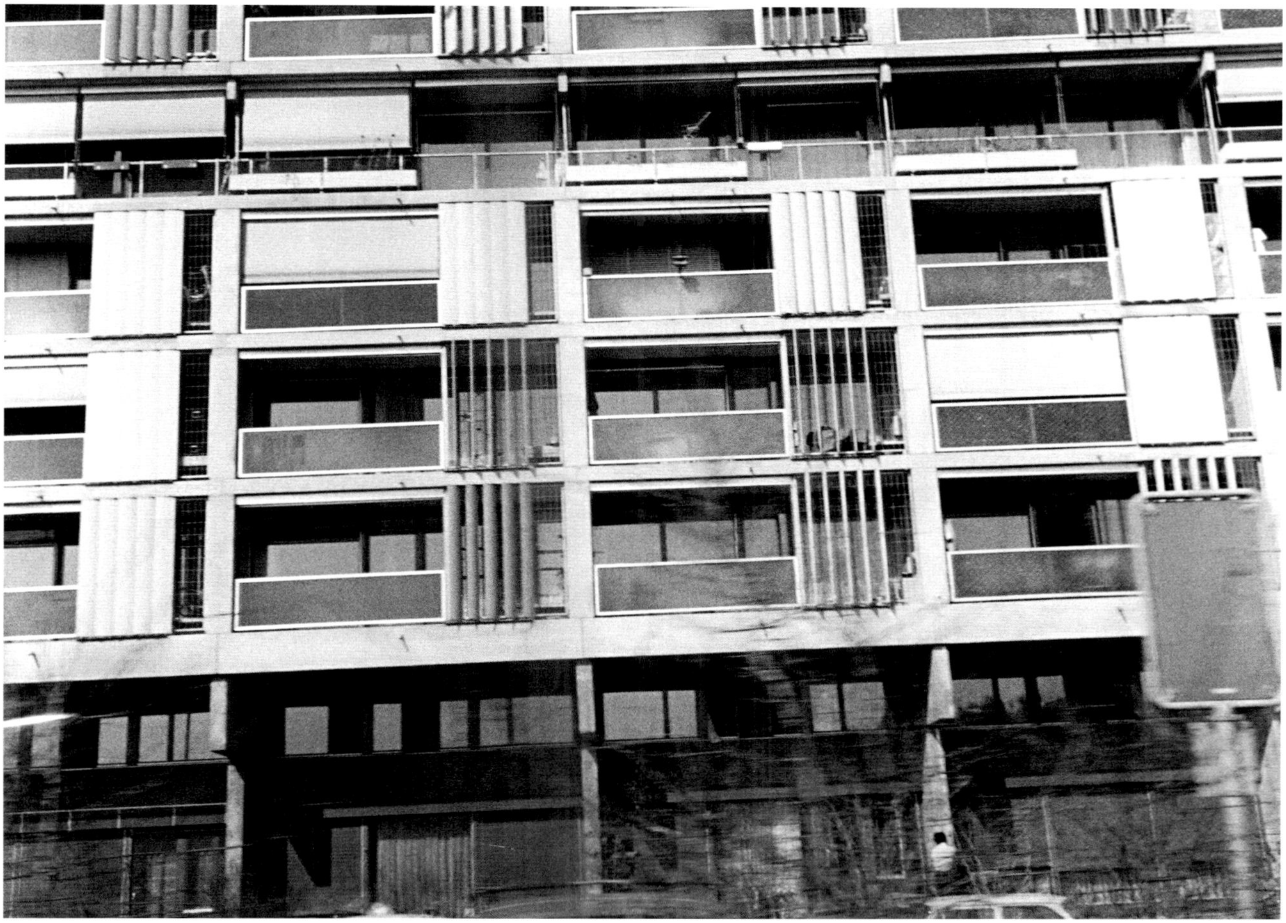

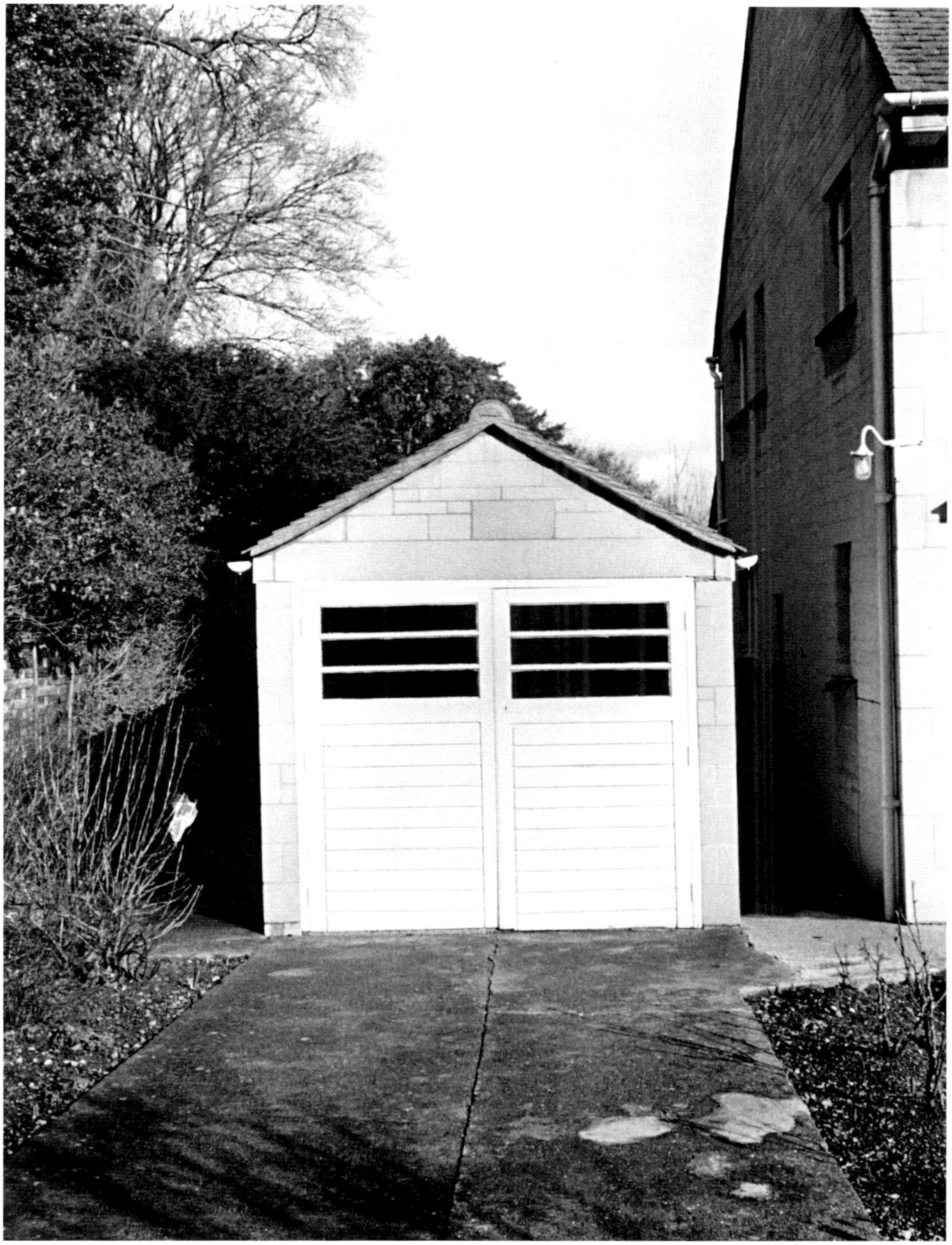

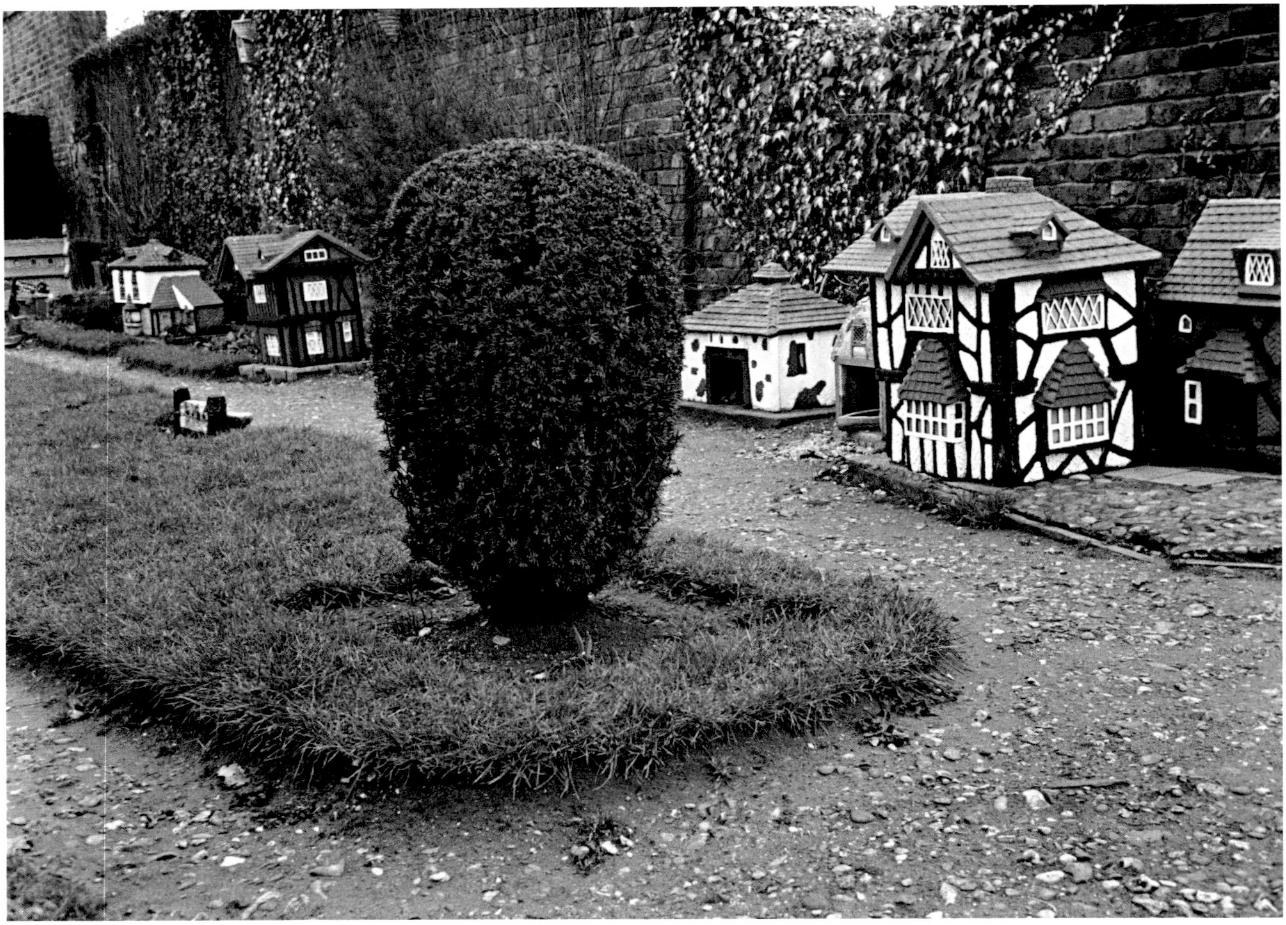

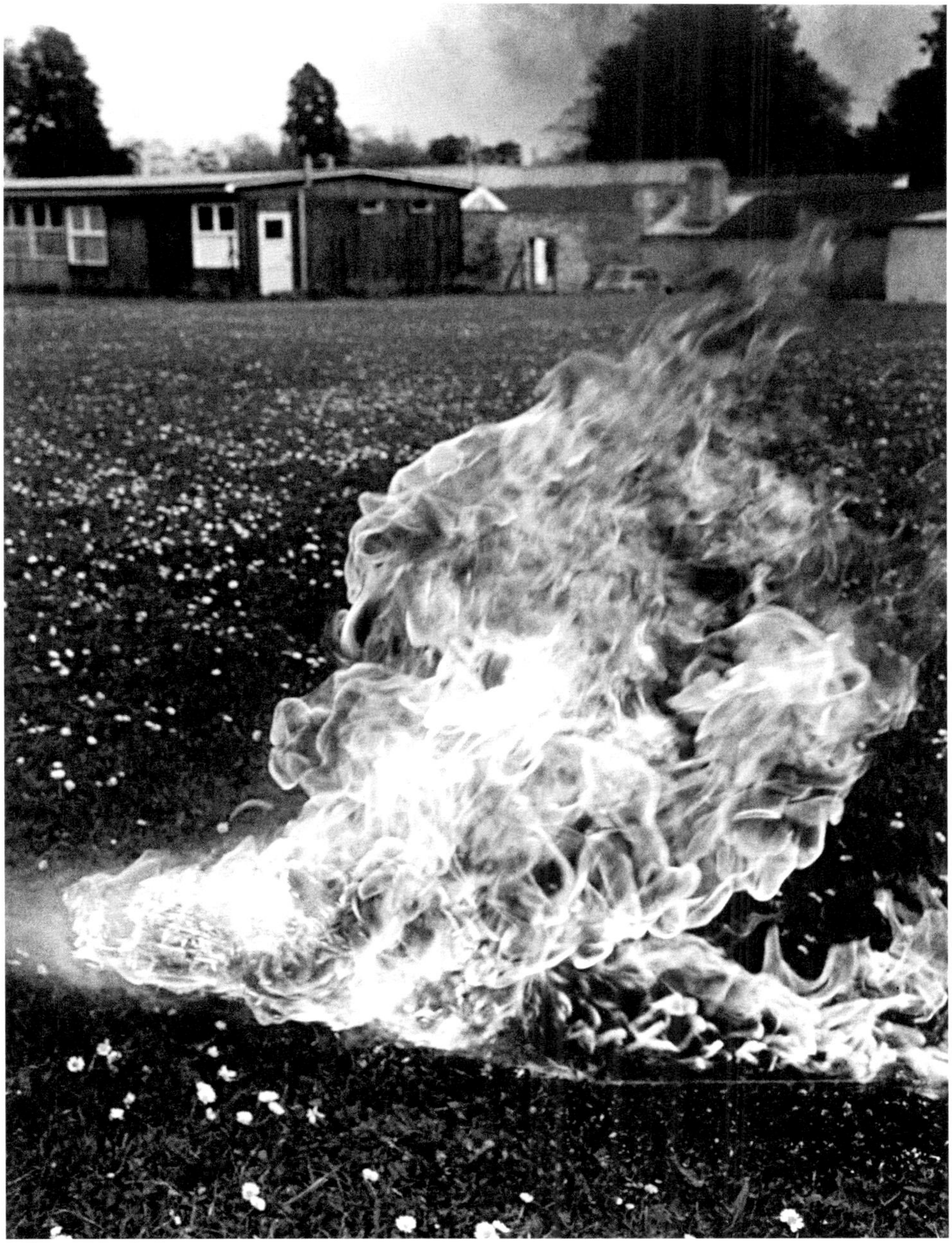

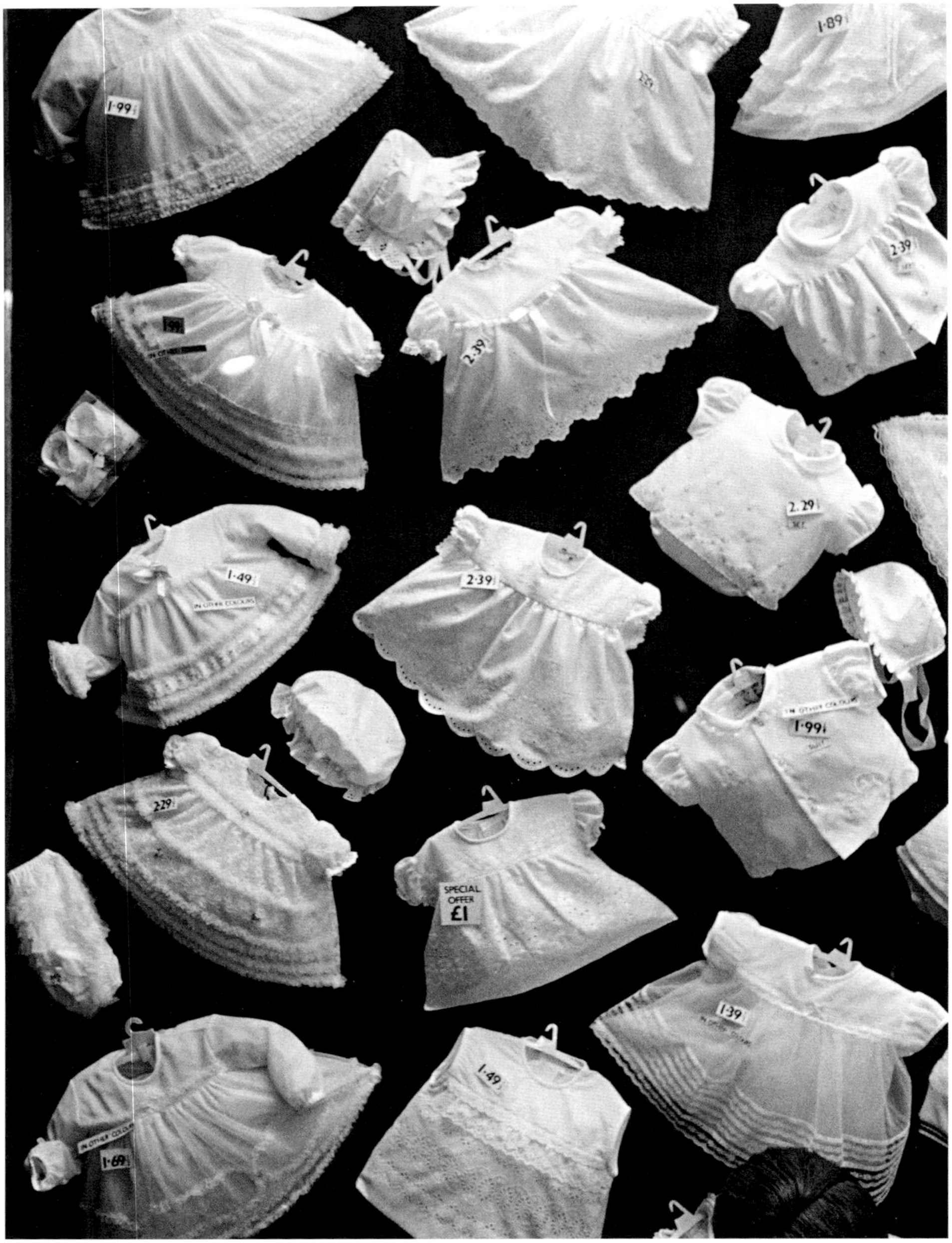
1·99
1·89
2·39
2·39
2·39
2. 29
1·49
IN OTHER COLOURS
2·39
IN OTHER COLOURS
1·99
2·29
SPECIAL
OFFER
£1
1·39
1·49
1·69

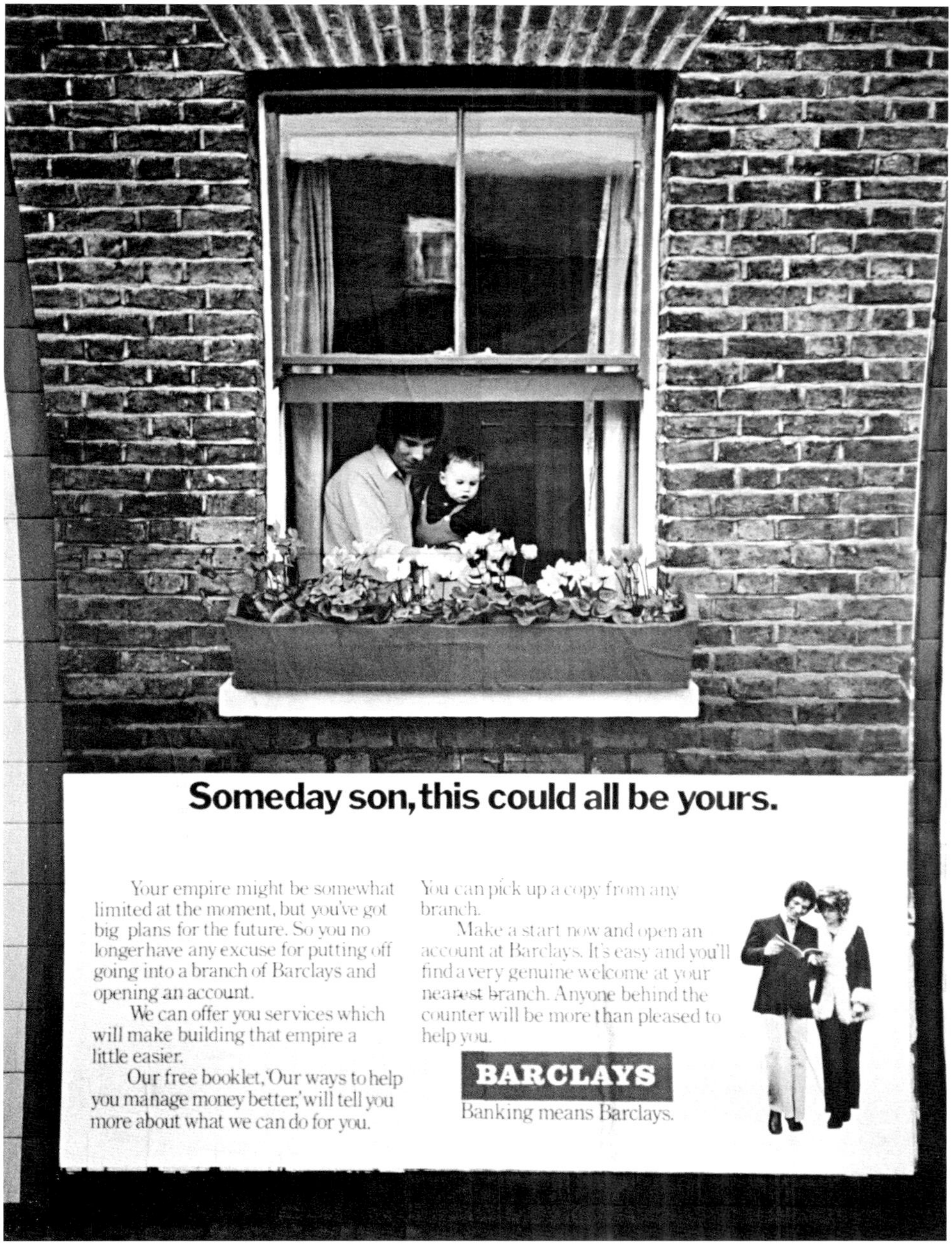
Someday son, this could all be yours.
Your empire might be somewhat limited at the moment, but you've got big plans for the future. So you no longer have any excuse for putting off going into a branch of Barclays and opening an account.
We can offer you services which will make building that empire a little easier.
Our free booklet, 'Our ways to help you manage money better,' will tell you more about what we can do for you.
You can pick up a copy from any branch.
Make a start now and open an account at Barclays. It's easy and you'll find a very genuine welcome at your nearest branch. Anyone behind the counter will be more than pleased to help you.
BARCLAYS
Banking means Barclays.

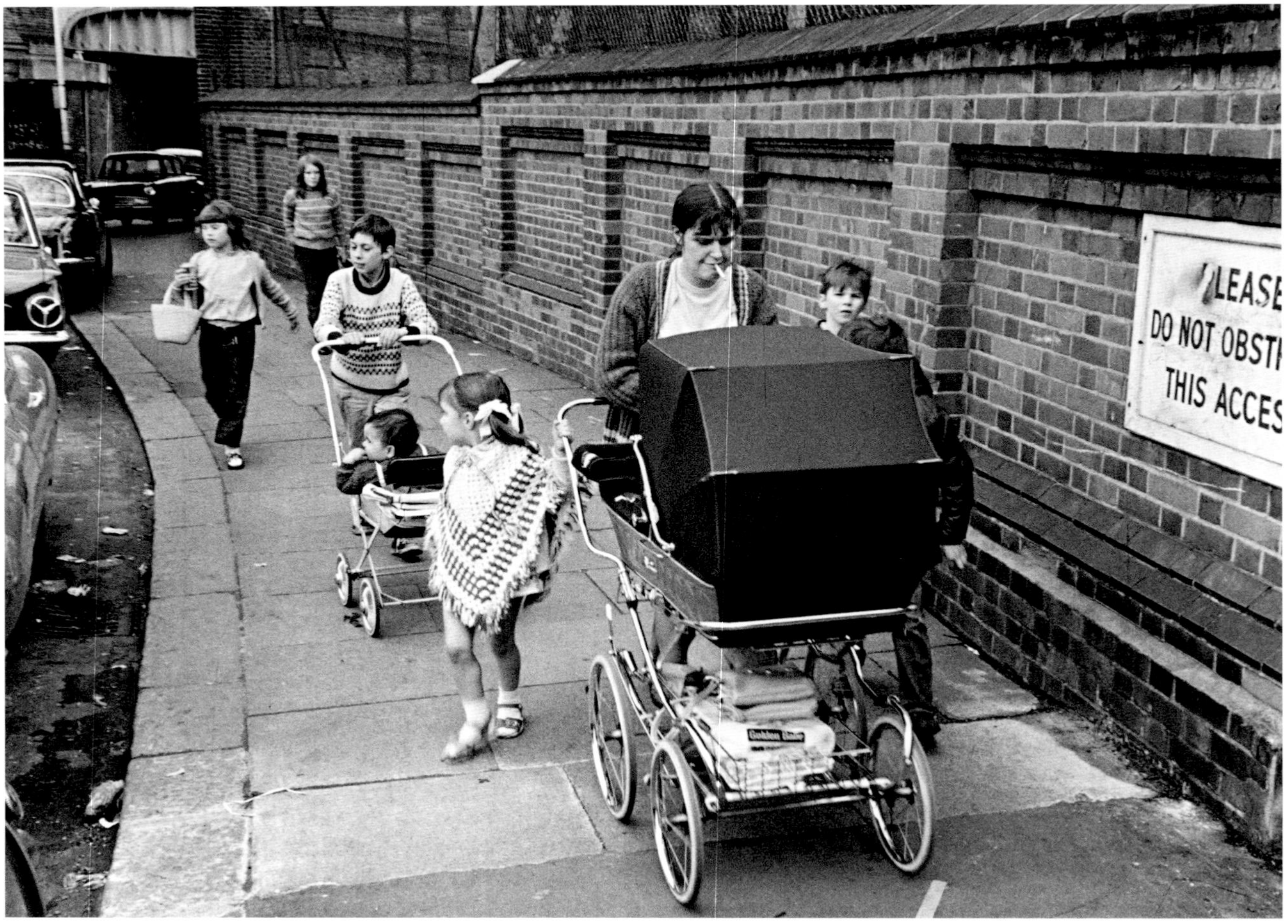
LEASE
DO NOT OBST
THIS ACCES

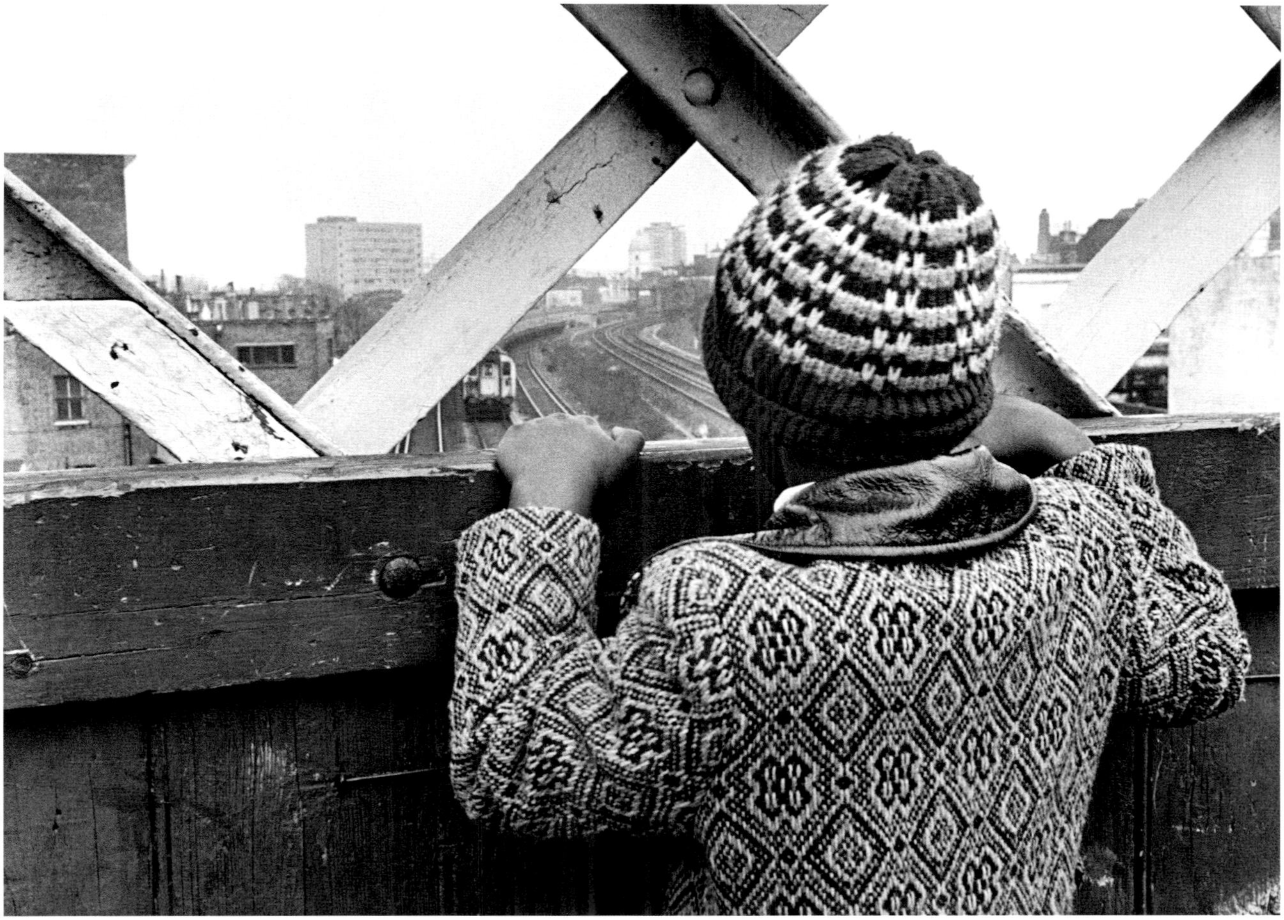

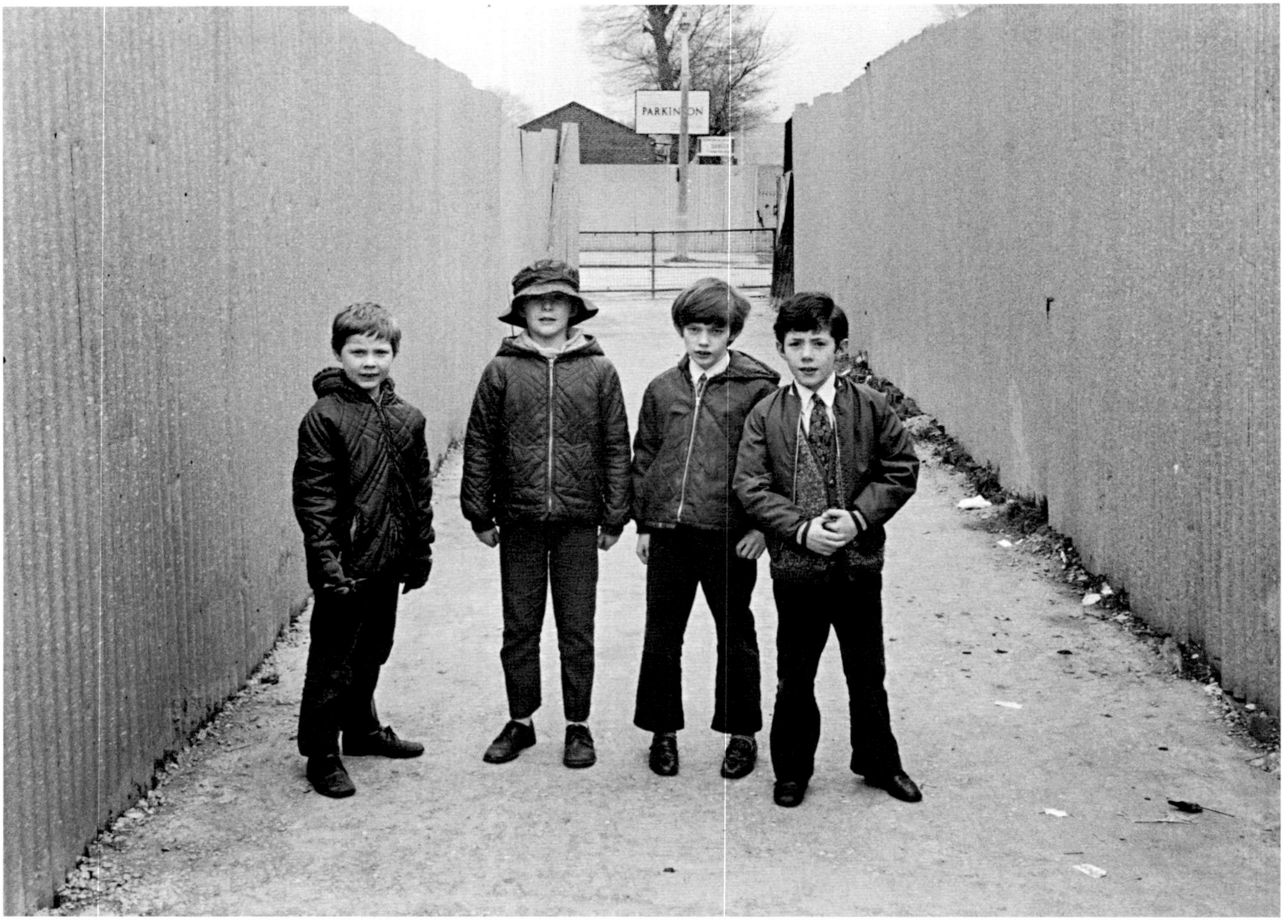

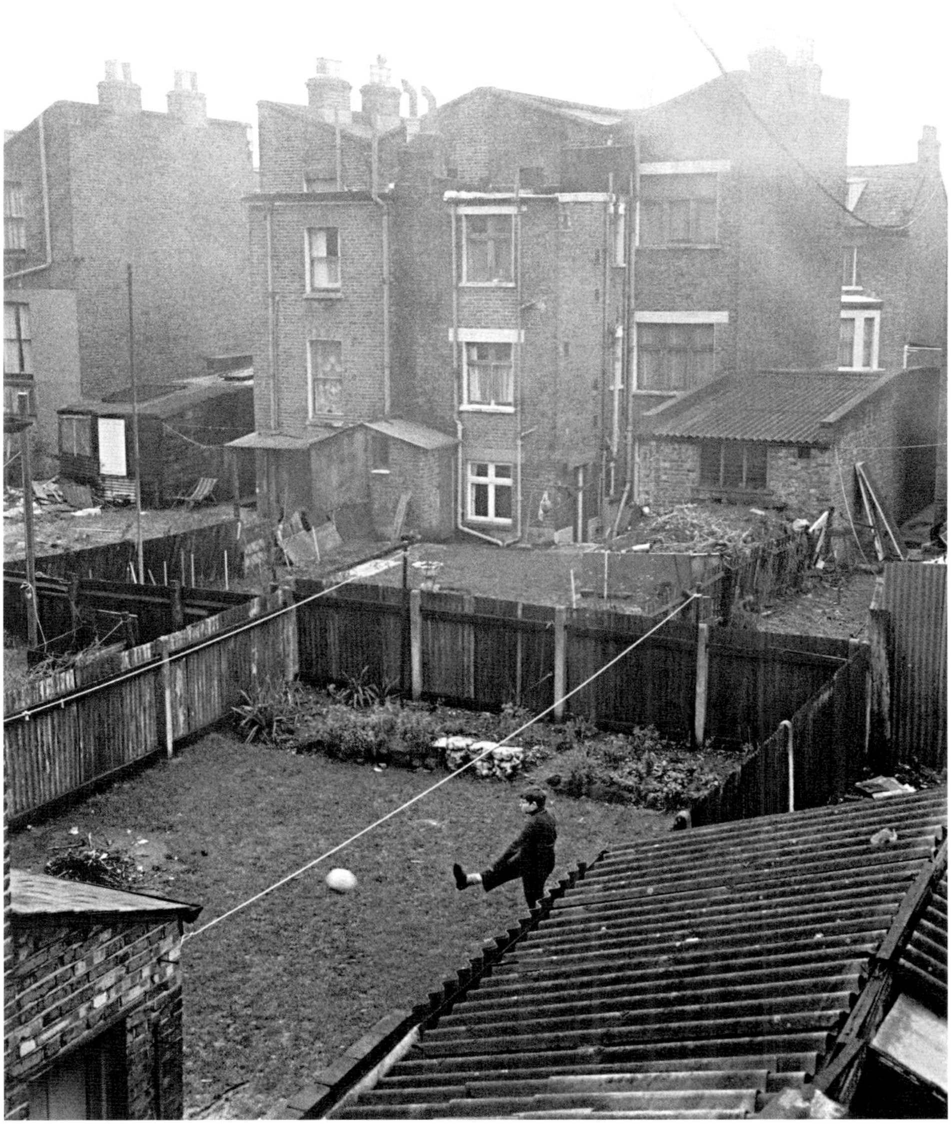

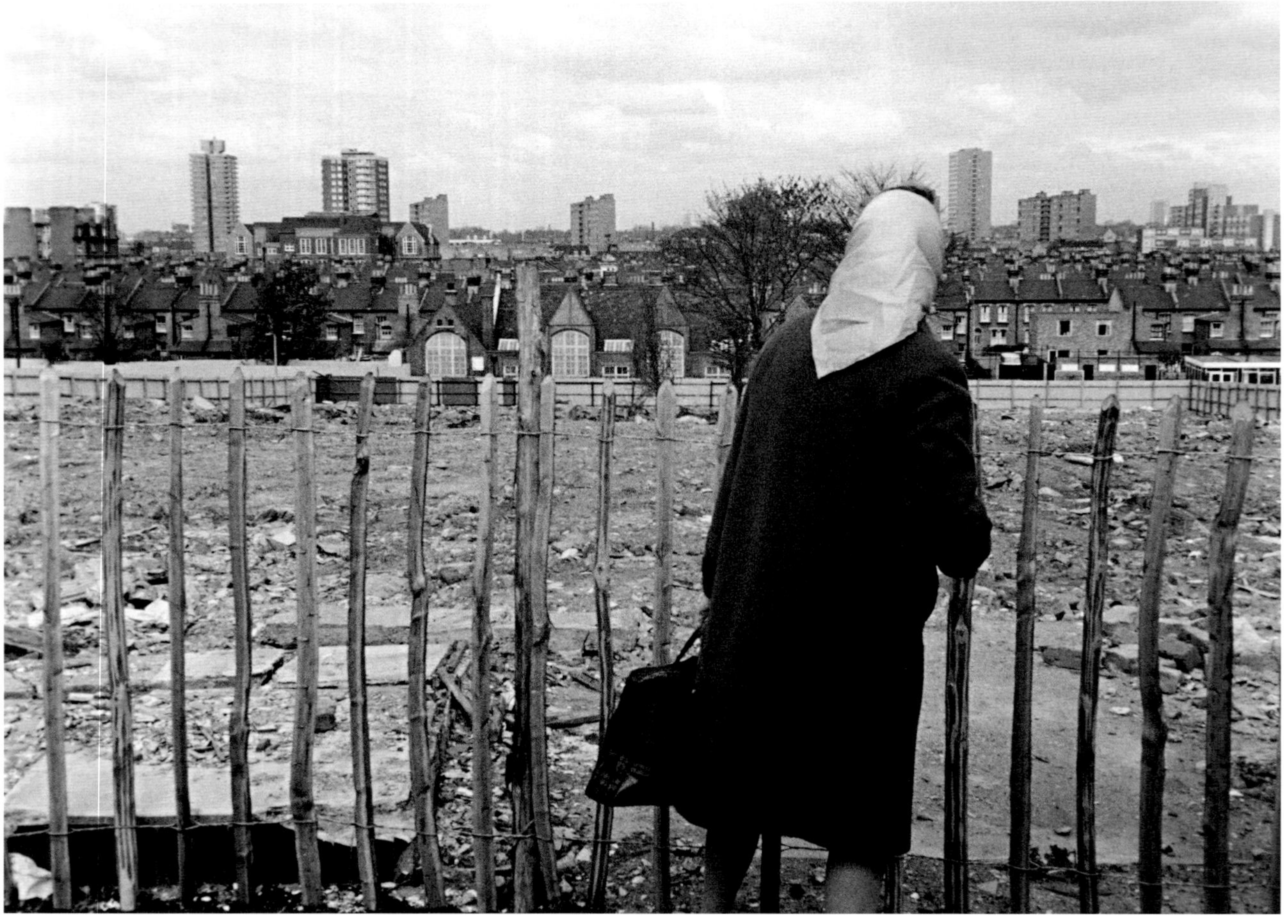

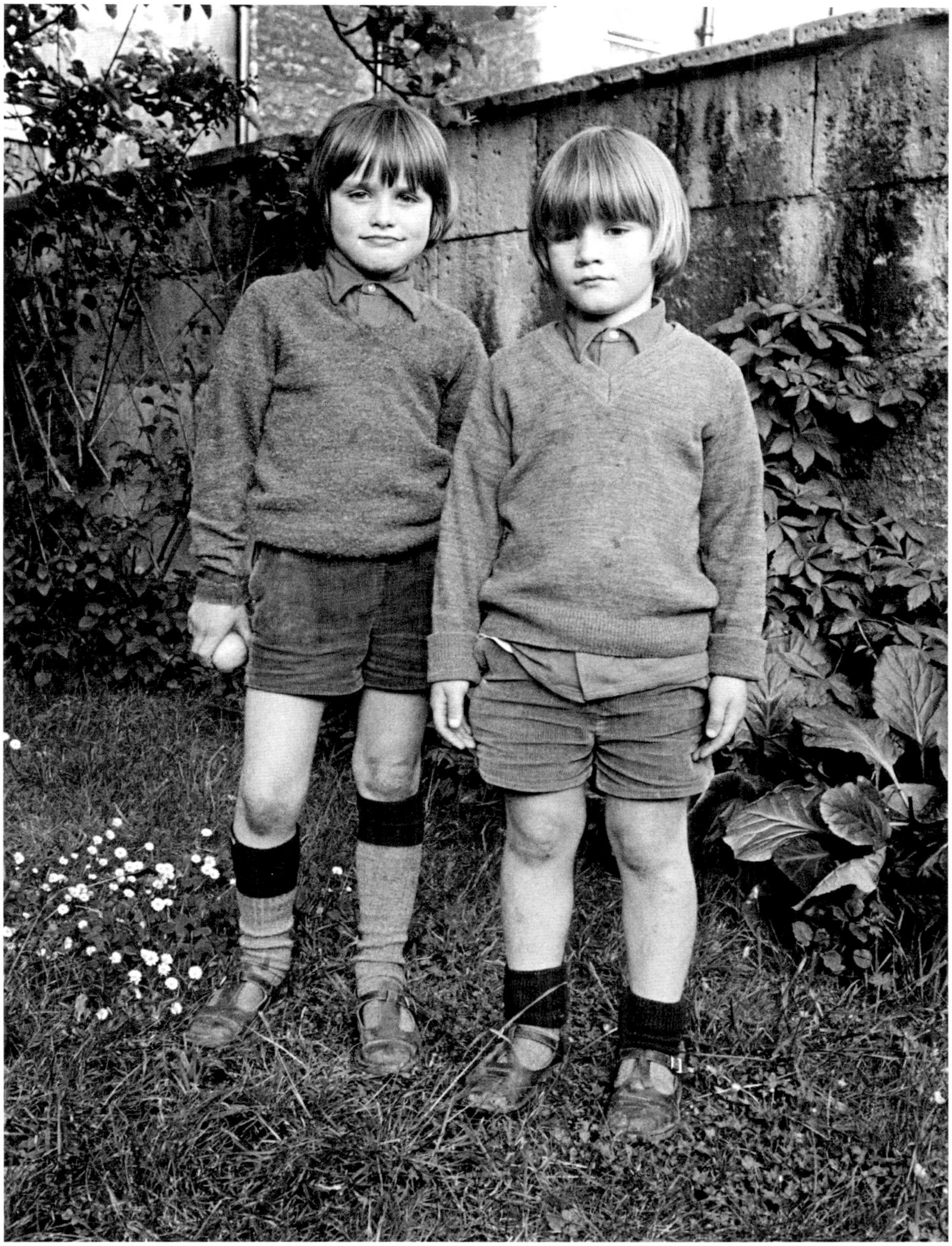

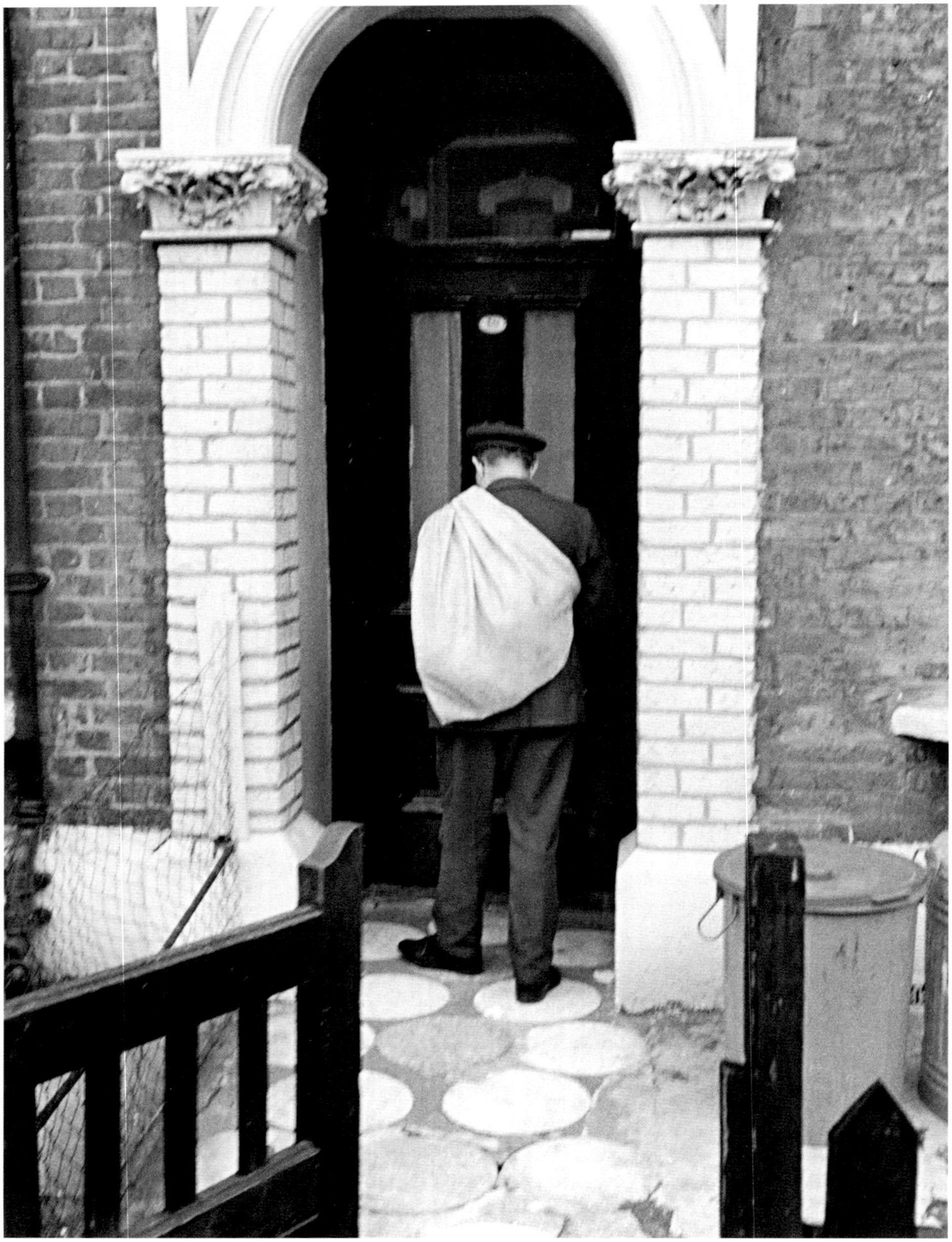

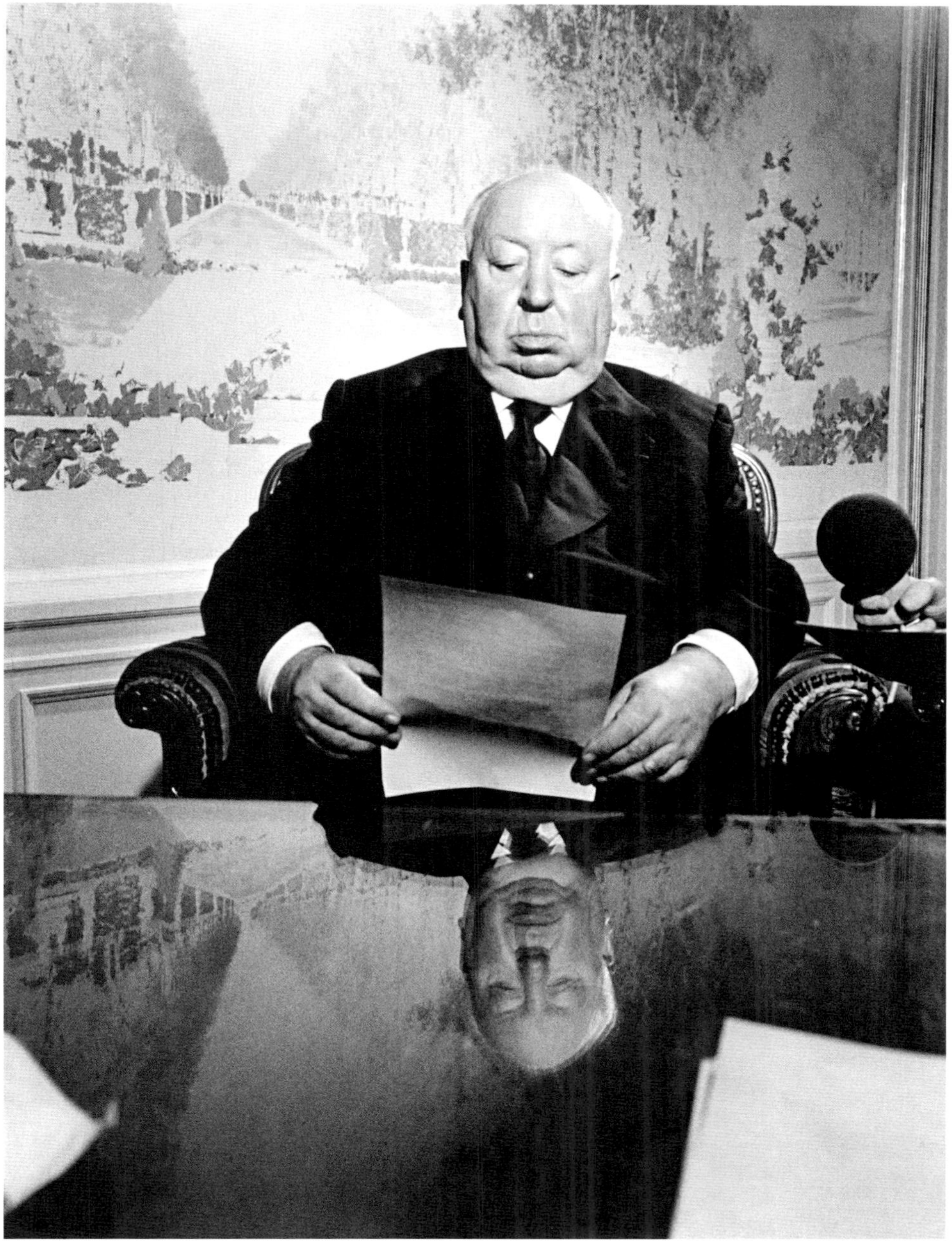

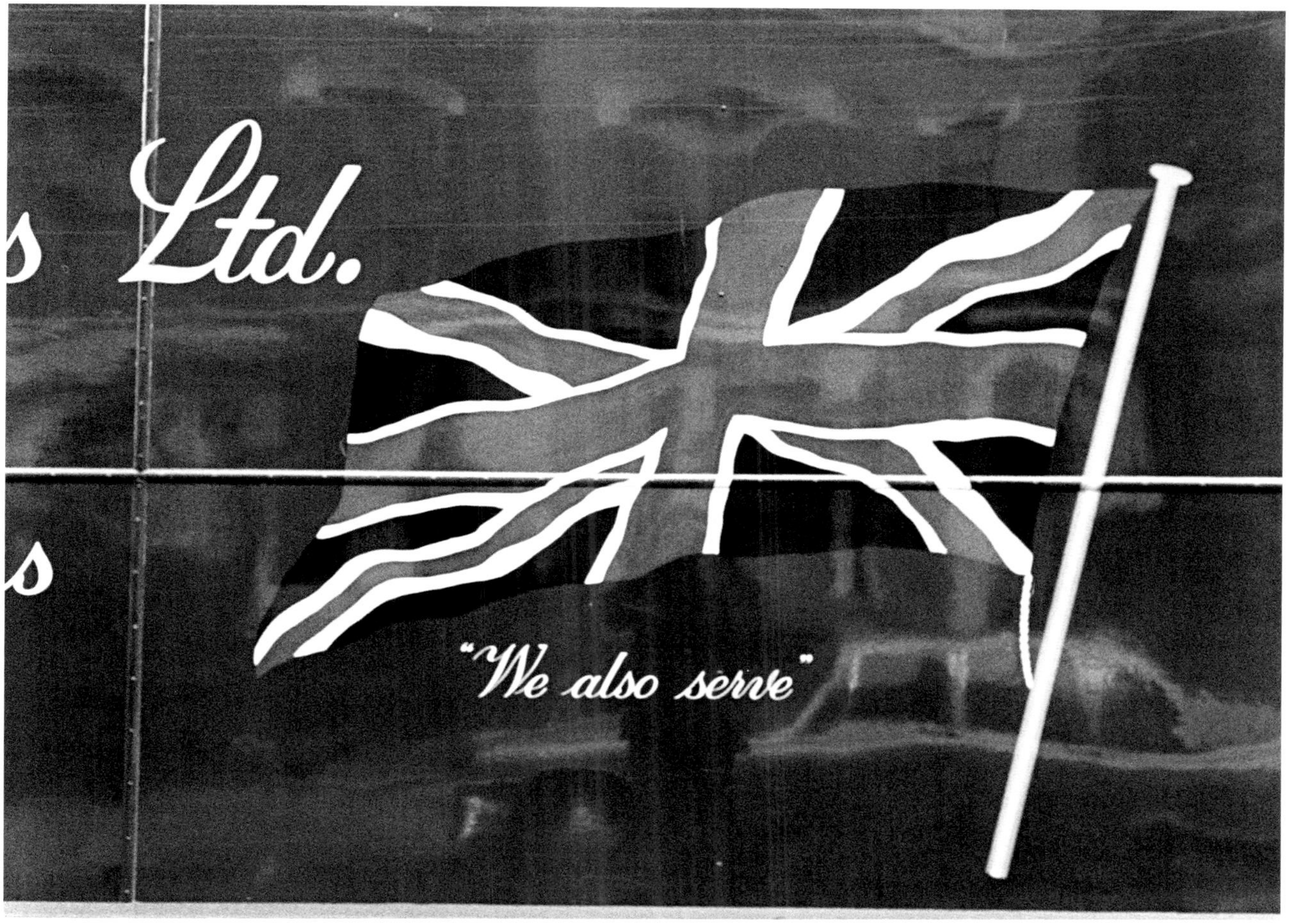
s Ltd.
s
"We also serve"

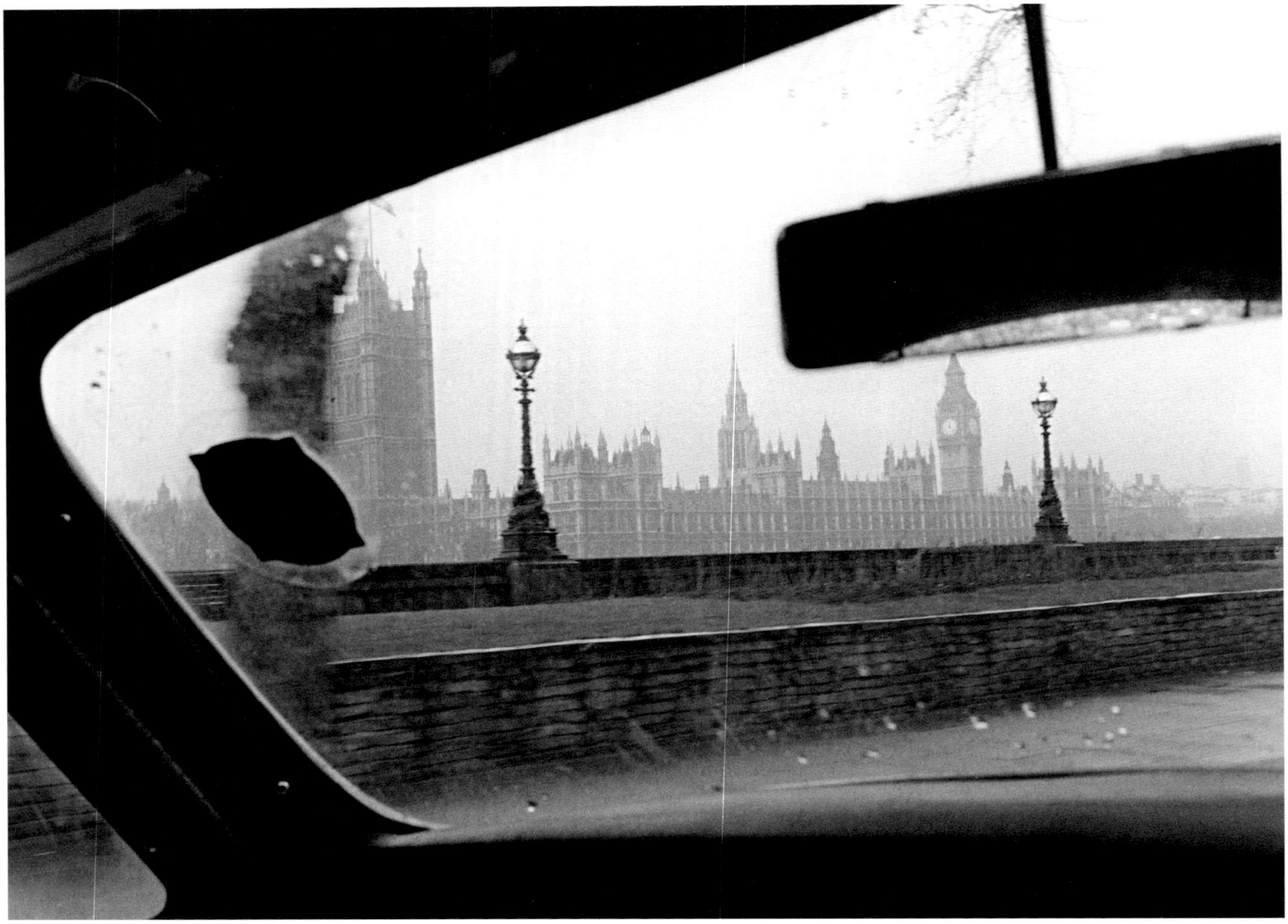

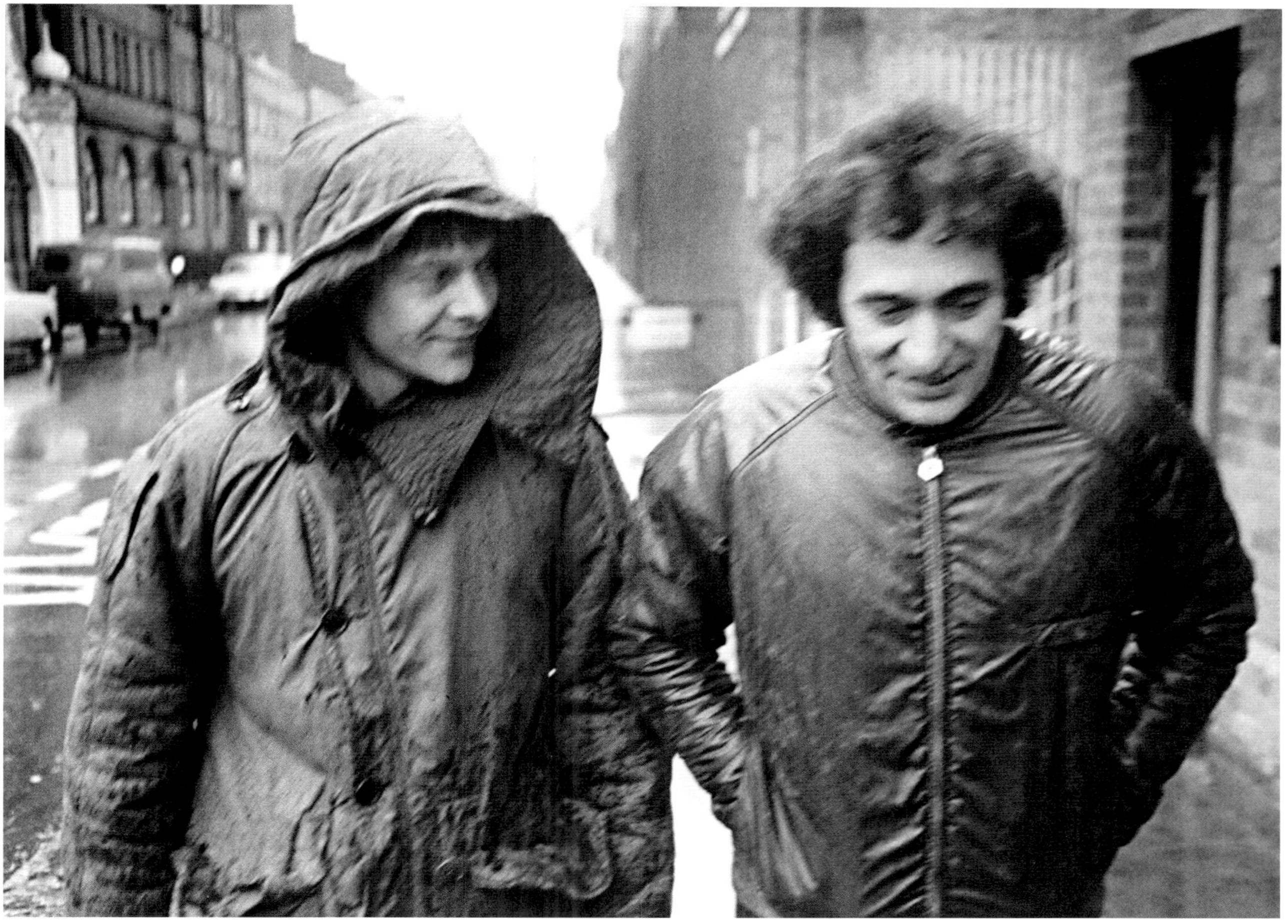

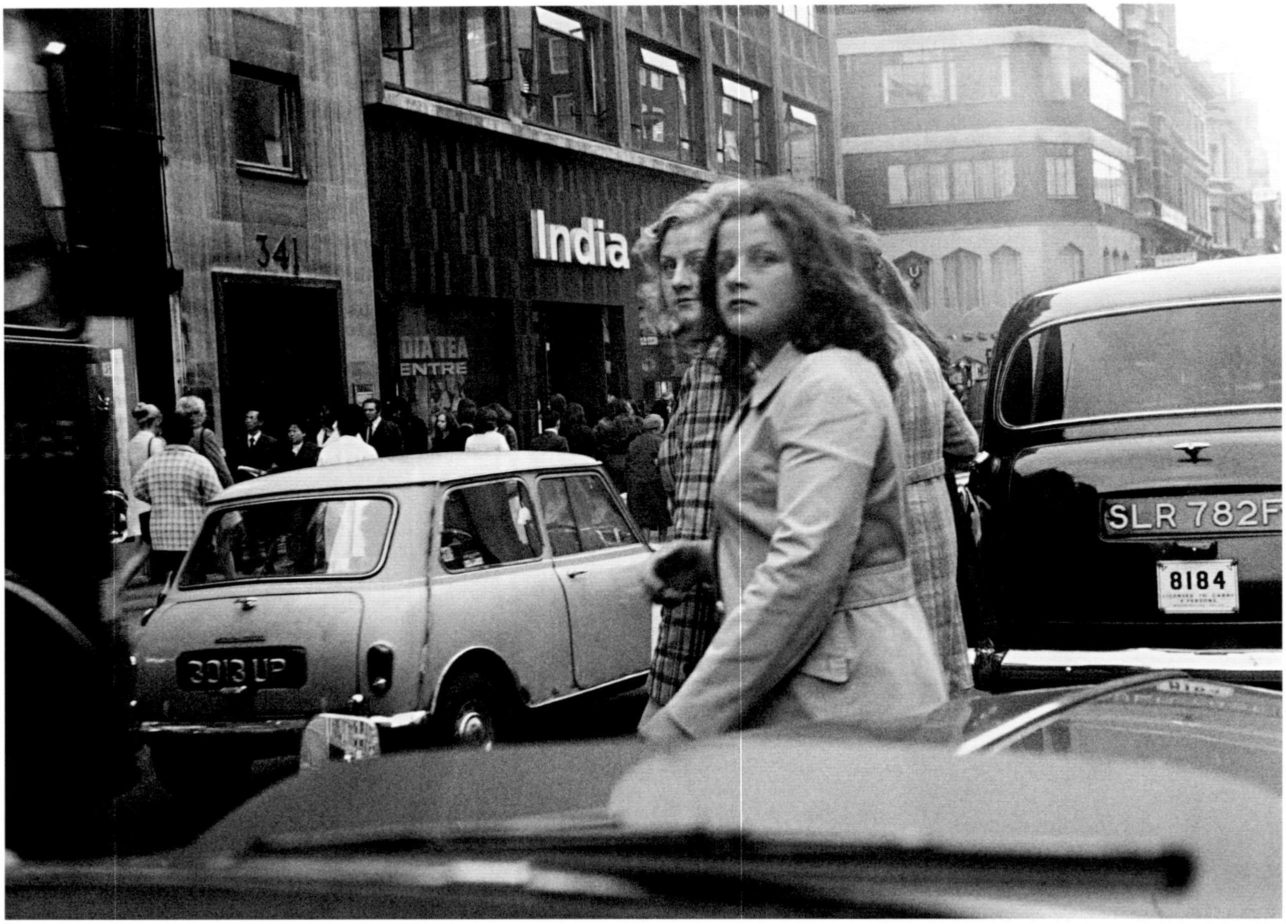
341
India
DIA TEA
ENTRE
3013 UP
SLR 782F
8184

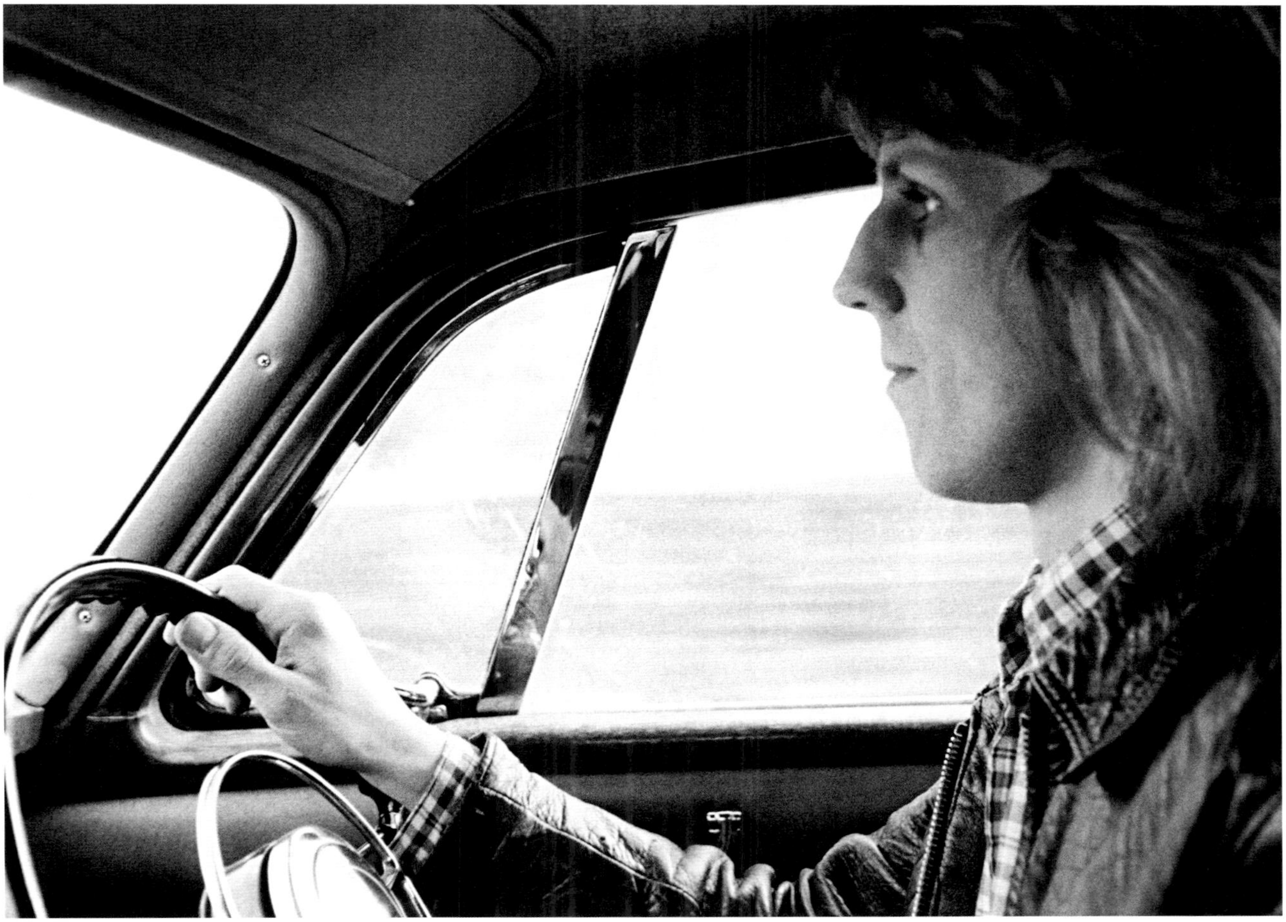

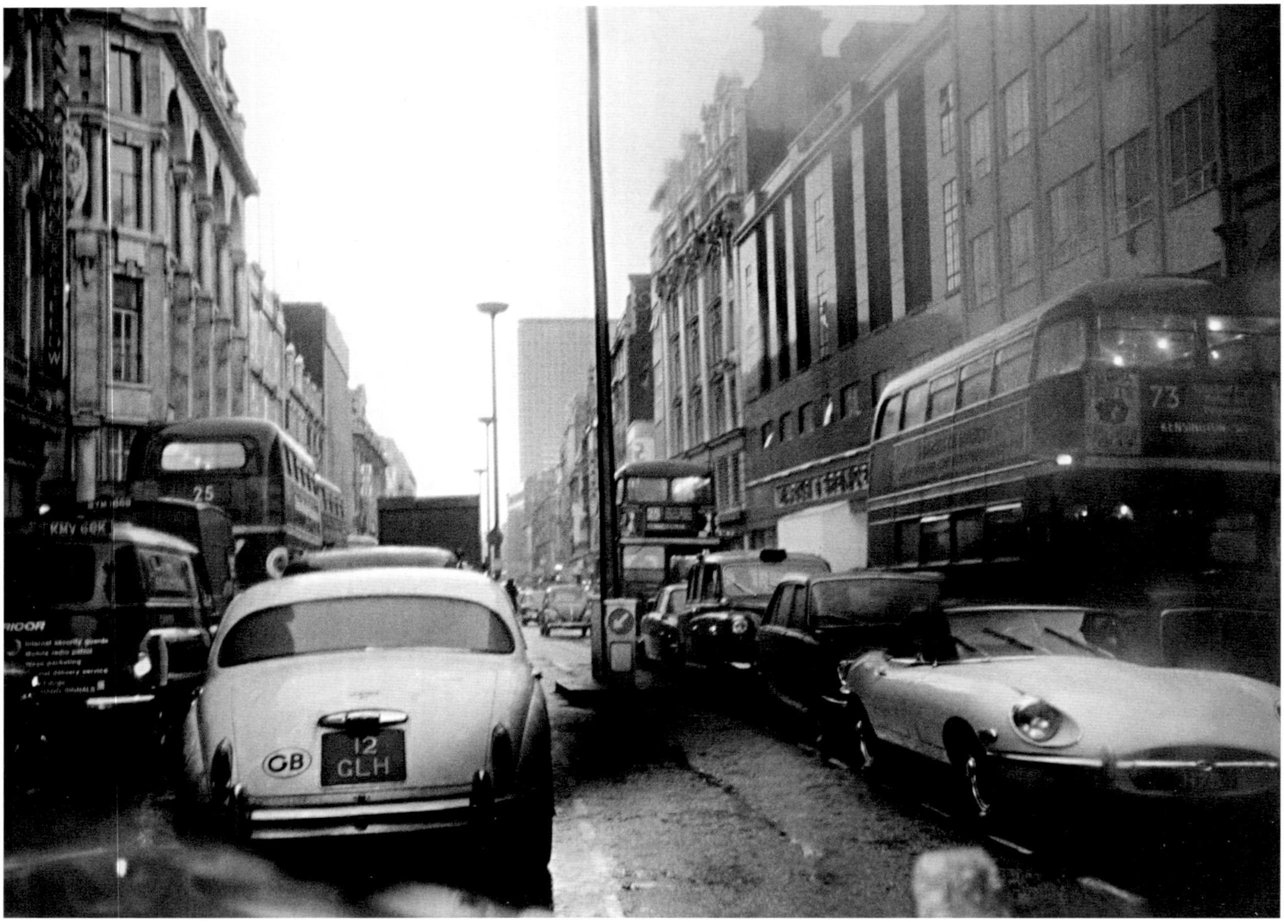
25
73
GB
12
GLH

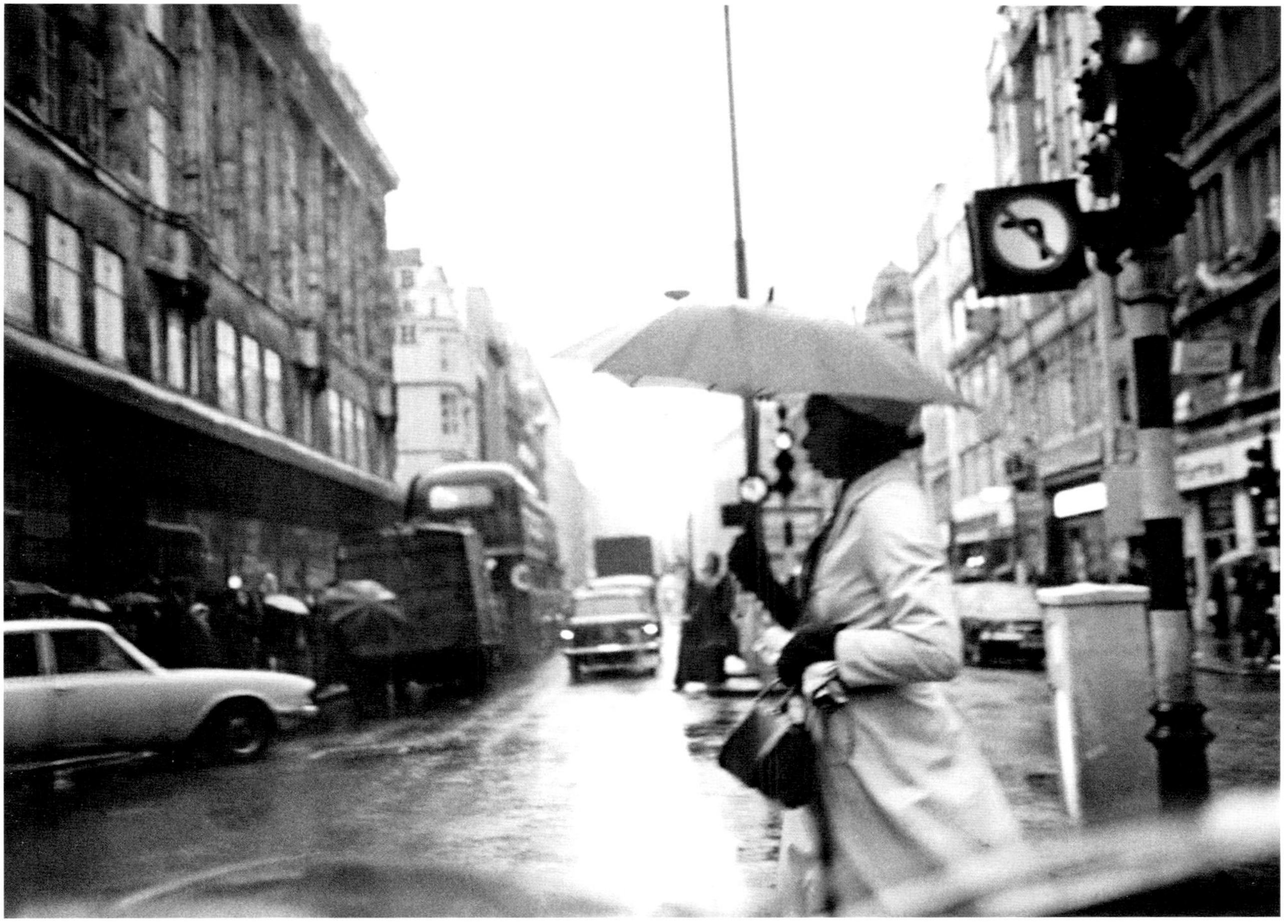

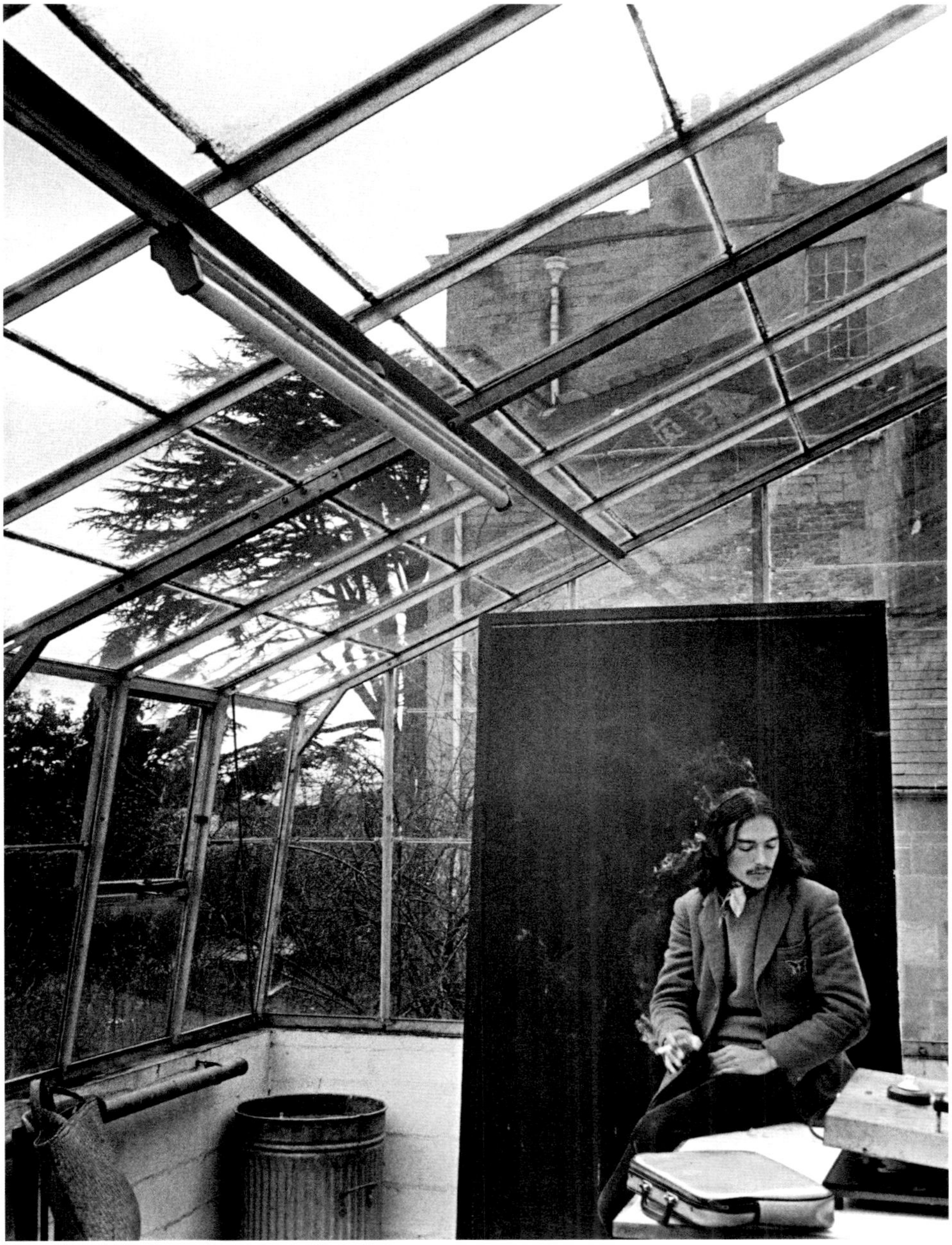

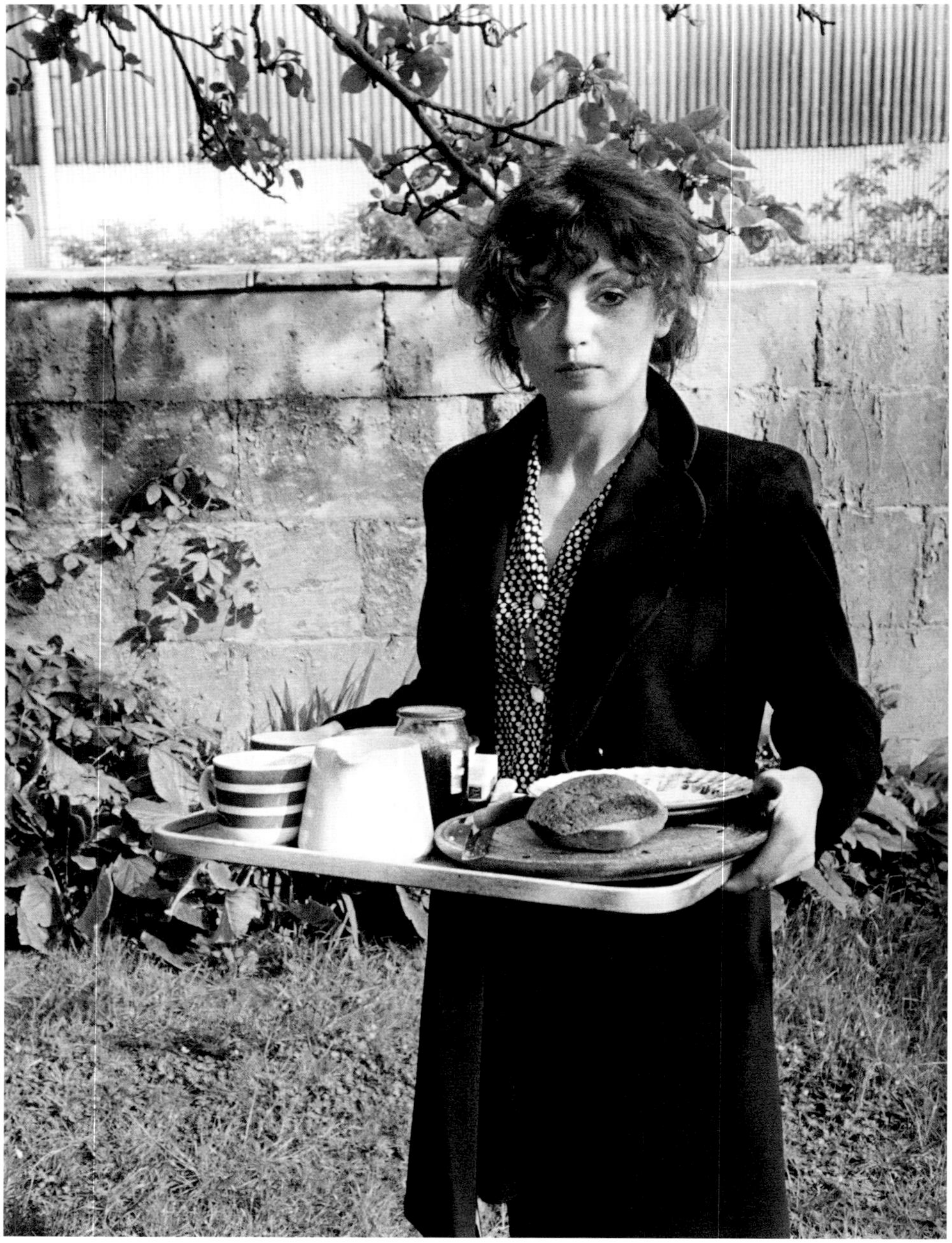

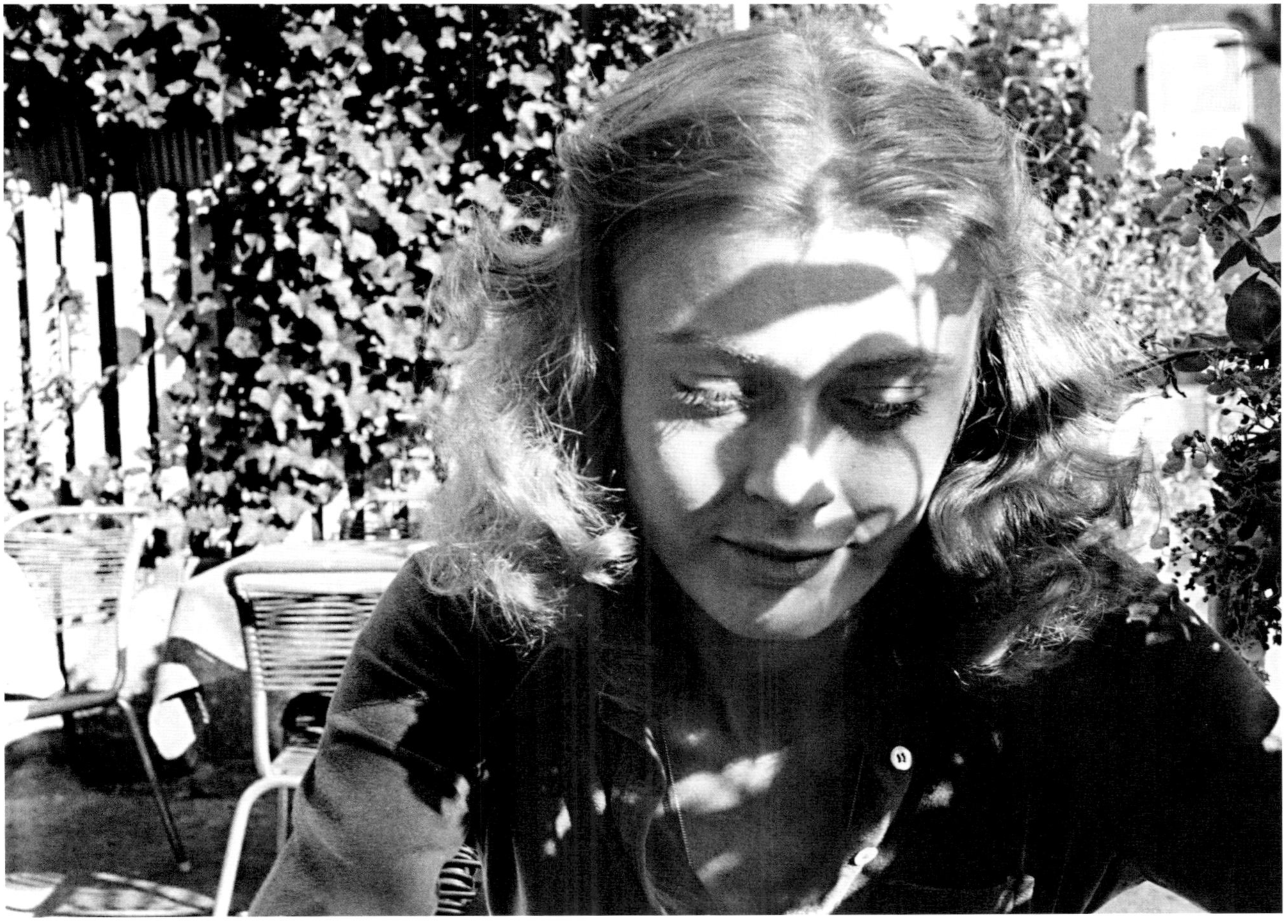

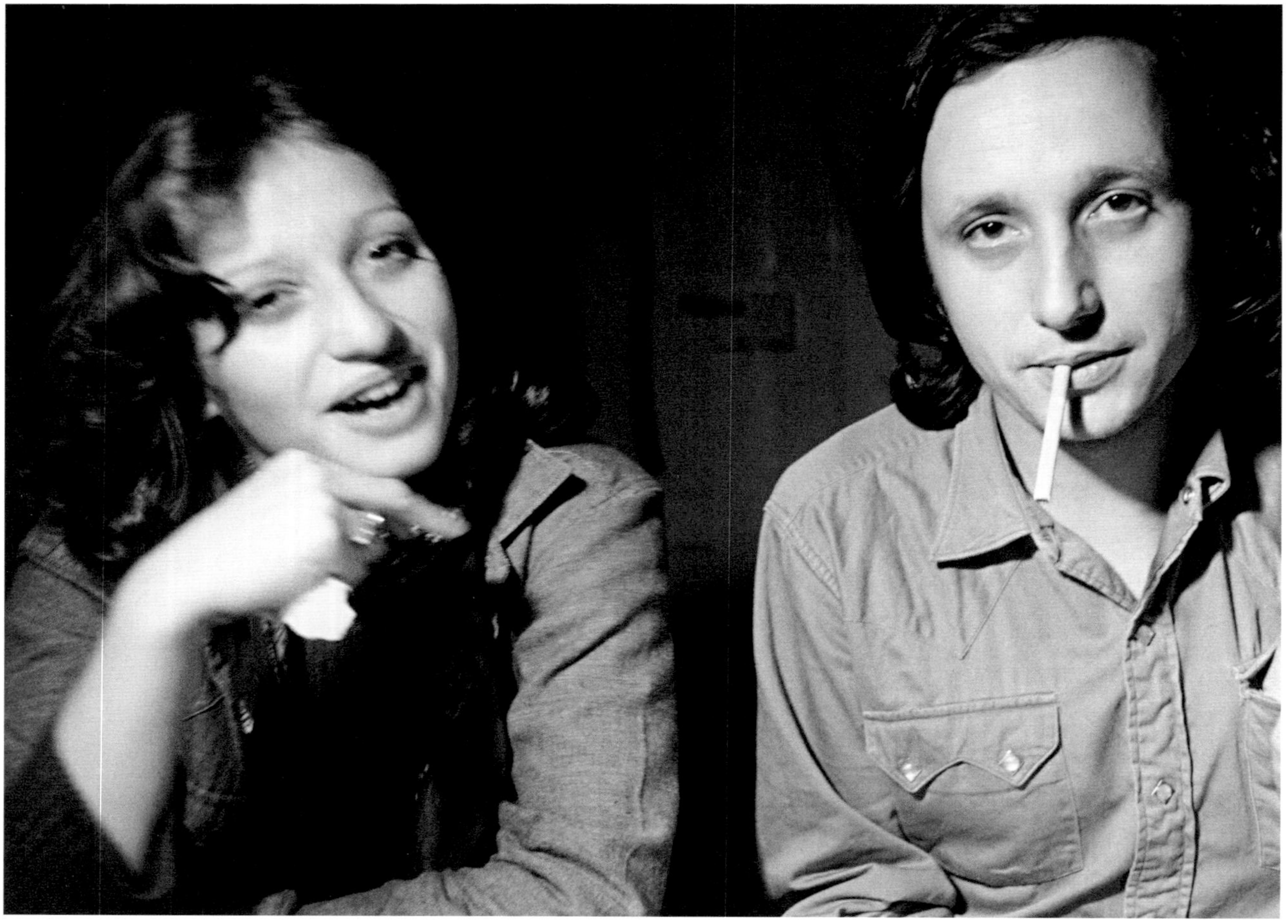

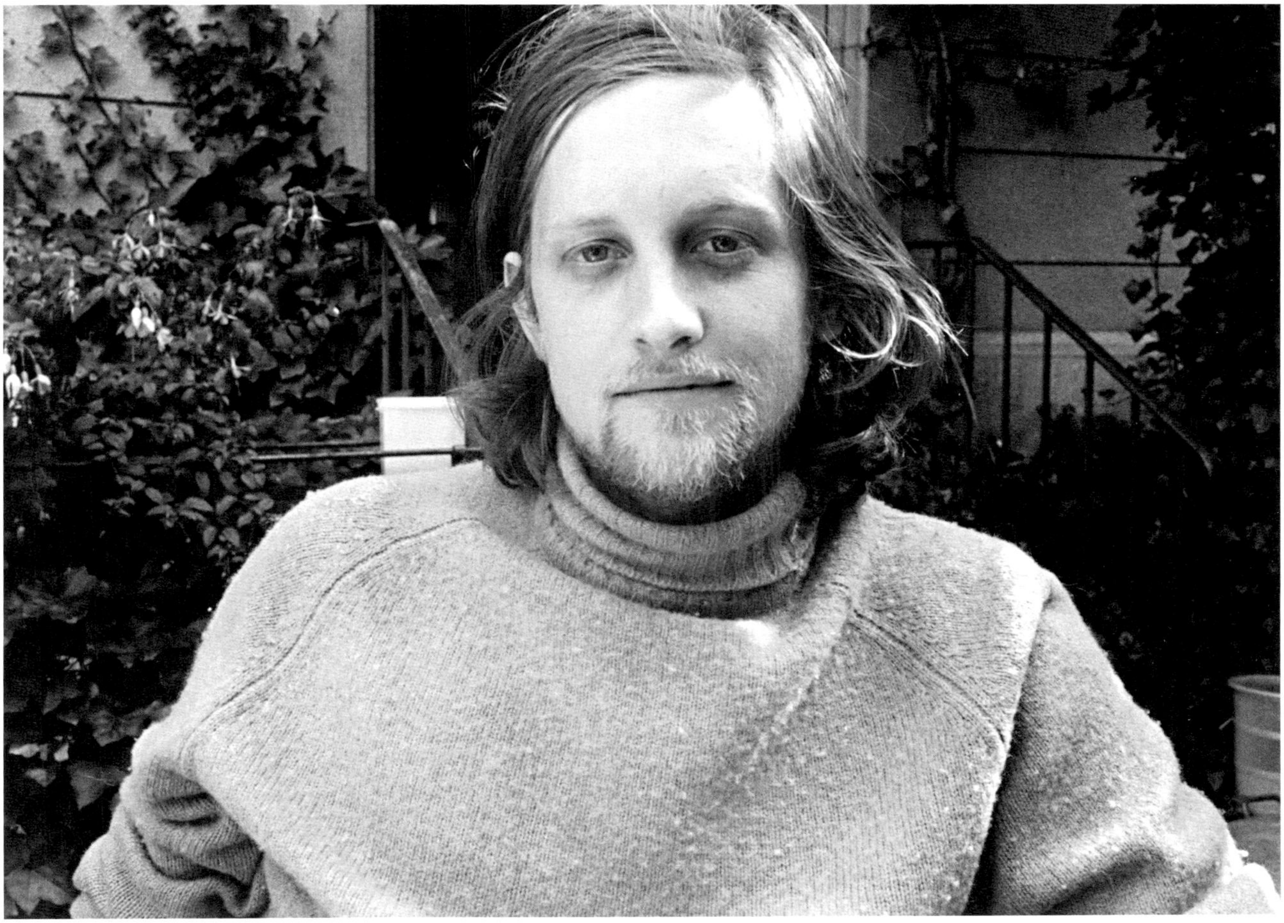

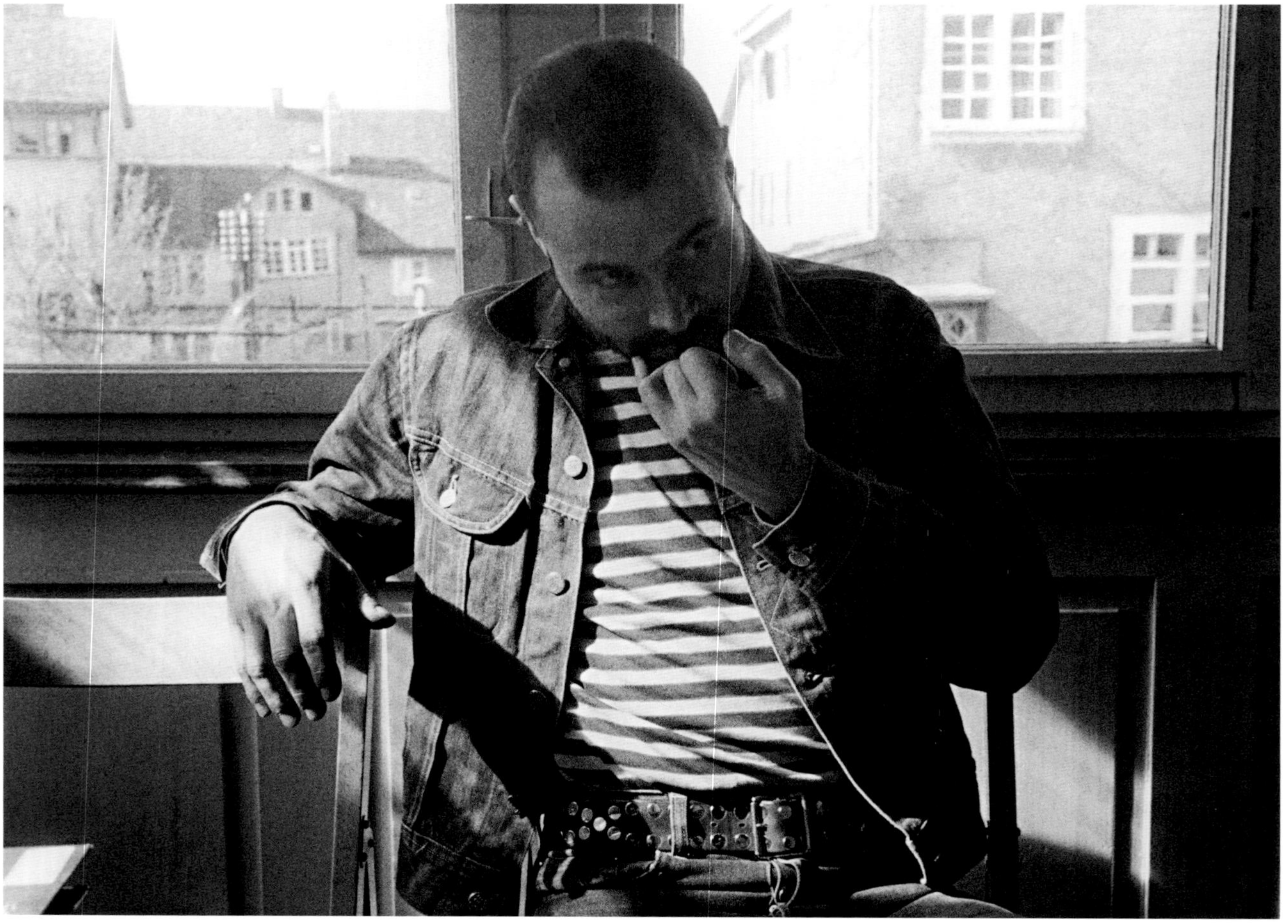

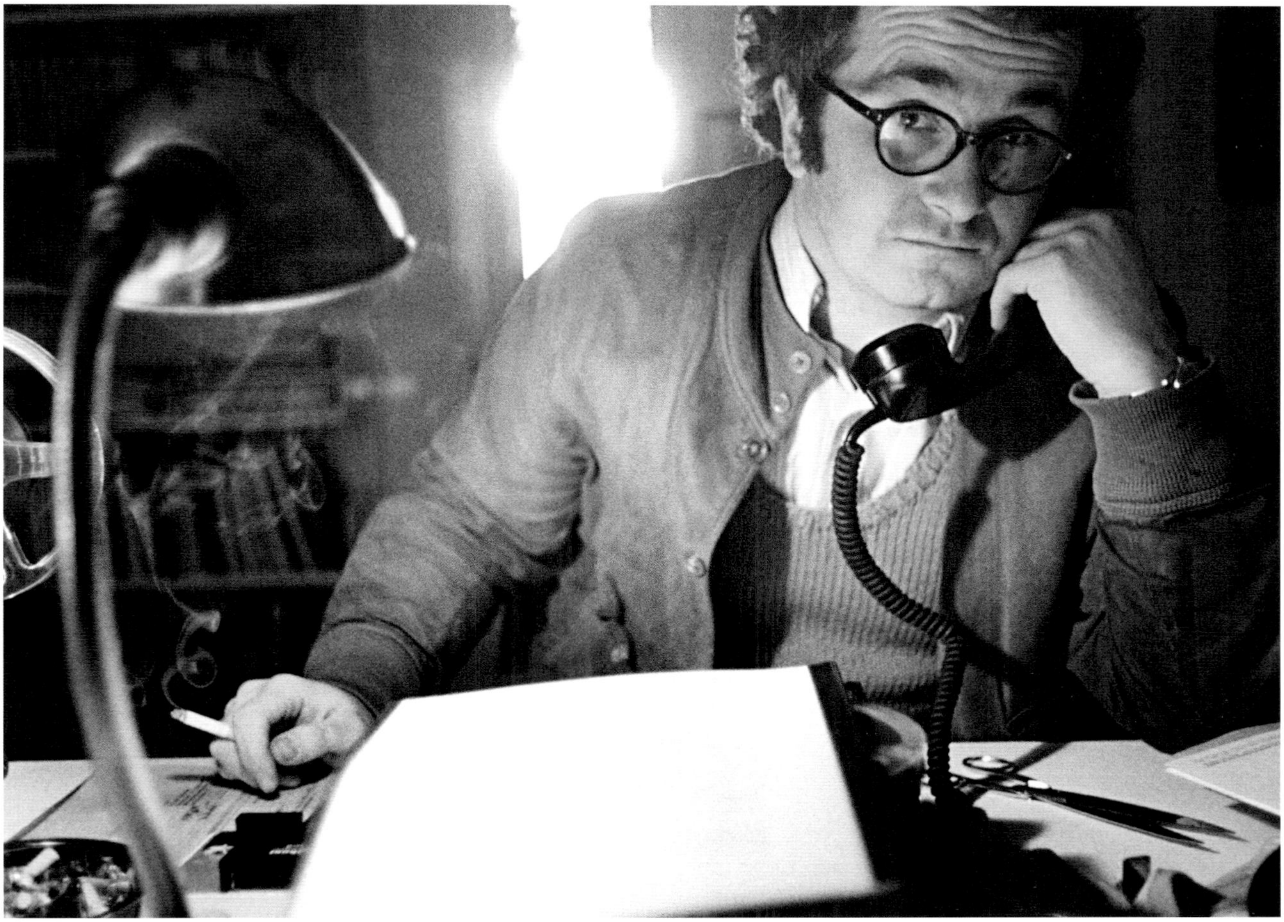

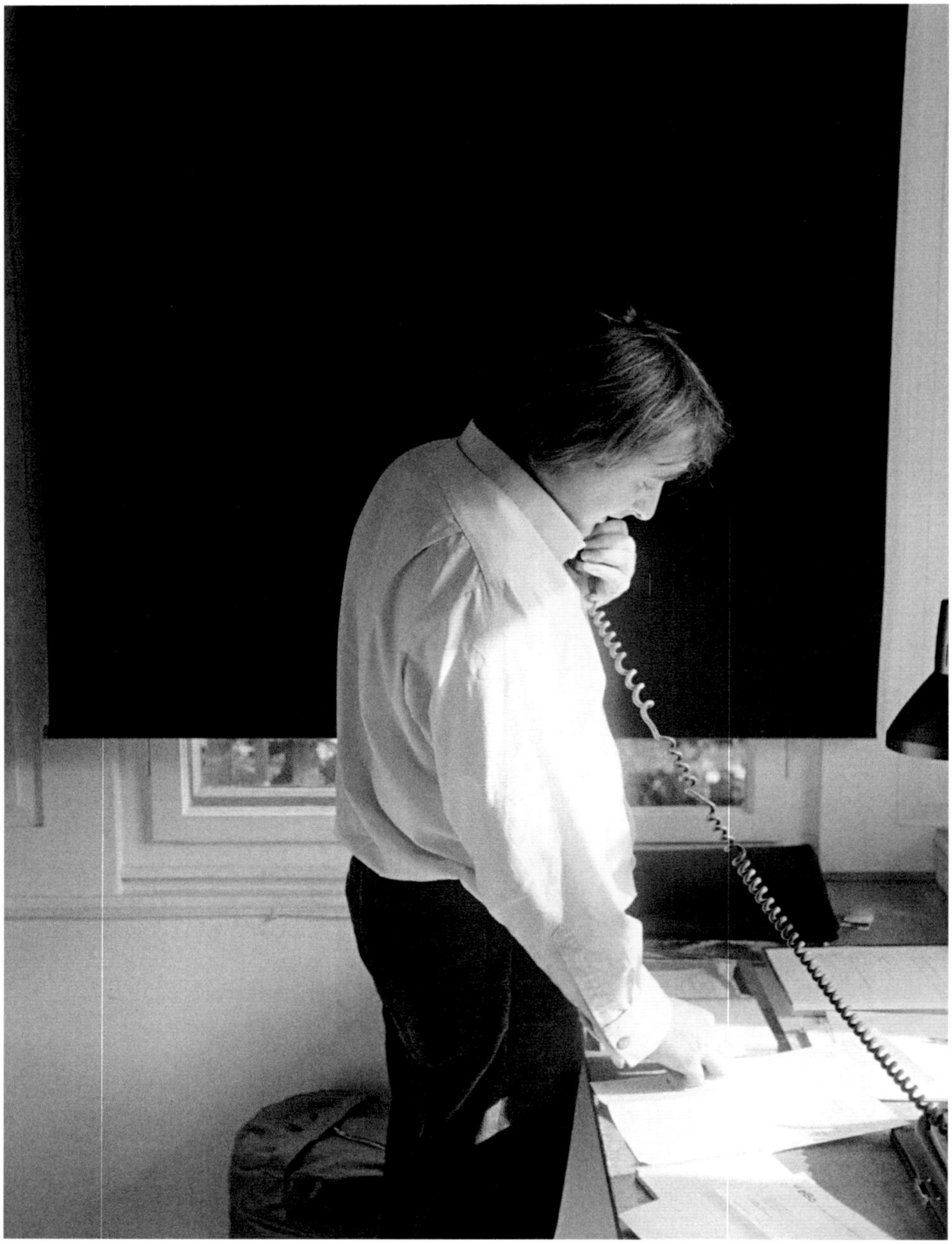

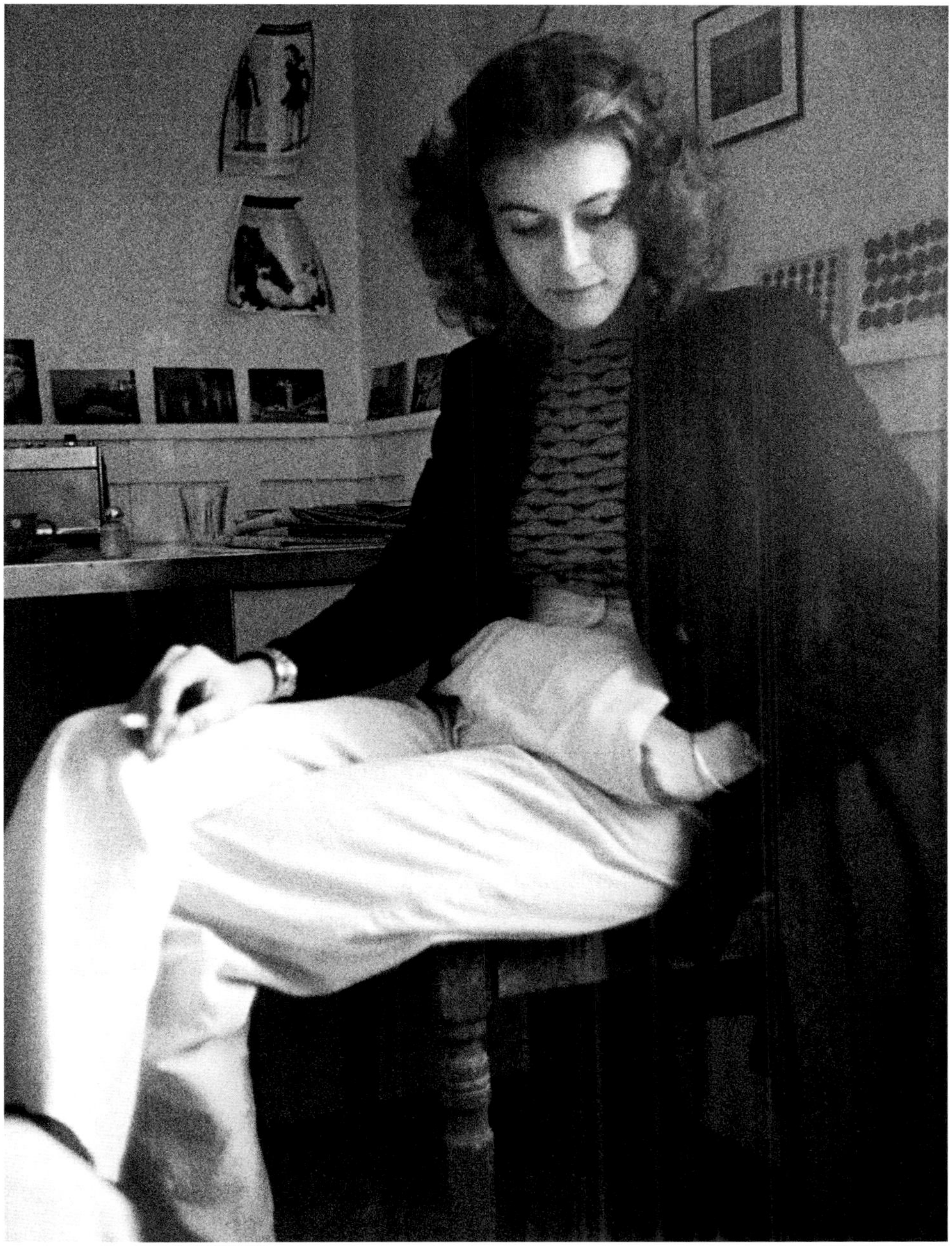

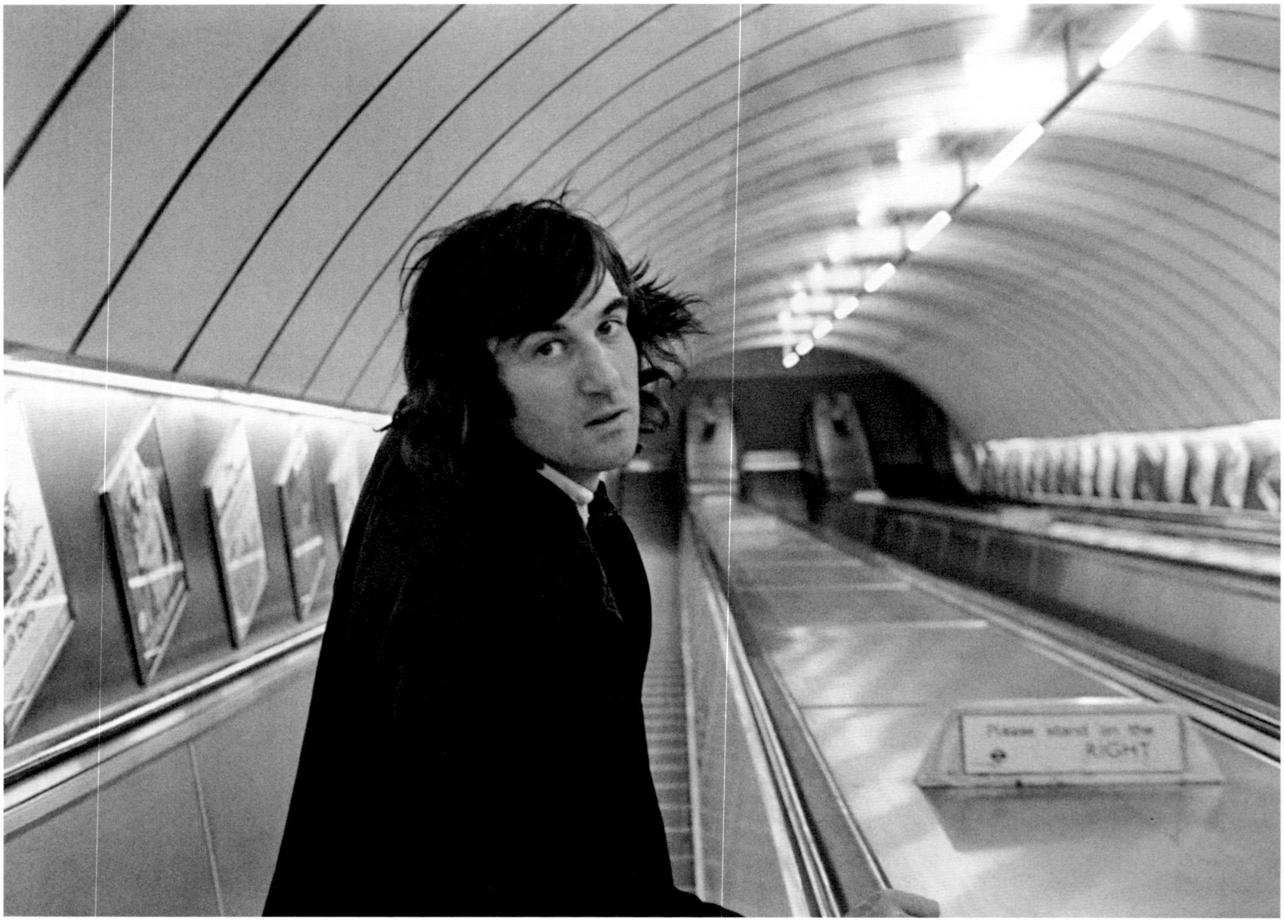
Please stand on the
RIGHT

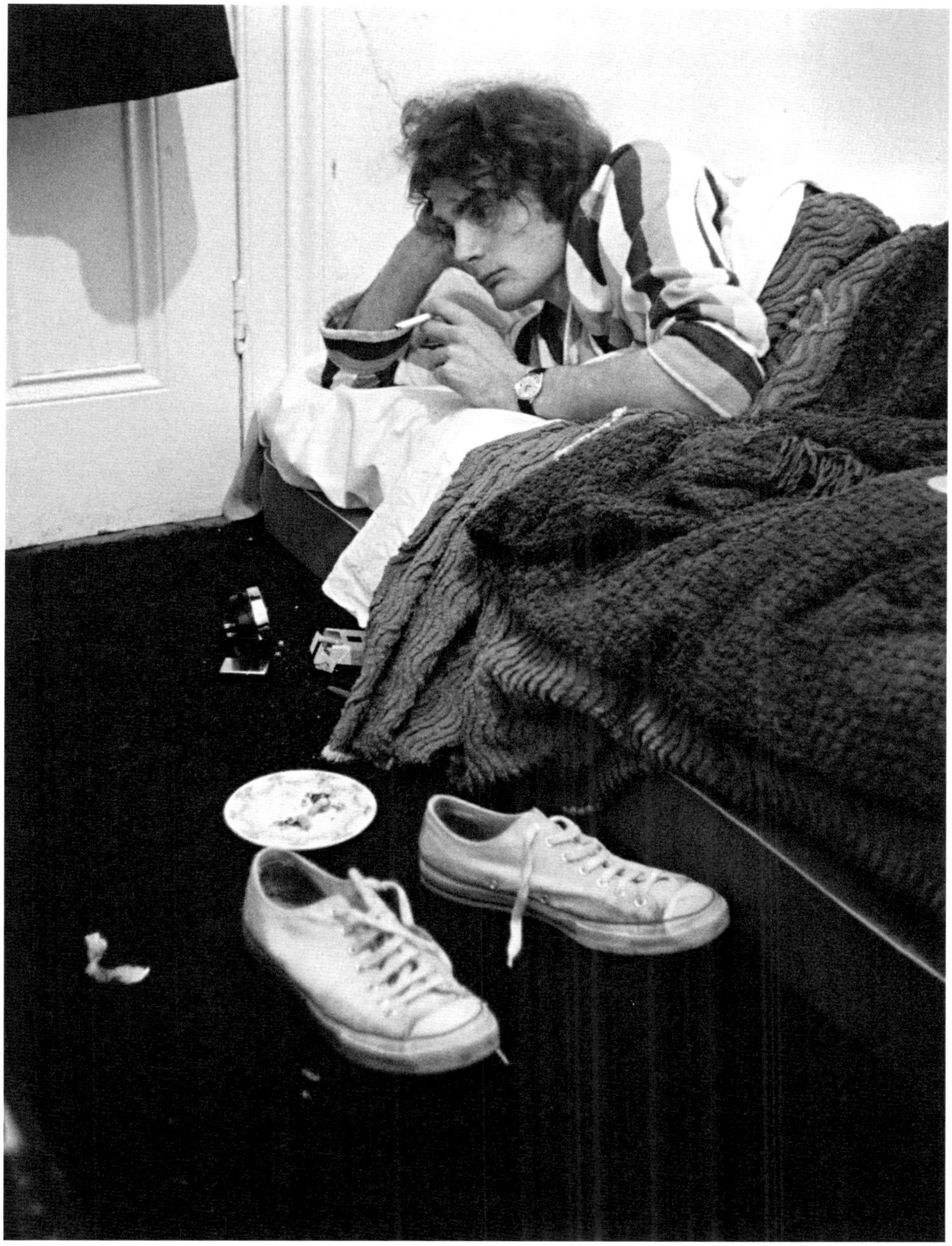

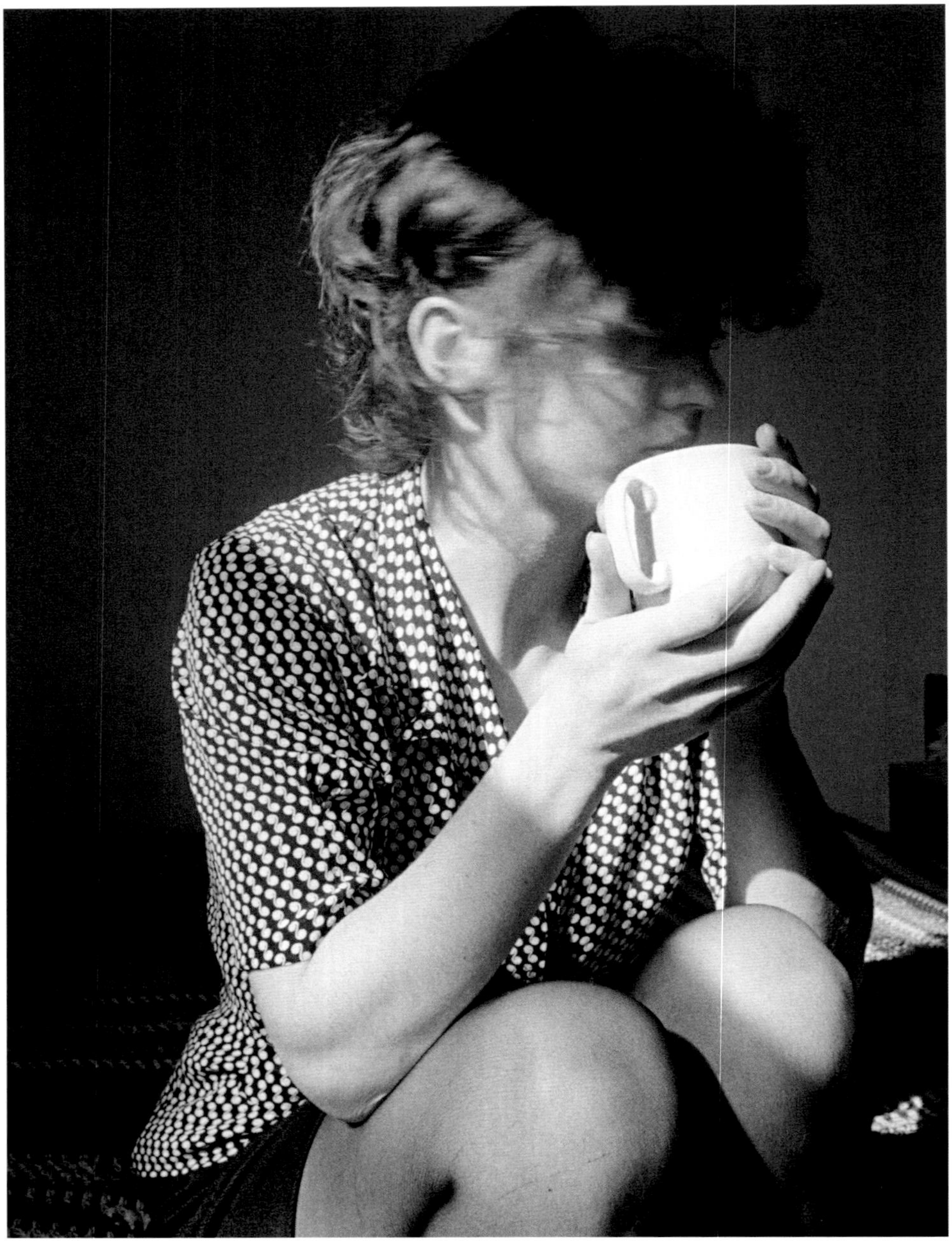

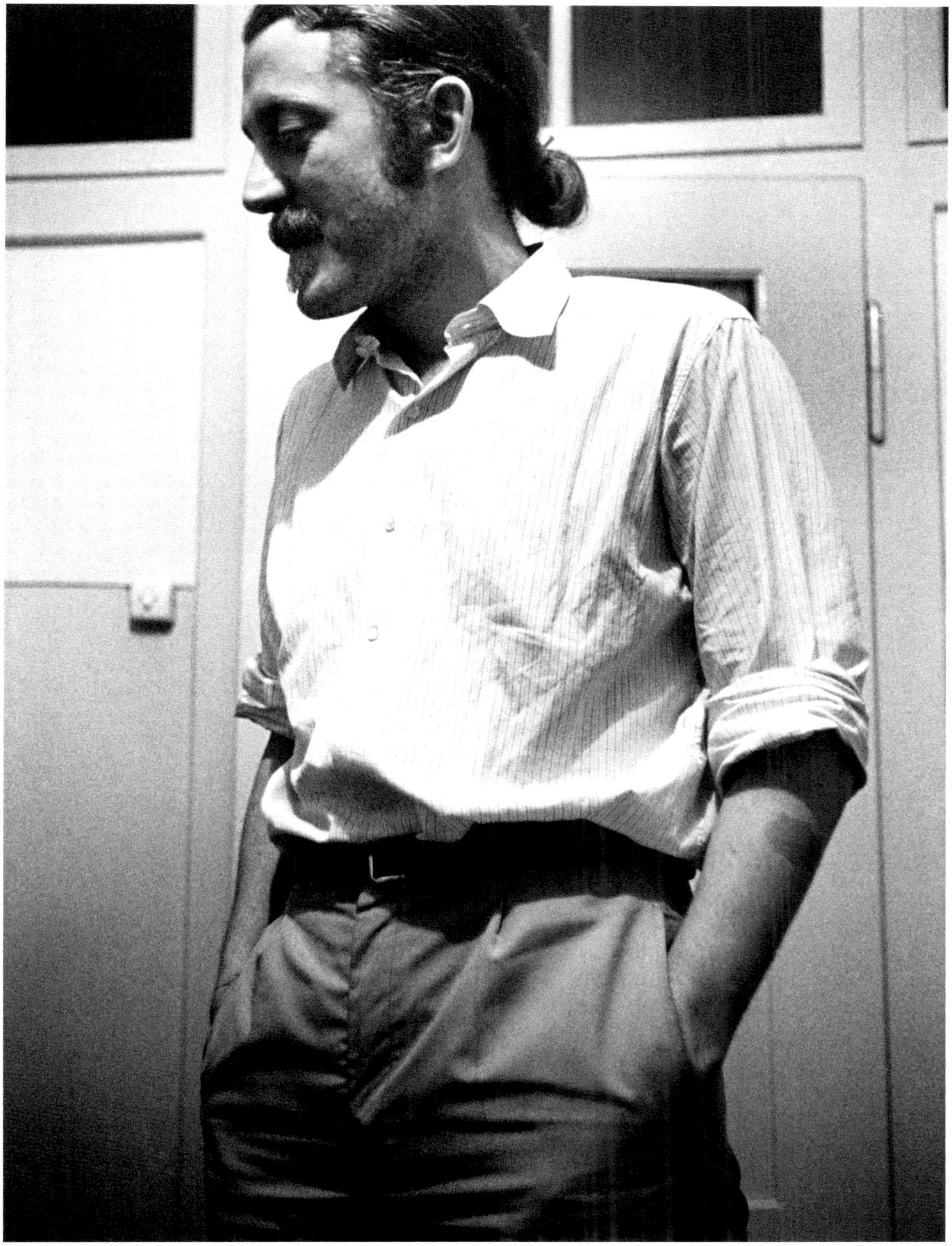

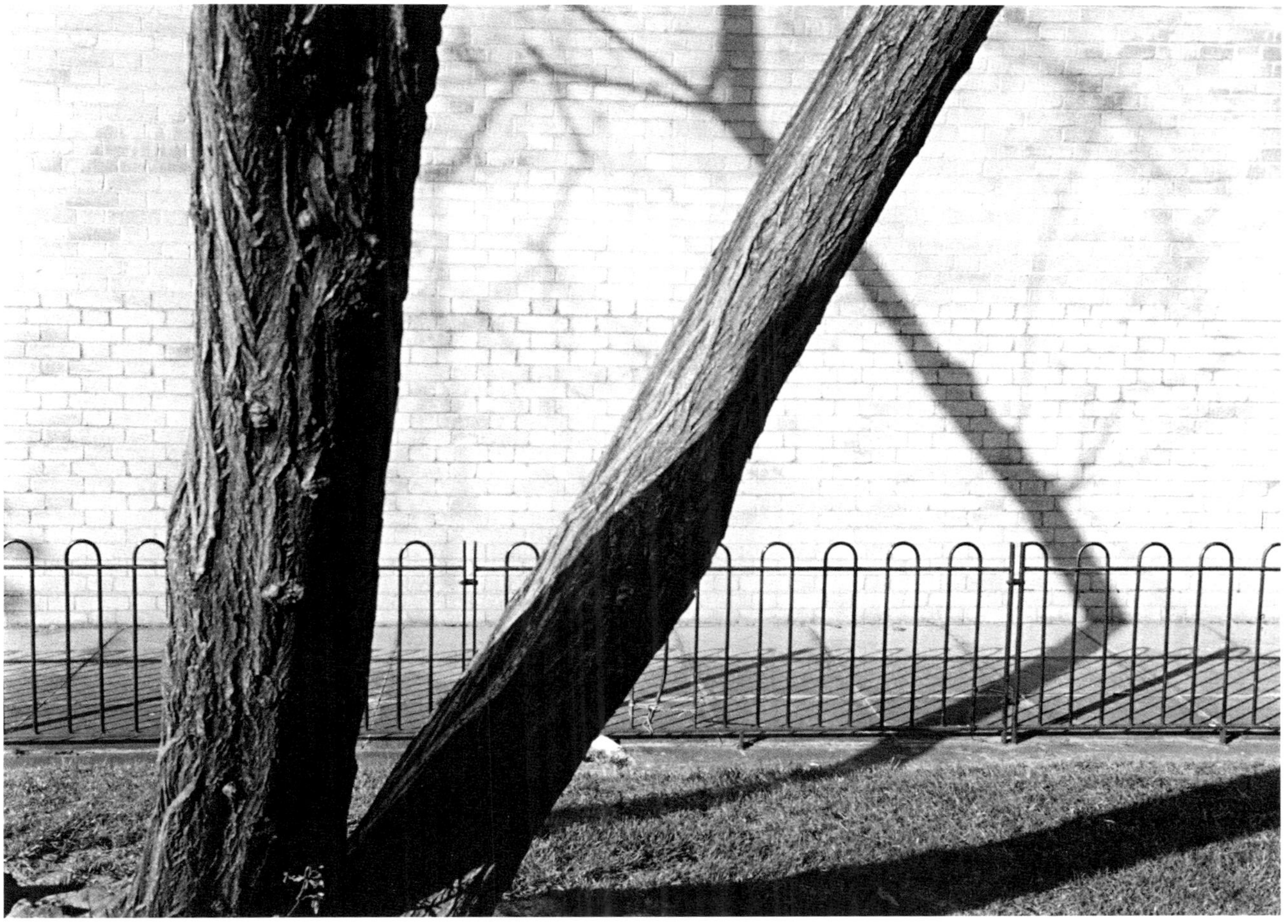

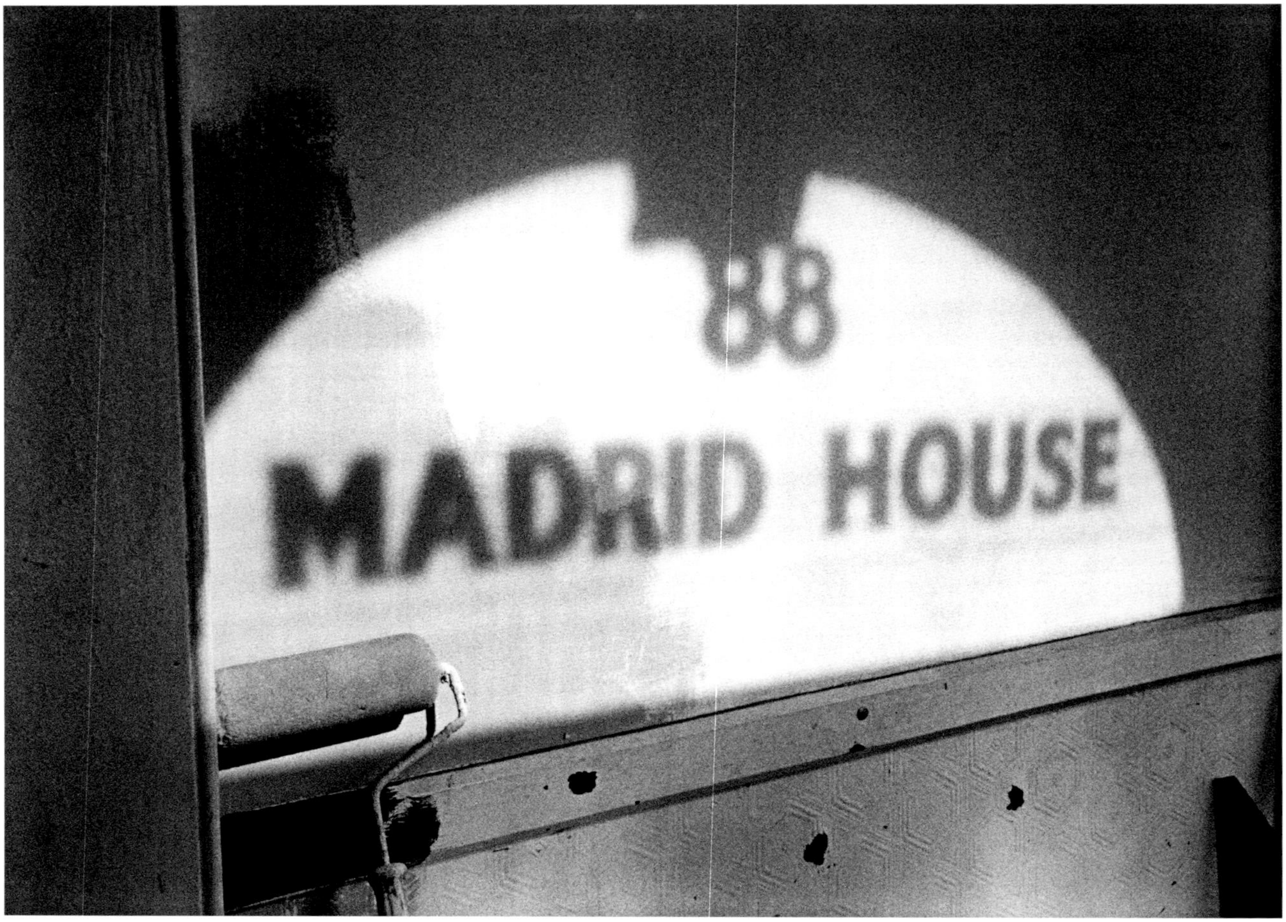
88
MADRID HOUSE

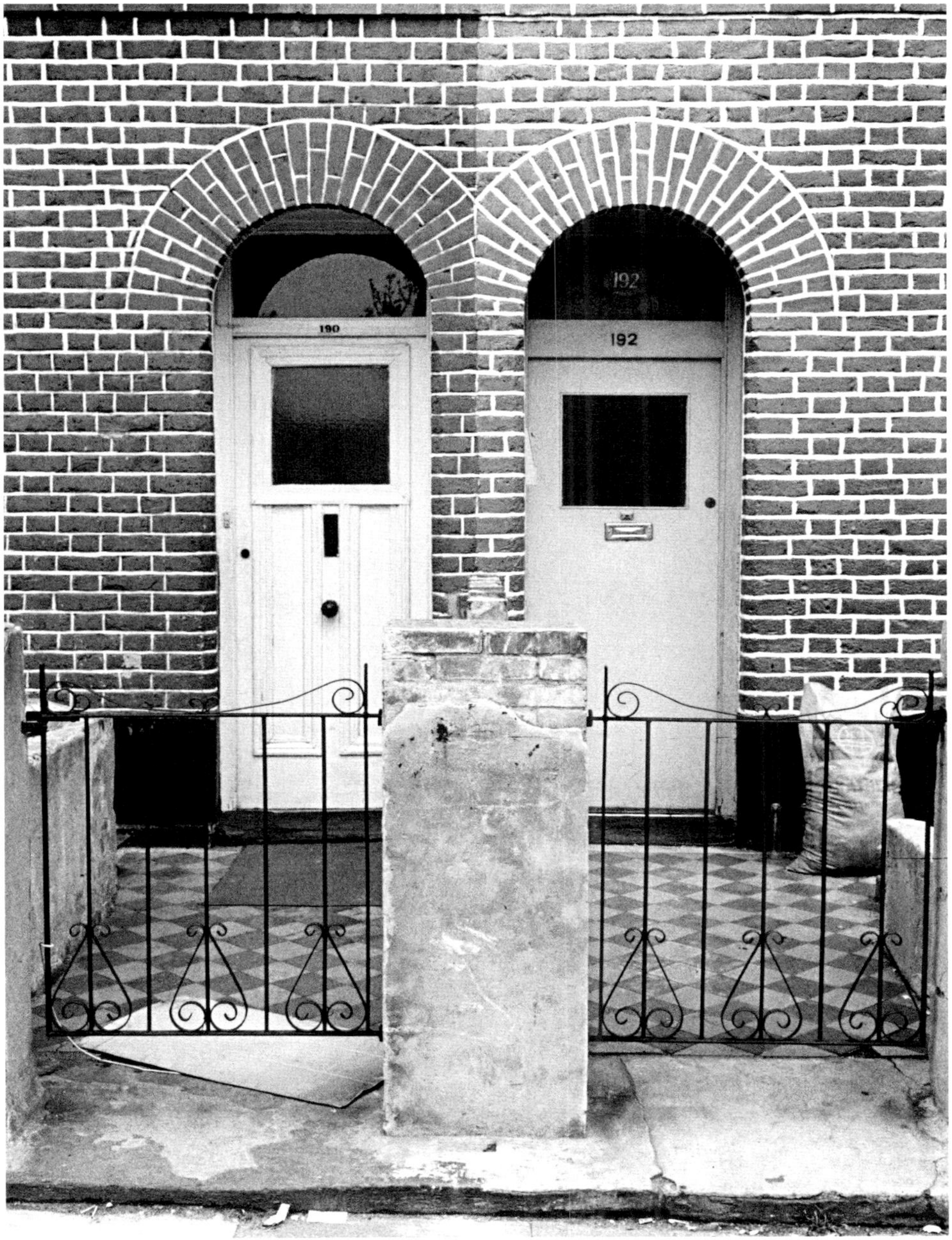
190
192
192

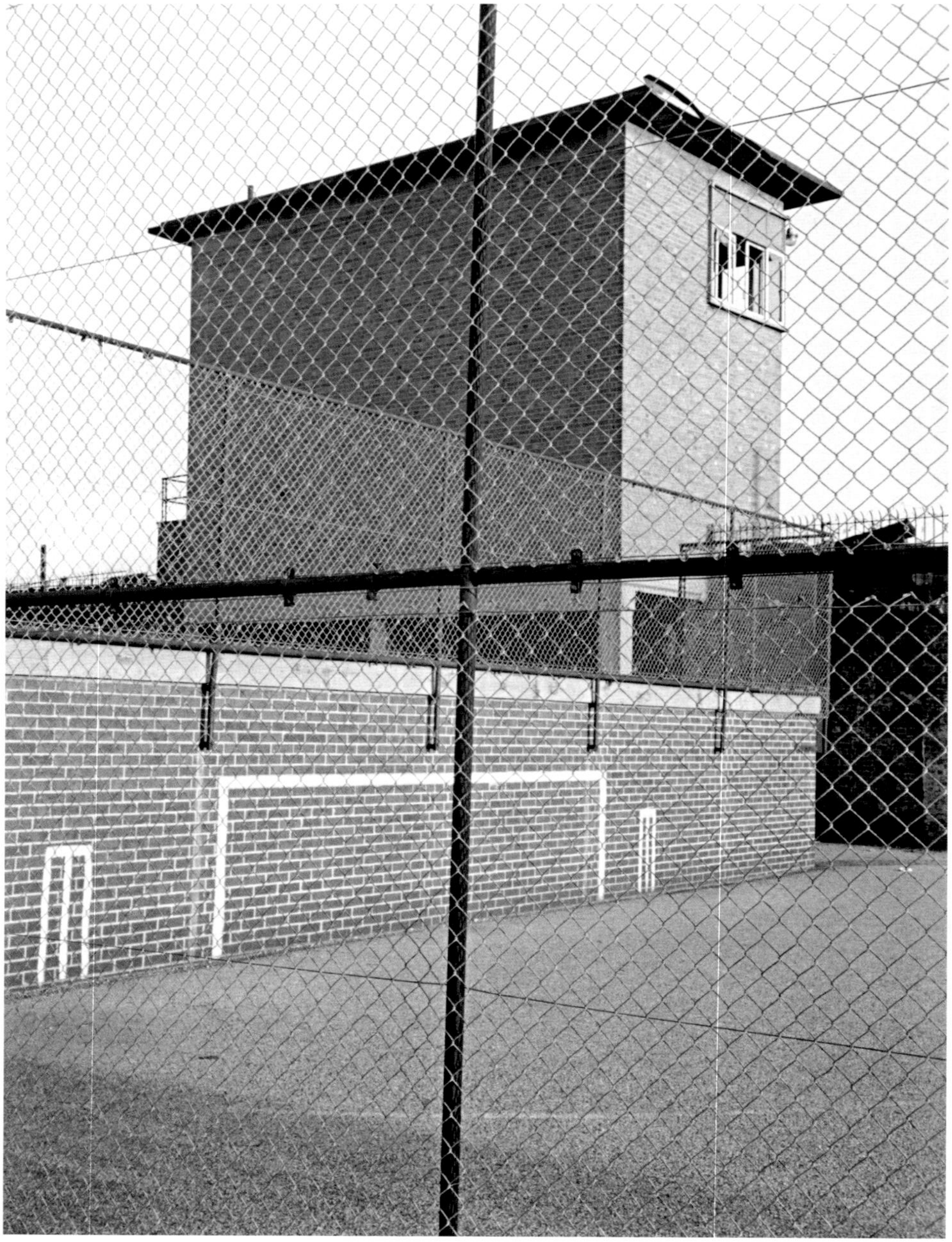

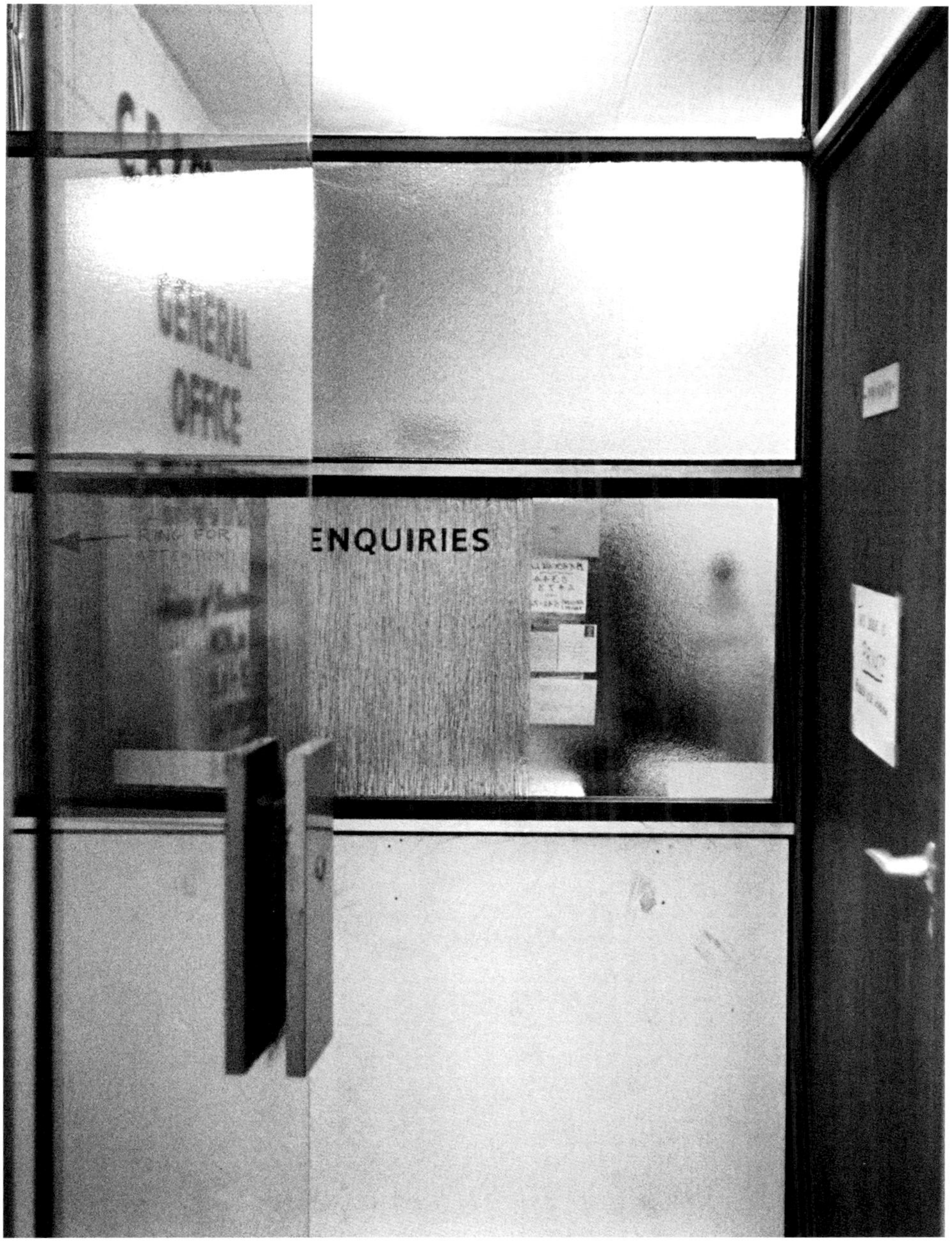
GENERAL
OFFICE
ENQUIRIES

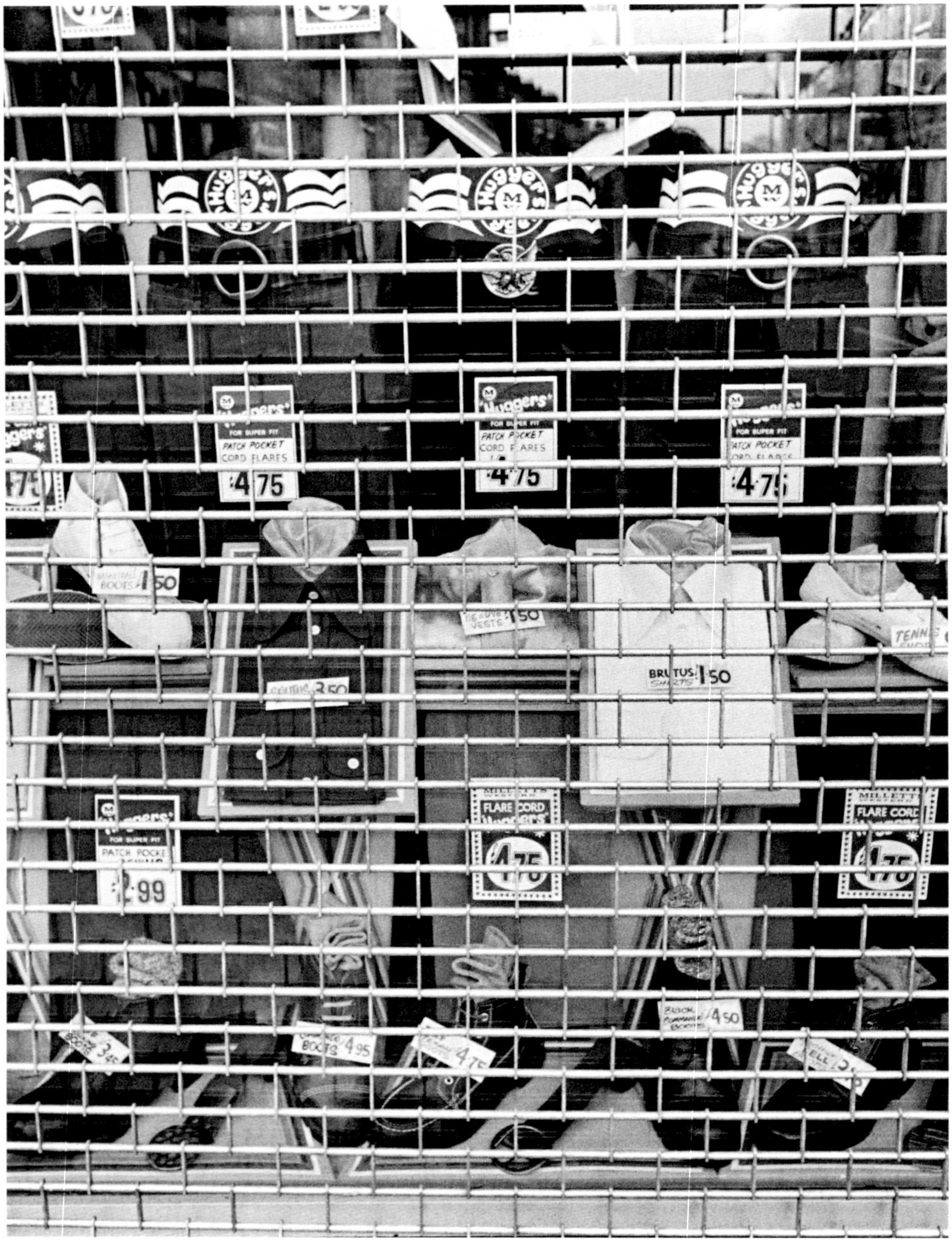
Huggers
FOR SUPER FIT
PATCH POCKET
CORD FLARES
4·75
BRUTUS SHIRTS 1·50
FLARE CORD
2·99

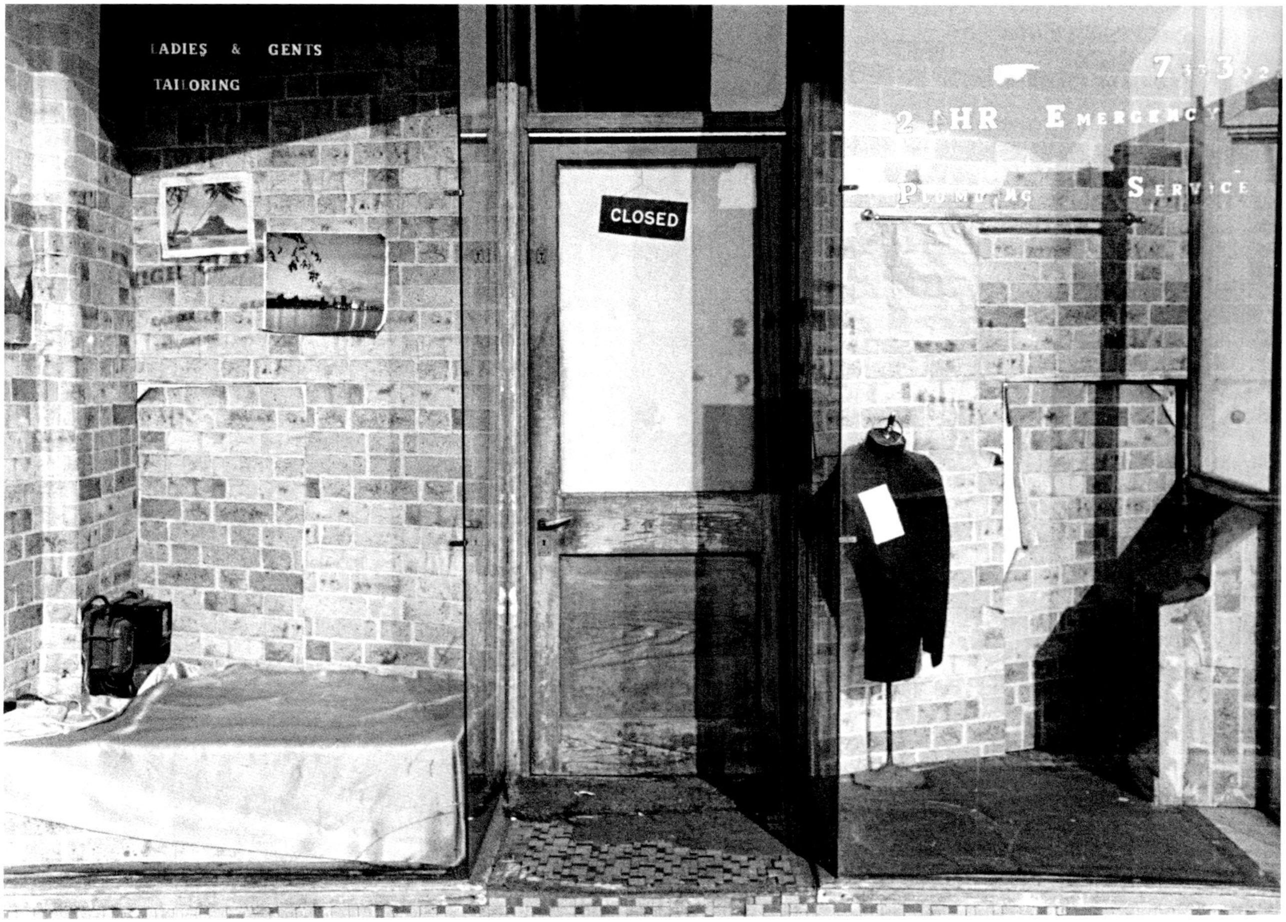
LADIES & GENTS
TAILORING
CLOSED

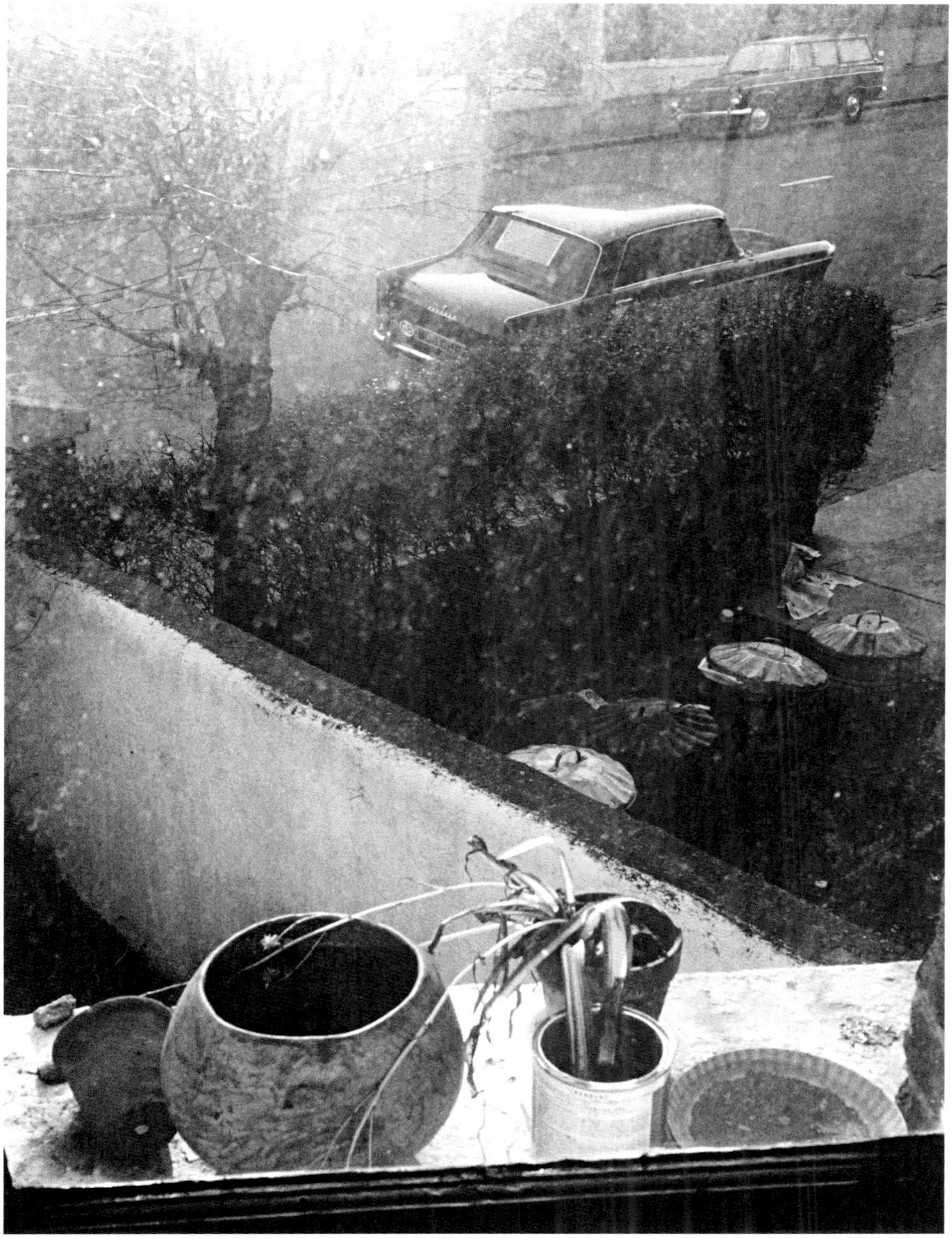

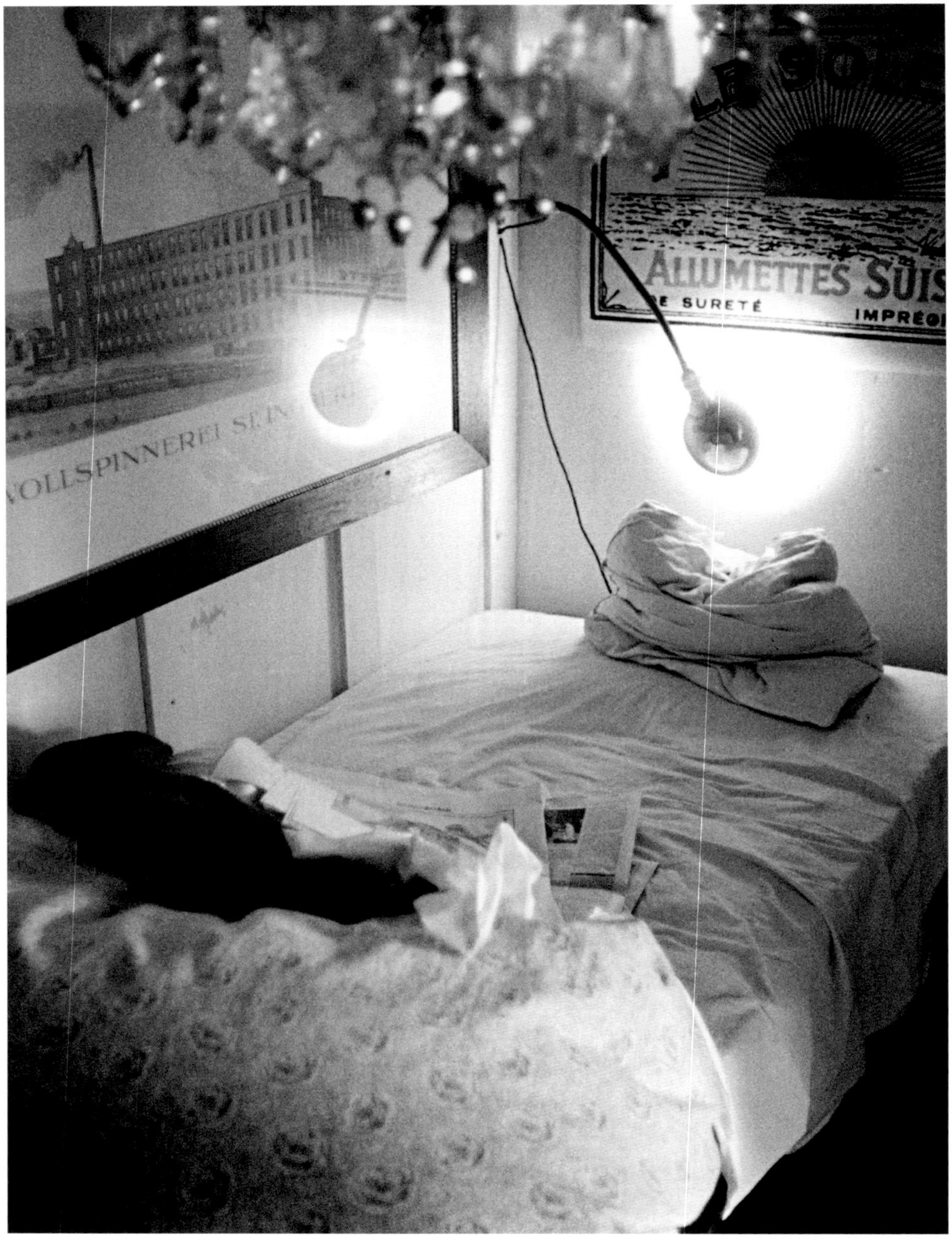

WOLLSPINNEREI
ALLUMETTES SUIS
SURETÉ
IMPRÉG

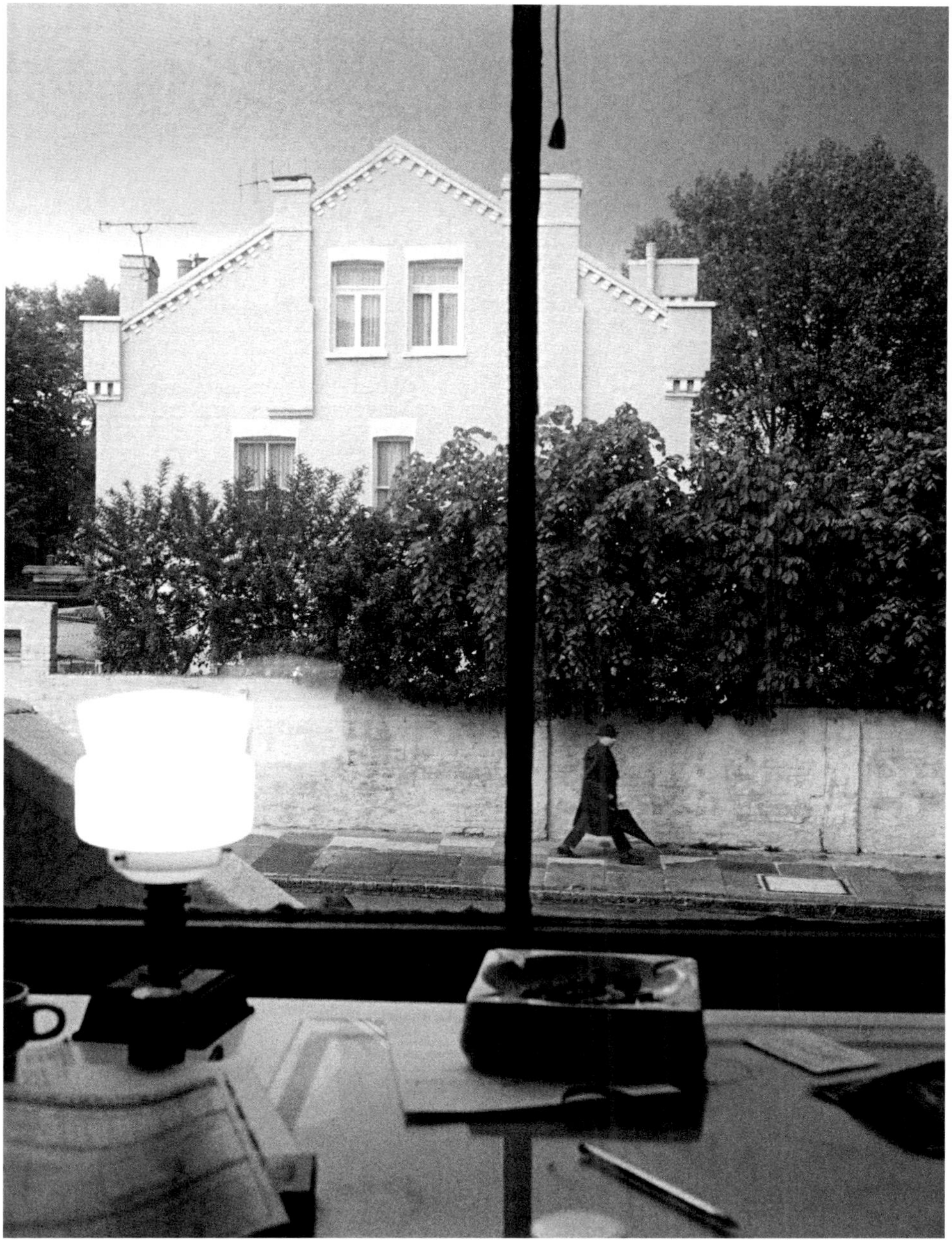

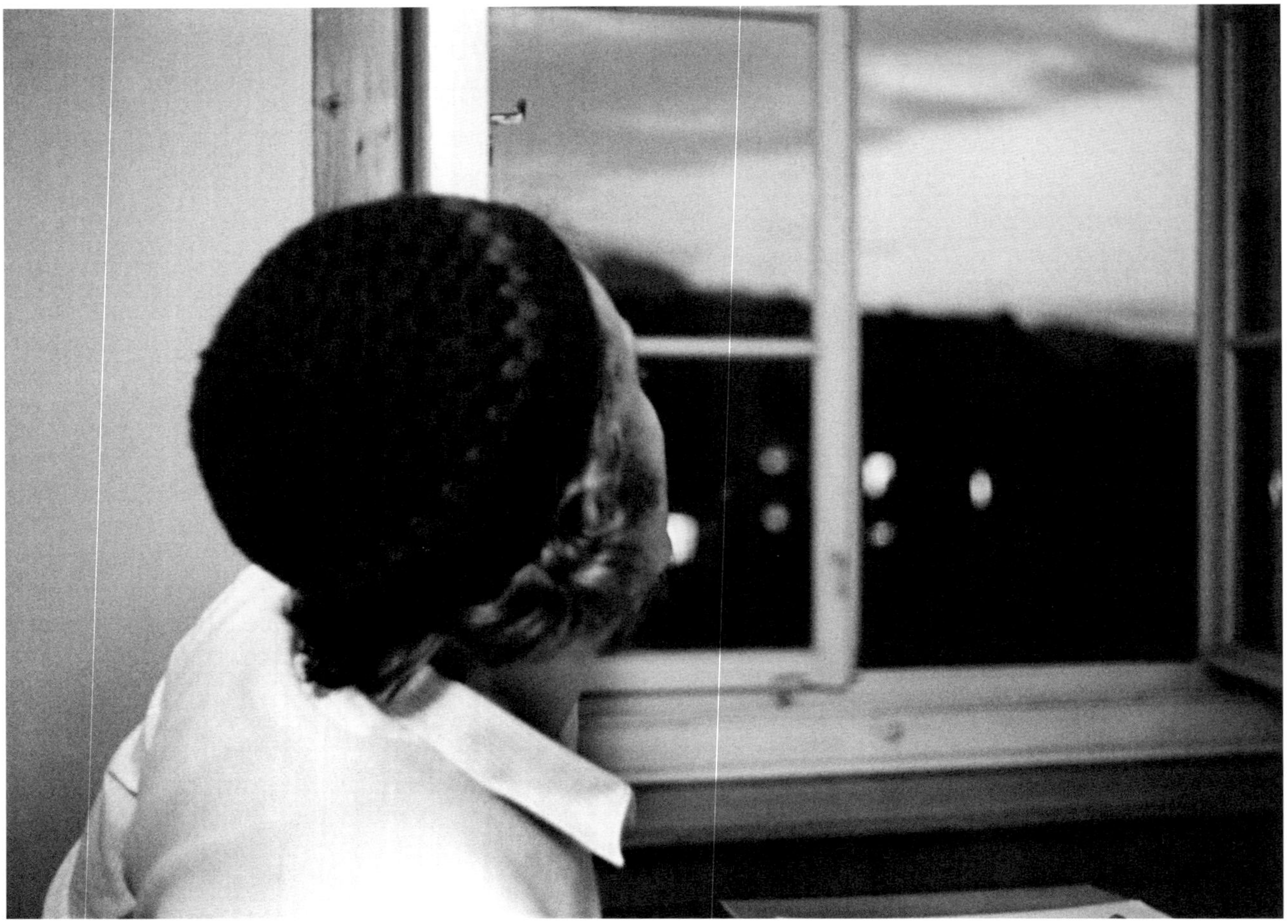

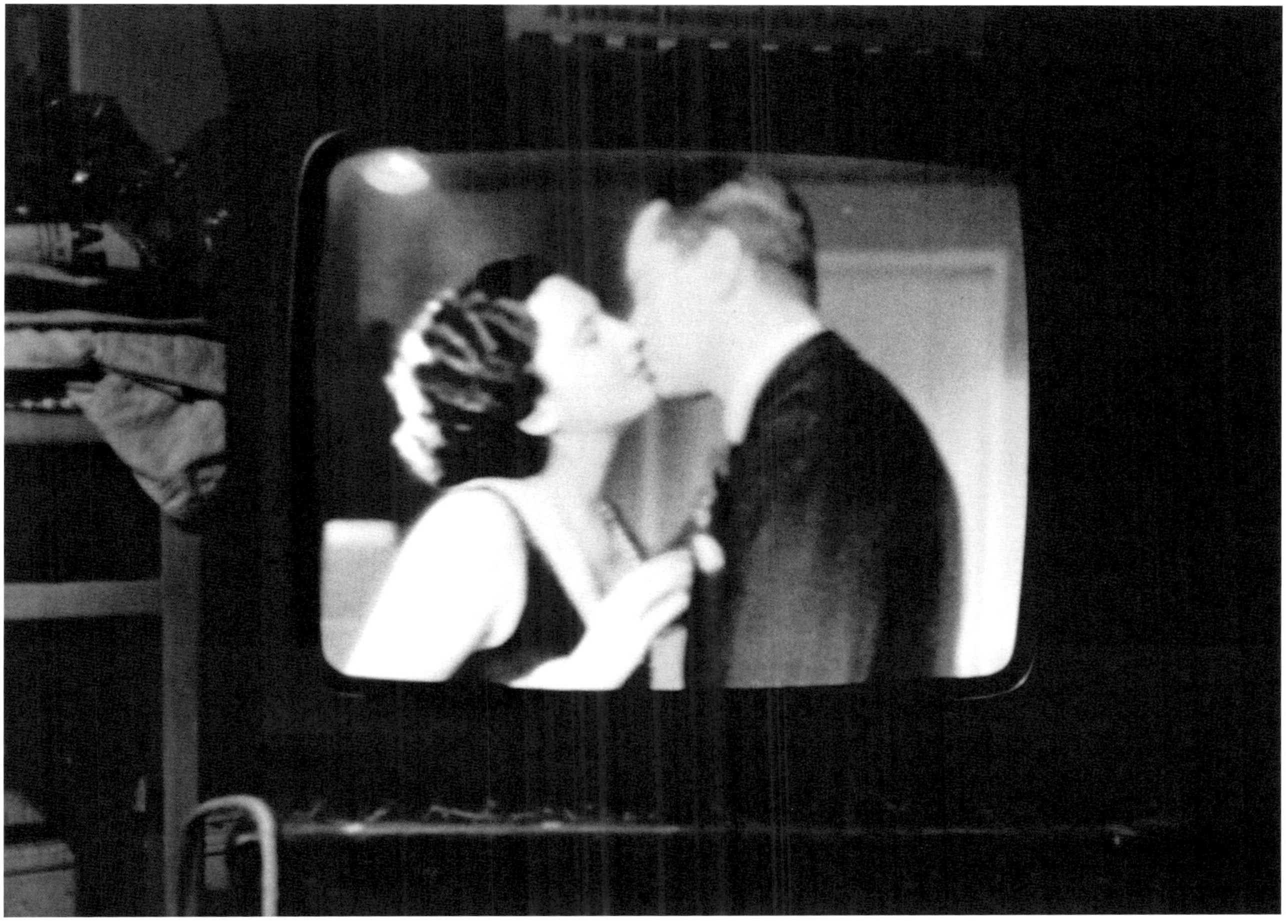

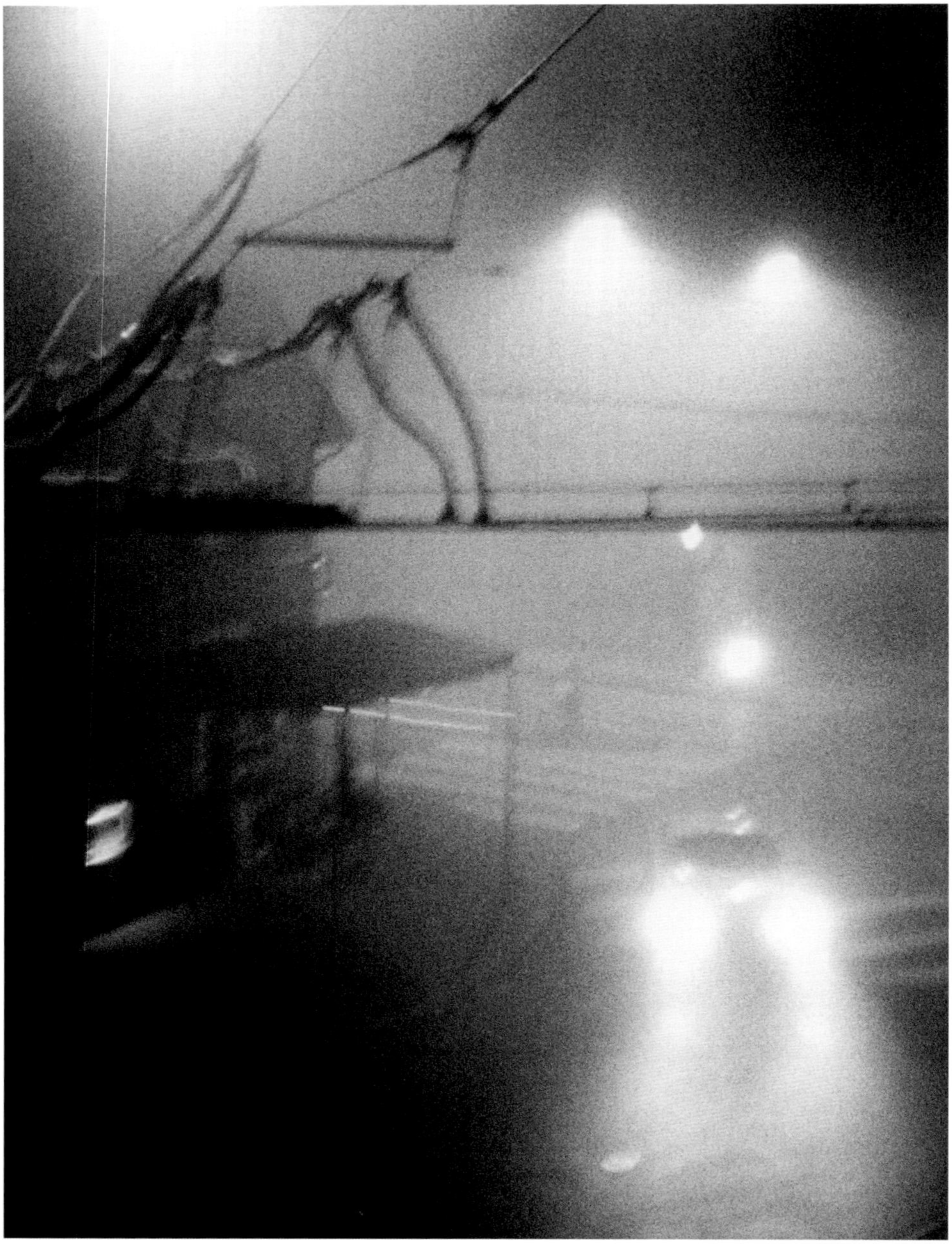

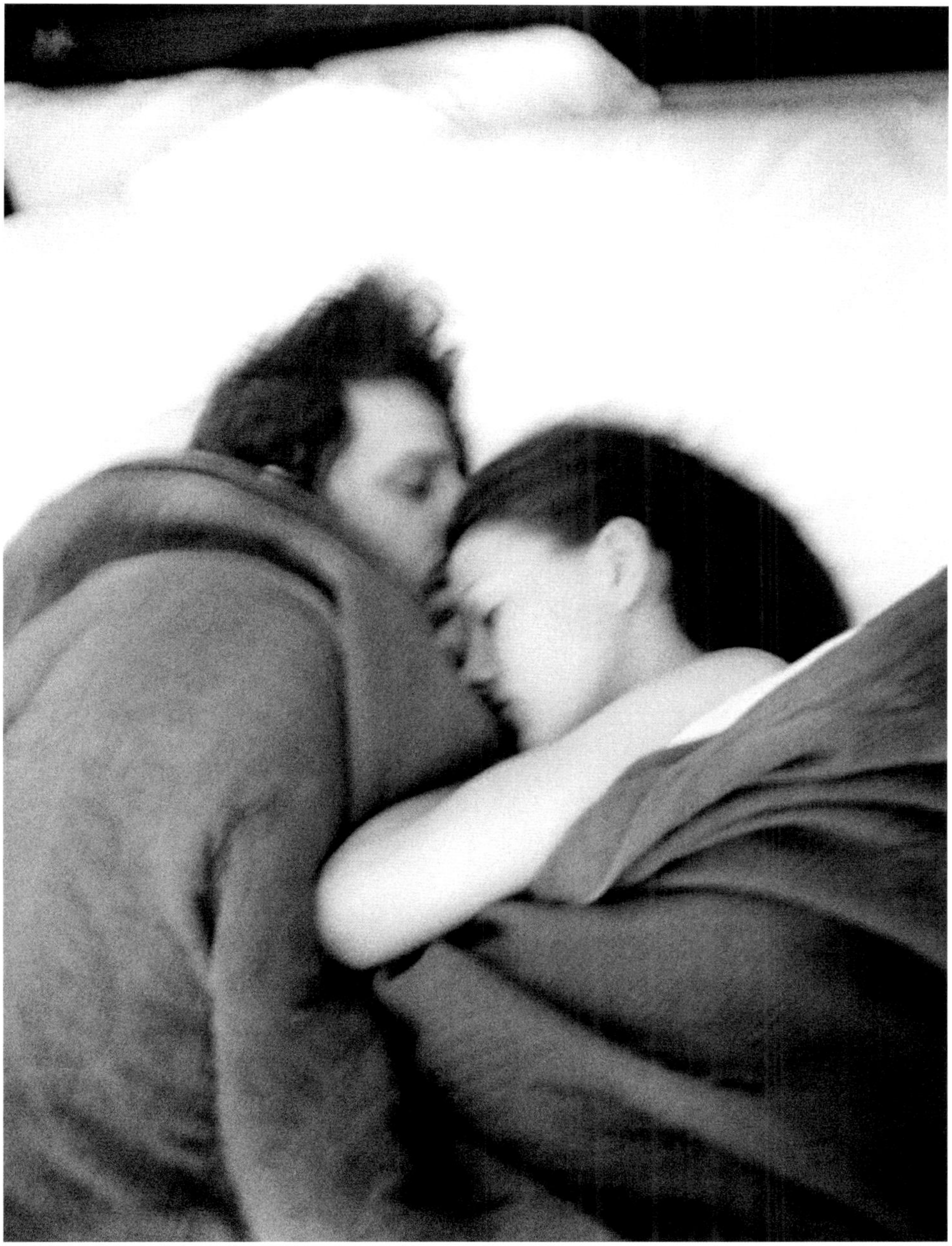

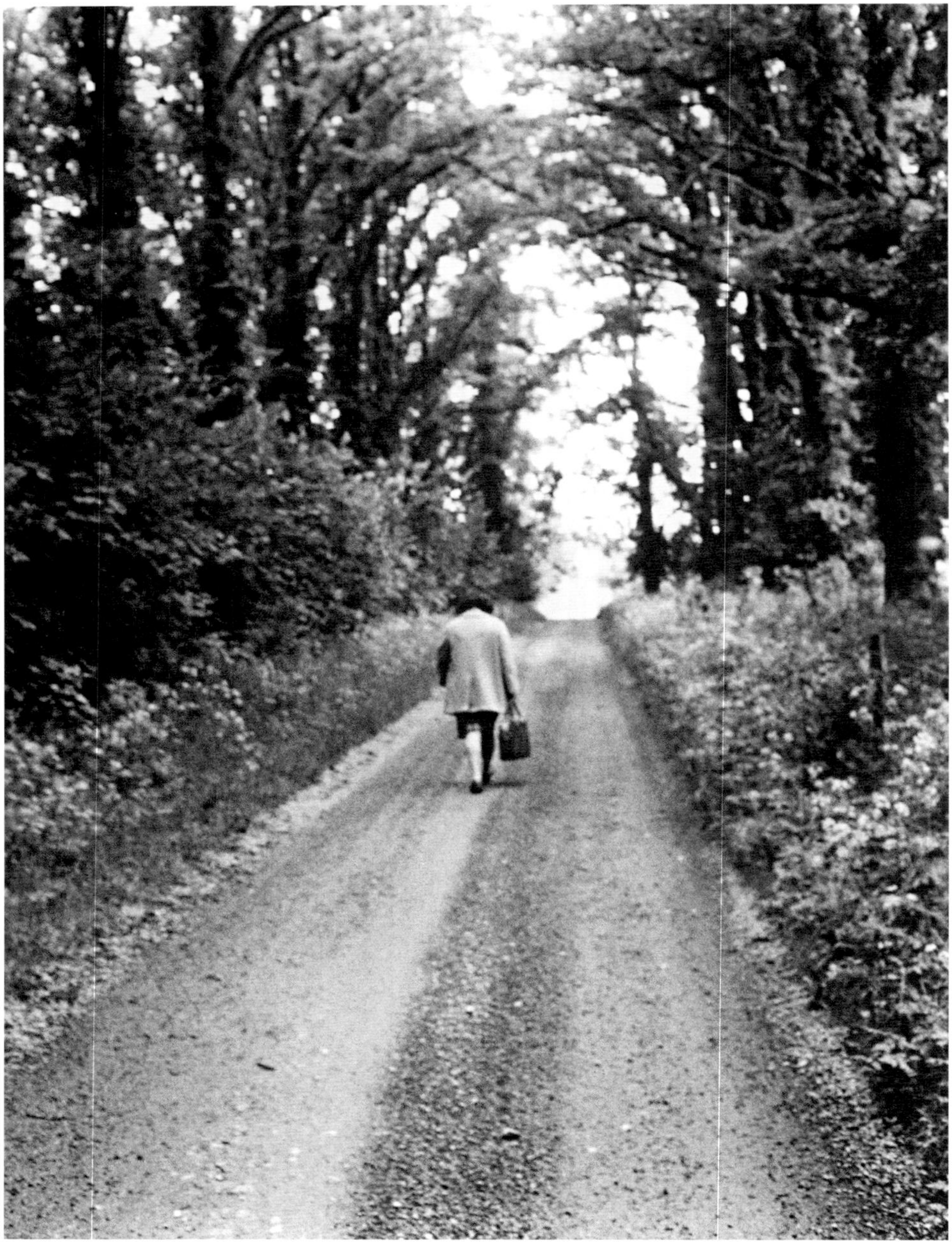

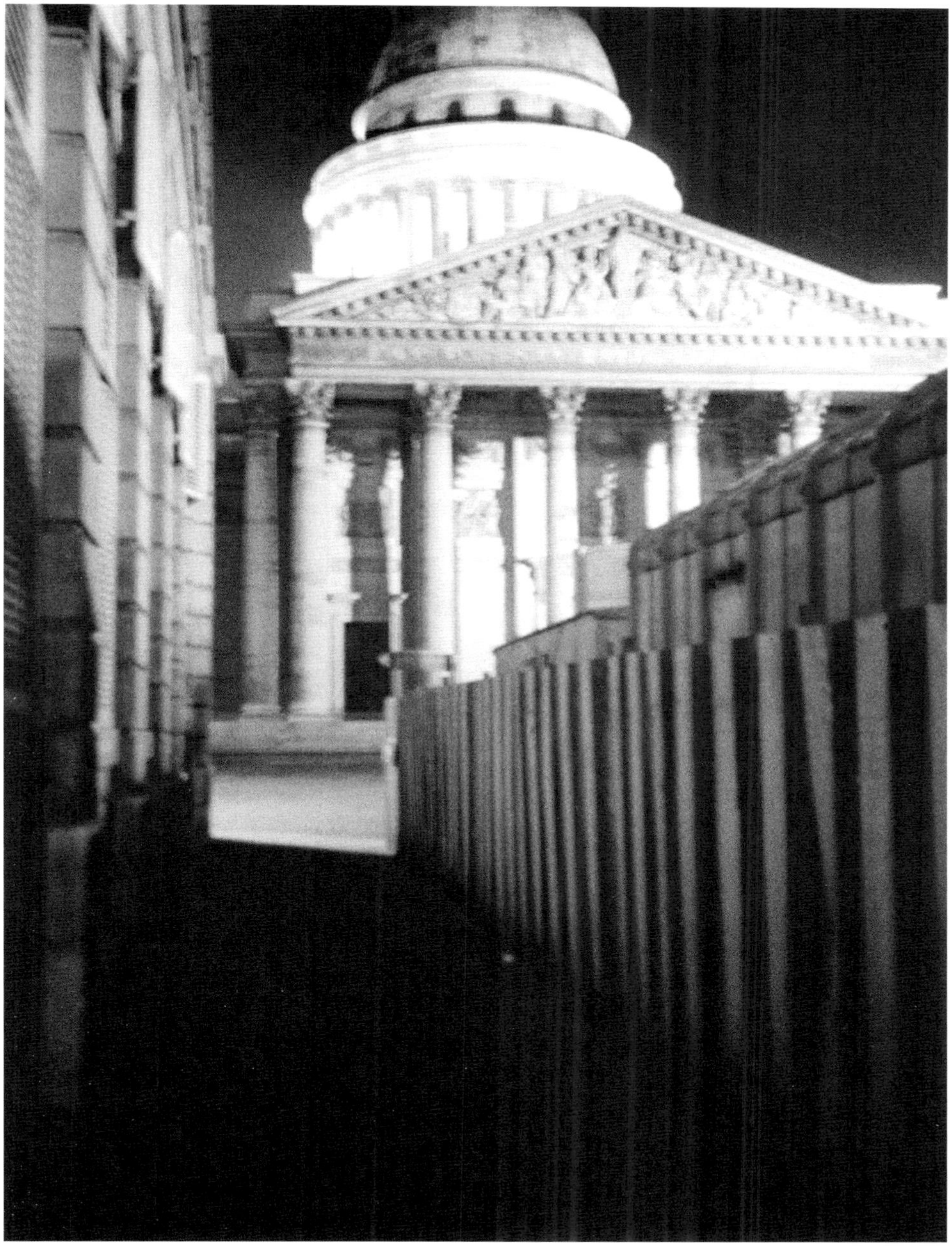

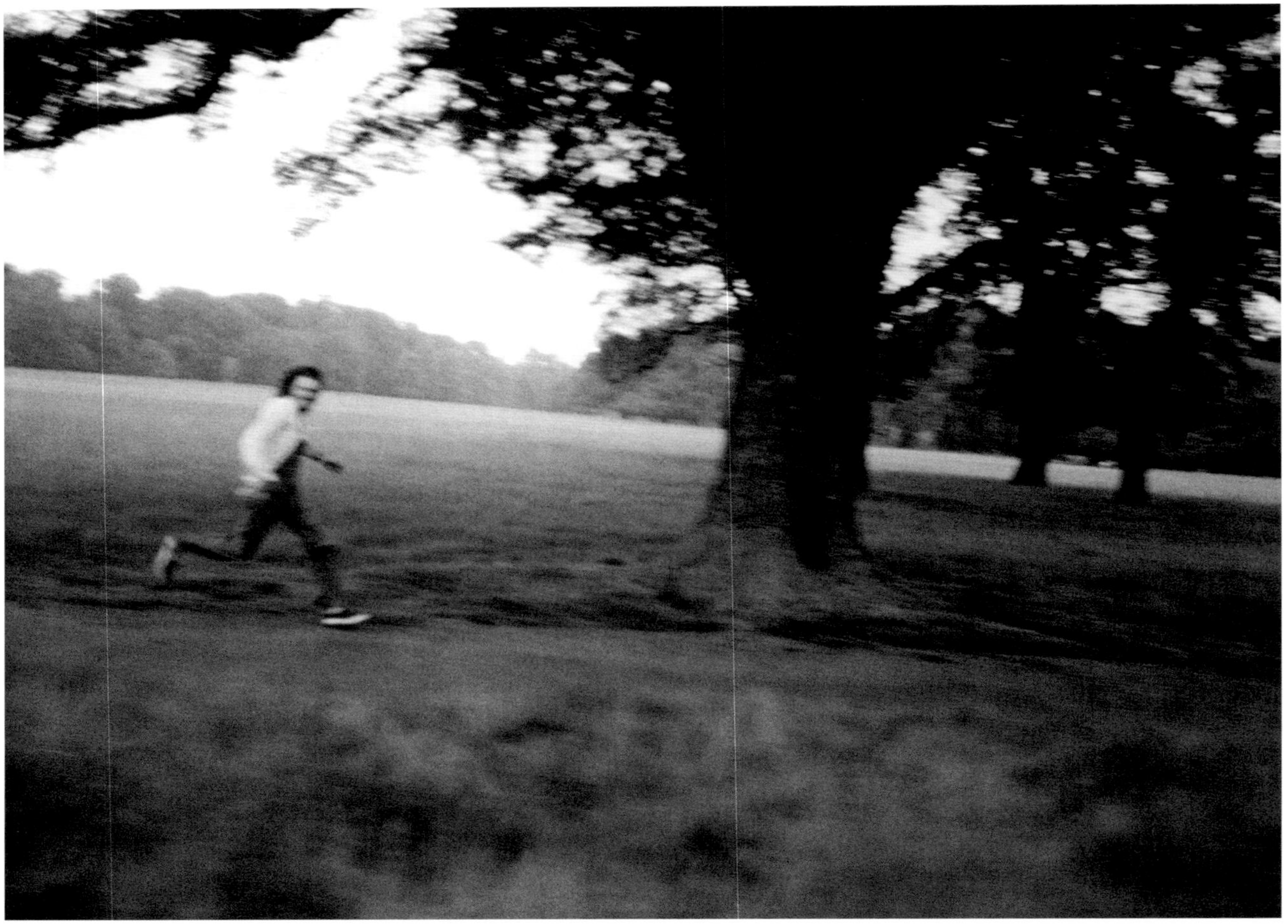

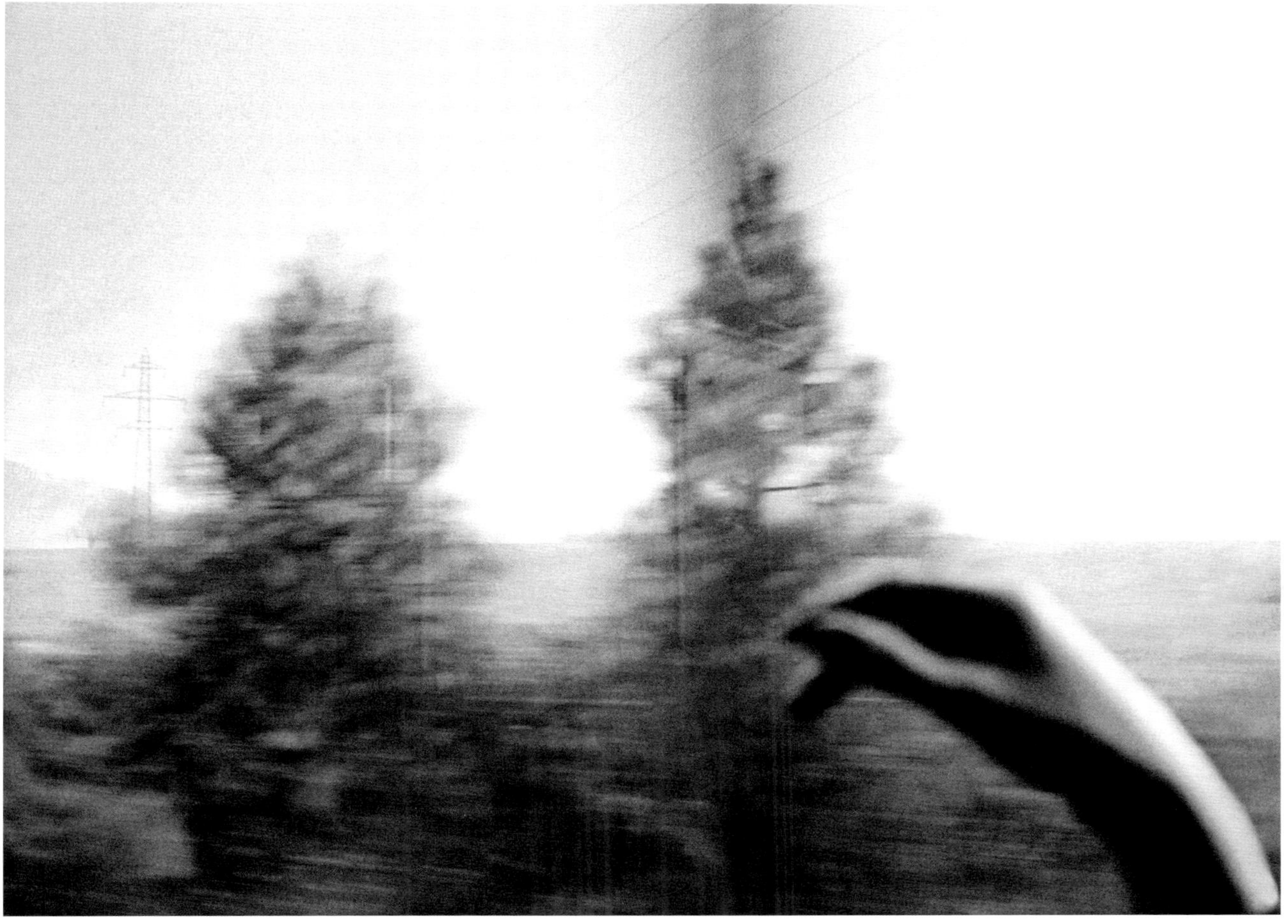

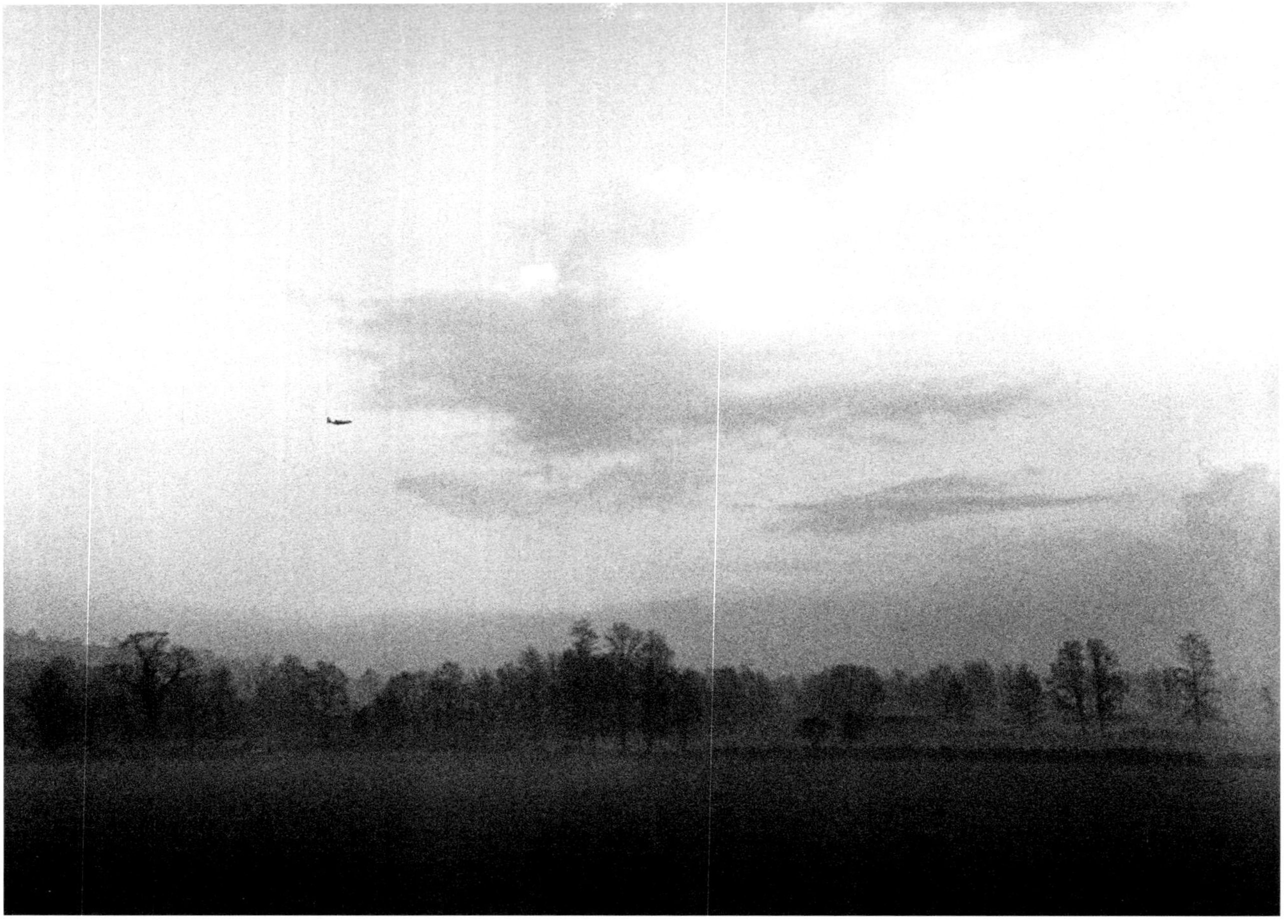

Ich hatte immer den Wunsch, wenn ich einem Regenbogen begegne, den fotografieren zu können

Gespräch zwischen Iwan Schumacher (IS)
und Martin Jaeggi (MJ)

M J Was zeigt dieses Buch?

I S Es zeigt 124 Fotografien, die alle 1972 entstanden. Ich kaufte mir Anfang 1972 eine Canon-Halbformatkamera, bei der auf einem regulären Kleinbildfilm 72 Fotos statt der üblichen 36 Platz hatten. Die Kamera war so klein, dass ich sie immer bei mir tragen konnte. Damit erfüllte ich mir einen Traum: Ich hatte immer den Wunsch, wenn ich einem Regenbogen begegne, den fotografieren zu können. Das war vorher nicht möglich gewesen, als ich mit einer Leica arbeitete und ständig eine Tasche mit mehreren Objektiven und einem Belichtungsmesser mit mir herumtrug.

M J Hast du die Bilder in der Absicht aufgenommen, ein Buch daraus zu machen? Oder kam dir diese Idee erst später? Es gibt aus jener Zeit ja eine erste Version.

I S Eigentlich steckte kein Plan dahinter, im Gegenteil. Meine Absicht war es, absichtslos zu fotografieren. Ich hatte vier Jahre vorher die Fotoklasse an der Kunstgewerbeschule Zürich abgeschlossen. Freie Fotografie oder Kunstfotografie, wie man sie heute kennt, gab es damals noch nicht. Die Fotoklasse war dem Bundesamt für Industrie, Gewerbe und Arbeit (BIGA) unterstellt, entsprechend mussten wir beim Abschluss der Ausbildung eine BIGA-Prüfung ablegen. Alles war auf Auftragsfotografie ausgerichtet. Freie Fotografie gab es am ehesten noch in der Reportage, wo einem ein Thema gestellt wurde oder man sich selbst eines stellte. Aber auch da zückte man die Kamera erst, wenn ungefähr klar war, was man fotografieren wollte. Zumindest mir ging es so, dass ich nie ohne Konzept fotografierte.

Jetzt mit diesem kleinen Apparat war etwas ganz anderes möglich. Ich konnte die Dinge an mich herantreten lassen. Ich porträtierte Freundinnen und Freunde und fotografierte Dinge in meiner unmittelbaren Umgebung. Viele Aufnahmen nahm ich aus den Fenstern von fahrenden Zügen oder Autos auf. Die Aufnahmen mussten nicht unbedingt scharf sein, wichtig war, dass sie eine gewisse Stimmung wiedergaben. Die Idee eines Buches kam erst zum Schluss.

M J Du sagst, du hättest absichtslos fotografiert: Was war die Absicht dahinter – denn die gibt es ja immer.

I S Ich wollte wegkommen von der Art und Weise, wie ich bislang fotografiert hatte: vorgefassten Ideen und Konzepten folgend. Ich hoffte, dass aus dieser Art des Sehens, der Offenheit für Begegnungen, eine neue Bildsprache entstehen könnte. Es ging um die Fähigkeit, sich visuell auf vorgefundene Dinge einzulassen – die Kamera als Notizblock. Dass ich mit diesen Bildern nicht meinen Lebensunterhalt verdienen musste, half natürlich.

M J Kannst du über die Phase deines Lebens erzählen, in der die Bilder entstanden?

I S Ich zog im Herbst 1970 mit 23 Jahren nach England, weil ich dort einen Job an einer Kunstschule hatte. Ich unterrichtete Fotografie an der Bath Academy of Art in Corsham, mitten auf dem Land, zwei Autostunden von London entfernt. Es war so etwas wie eine Tradition, dass Absolventen der Fotoklasse dort ihr Wissen weitergaben. Die meisten gingen für ein Semester hin, ich blieb gleich zwei Jahre. Ein Teil der Schule befand sich in Corsham Court, einem Schloss mit einem echten Lord, mitten in einem prächtigen Park gelegen. Die Studios hingegen waren in Baracken eines ehemaligen Militärcamps außerhalb des Dorfes untergebracht, eine recht eigenartige Situation. Als Lehrer hatte ich nicht einmal einen Haken, um meinen Mantel aufzuhängen. Wenn ich die Schüler zusammen sehen wollte, um ihnen eine Aufgabe zu stellen, musste ich in der Woche davor einen Brief verfassen, der dann vom Sekretariat vervielfältigt und verteilt wurde. Ich unterrichtete zwei bis drei Tage in der Woche und verbrachte den Rest meiner Zeit in London.

Als ich nach den Weihnachtsferien im Januar 1972 wieder nach England zurückkehrte, wusste ich, dass dies mein letztes halbes Jahr dort sein würde. Ich nutzte die Schule für meine Zwecke, entwickelte meine Negative und zog Blattkopien. Ich traf eine Auswahl von 9 × 12 cm-Vergrößerungen und zog diese auf Karton auf. Am Ende des Jahres hatte ich fünf Bundesordner mit Fotografien in chronologischer Reihenfolge.

Damals wohnte ich im Süden von London, zwischen den U-Bahn-Stationen Stockwell und Clapham North. Die Zeiten von *Swinging London* waren vorbei, England war durch Streiks und Stromausfälle wie gelähmt. Erstmals seit 1930 überstieg im Januar 1972 die Zahl der Arbeitslosen die Millionengrenze (Seite 5). Obwohl ich absichtslos fotografierte, gab es wiederkehrende Themen. Die Battersea Power Station war ganz in der Nähe und faszinierte mich als gigantisches Backsteingebäude aus den dreißiger Jahren (Seiten 67–75). Wenn ich zu Fuß durchs Quartier lief oder mit dem Auto fuhr, tauchte sie immer wieder vor mir auf. Dies erinnerte mich an die *100 Ansichten des Berges Fuji* von Hokusai. Wenn ich sage, Themen kristallisierten sich heraus, war es aber nicht so, dass ich mir gesagt hätte: „Ah, die Battersea Power Station ist mein Thema, ich spaziere jetzt einen Monat lang herum und mache bei jeder Tages- und Nachtzeit eine Aufnahme." Ich versuchte, die Absichtslosigkeit beizubehalten.

Ein anderes Thema waren Ansichten aus den Fenstern des Madrid House an der Bromfelde Road 88 in Südlondon, wo ich mit Freunden wohnte (Seiten 13, 22, 51, 122, 129, 131). Ich habe erst kürzlich auf Google Maps nachgeschaut, und es sieht dort tatsächlich noch immer so aus wie damals. Im Gegensatz zur Gegend um die Battersea Power Station, die inzwischen total mit Hochhäusern zugebaut ist.

In der zweiten Hälfte des Jahres 1972 kehrte ich in die Schweiz zurück. Ich hatte bereits während meiner Zeit an der Kunstgewerbeschule ein Interesse an Film entwickelt. In London ging ich fast täglich ins Kino. In England selber Filme zu machen war mir aber nicht möglich – es sei denn, ich hätte eine Filmschule besucht, das konnte ich mir nicht leisten, und ich hatte auch keine Lust, nochmals vier Jahre die Schulbank zu drücken. In Zürich existierte bereits ein kleines Netzwerk von Absolventen der Fotoklasse, Leute, die Filme machten, wie beispielsweise Fredi Murer (Seite 114) und Georg Radanowicz

(Seite 113), für den ich 1968 für sein Porträt über Max Bill die Kamera geführt hatte. Dies erlaubte mir einen Wiedereinstieg in den Film. Kurz nach meiner Rückkehr arbeitete ich als Assistent bei dem Dokumentarfilm *Wer einmal lügt oder Viktor und die Erziehung* von June Kovac mit Sebastian C. Schroeder an der Kamera (Seiten 6 und 7) und begann, ein eigenes Filmprojekt voranzutreiben. Ich fotografierte weiter mit meiner kleinen Kamera, fand jedoch gegen Ende des Jahres, dass sich die Motive zu wiederholen begannen. Trotz des in der Fremde geschärften Blicks, um es mal etwas hochgestochen zu formulieren, faszinierten mich Zürich oder die Schweiz visuell weit weniger als England. Meine Tagebuch-Aufnahmen begannen mich zu langweilen, und ich vermisste zusehends die Farbe. Ich machte noch einen Versuch mit Farbfotografie, der aber scheiterte, weil Dias zu teuer und beim Negativfilm die Abzüge sehr unbefriedigend waren. Erst mit den Handys ist Farbfotografie für mich wieder interessant geworden. Die Fotos von 1972 nehmen in gewisser Weise vorweg, wie wir heute mit Smartphones fotografieren.

M J Du sagst, diese absichtslose Art zu fotografieren sei auch eine Abgrenzung zu deiner früheren Arbeitsweise gewesen. Was hast du vorher fotografiert?

I S Die beiden wichtigsten Arbeiten nach der Schule waren einerseits eine Serie, die 1970 anlässlich einer DDR-Reise entstand. Sie zeigte die zwanzigjährige Geschichte der DDR anhand von Skulpturen und Monumenten. Die Reise wurde vom Buchhändler Theo Pinkus organisiert, es waren drei Journalistinnen mit von der Partie und ich als Fotograf. Wir reisten durch die DDR und arbeiteten an verschiedenen Geschichten. Mit Sil Schmid machte ich eine Reportage über Schweizer hinter der Mauer, die helfen wollten, den Sozialismus aufzubauen, wie beispielsweise der Theaterregisseur Benno Besson. Wenn wir herumreisten, sahen wir immer wieder Monumente, nicht zuletzt die Mauer, die ich auch als Monument behandelt habe. Diese fotografierte ich. Daraus entstand später eine Serie, in der ich die Fotografien bearbeitete und kolorierte. Diese erschien wiederum mit Texten von Sil Schmid im *Weltwoche-Magazin.*

Die andere Arbeit ging von einer selbst gestellten Aufgabe aus. Ich dachte nach 1968, man sollte dem bürgerlichen Publikum der Zeitschrift *Du* die „heutige Jugend“ nahebringen, um gegen Vorurteile anzukämpfen. Geplant war pro Porträt eine Seite, perspektivisch so aufgenommen, dass der Kopf richtig gegenwärtig wirkte. David Weiss (Seite 111) verfasste die Kurzbiografien dazu. Das *Du* veröffentlichte die Arbeit tatsächlich, aber mit vier Bildern pro Seite, was deren Effekt abschwächte.

Die kleine Canon half mir, mit dieser eher konzeptuellen Arbeitsweise zu brechen. Ich begann, Bilder zu machen von Dingen, so wie sie sich mir in der Realität präsentierten. Dies half mir auch beim Filmen. Ein oder zwei Jahre später machte ich die Kamera für Fredi Murers *Wir Bergler*, wo einiges aus dieser Arbeit in die Kameraarbeit einfloss.

M J Was begann dich an der Fotografie zu frustrieren, und was am Film zog dich an?

I S Die Möglichkeit, Geschichten zu erzählen und mich länger mit einer Sache zu beschäftigen.

M J Inwiefern war das, was wir in diesem Buch sehen, auch ein Übergang zum Film?

I S Das habe ich nie so gesehen.

M J Du sagtest, du wolltest Geschichten erzählen. Aber hast du nicht genau das gemacht mit diesen Fotos – sie in einem Buch zu einer tagebuchartigen Geschichte gefügt? Was war die Motivation bei der ersten Fassung des Buches?

I S Es war ein Versuch, diese Arbeit zu einem Abschluss zu bringen – aus den 3000 Fotos eine Auswahl zu treffen und sie dann in eine Abfolge zu bringen. Dazu bot sich die Buchform an.

M J Hast du diese Version damals öffentlich gezeigt?

I S Ich habe die Fotografien damals fortlaufend gezeigt. Wenn ich Besuch hatte oder jemanden besuchte, nahm ich oft einen Bundesordner mit Fotografien mit. Insofern war diese Arbeit immer öffentlich. Auch die Maquette in zwei Exemplaren mit den 366 Aufnahmen – 1972 war ein Schaltjahr –, die ich am Schluss herstellte, war eigentlich als Buchveröffentlichung angedacht. Ich wusste zwar, dass ich keinen Verlag finden würde, hatte aber die Idee, das Buch im Eigenverlag mit Subskriptionen herauszubringen. Nach zwei oder drei Anläufen musste ich das allerdings aufgeben. Einerseits wurde ich es leid, Subskribenten aufzutreiben, und andererseits machte ich einen Offset-Testdruck, dessen Qualität enttäuschend war. Offset war jedoch das Einzige, was ich mir hätte leisten können. Schließlich reichte ich die Arbeit beim Bundesamt für Kultur ein und erhielt dafür ein Eidgenössisches Stipendium für angewandte Kunst.

M J Was brachte dich dazu, zu diesem Buch zurückzukehren?

I S Vielleicht ist es eine Alterserscheinung, dass man nochmals durchs Archiv geht, um aufzuräumen und zu sehen, was noch verwertet werden könnte. Es war, als ob ich einen Schatz gefunden hätte, als ich nach mehr als vierzig Jahren wieder über diese Bilder ging und feststellte: Doch, das ist was.

M J Weshalb hast du es nochmals editiert und nicht die erste Version übernommen?

I S Die Maquette hatte eher einen Albumcharakter mit bis zu vier Bildern pro Seite. Das Buch war aber damals schon in vier Kapitel gegliedert. Heute sind es 13. Ich ließ rund 300 neue Abzüge im Format 18 × 24 cm herstellen. Zusammen mit der Cutterin Anja Bombelli, die seit bald zwanzig Jahren meine Filme montiert und ein wunderbares Sensorium für Bildassoziationen besitzt, ordneten wir die Fotos und trafen eine Auswahl. Die 124 Bilder sollen in ihrer fast filmischen Abfolge mögliche Geschichten suggerieren. Bezeichnenderweise heißt das Buch immer noch *At Home and on the Way*, nun einfach mit dem Vorsatz *1972*.

I'd always wanted to be able to photograph a rainbow, if one should happen to appear

Conversation between Iwan Schumacher (IS) and Martin Jaeggi (MJ)

M J What's in this book?
I S 124 photographs, all from 1972. In early 1972 I bought a Canon half-frame camera, which lets you take 72 pictures, instead of the usual 36, on a normal 35mm cartridge. The camera was so small I could take it with me everywhere. It was a dream come true. I'd always wanted to be able to photograph a rainbow, if one should happen to appear. That had never been possible when I was working with a Leica and lugging a bag around with more lenses and a light meter.
M J Did you take those pictures with a book in mind? Or did that idea come later? There is a first version from back then.
I S I didn't have a plan, on the contrary. My idea was just to take photographs, with no specific intention. I'd graduated from the photography course at the School of Applied Arts in Zurich four years earlier. In those days there was no such thing as "free" photography, or art photography, as they call it now. The photography course was overseen by the Federal Office for Industry, Trade, and Labor (Bundesamt für Industrie, Gewerbe und Arbeit, or BIGA), so at the end of the course we had to sit a BIGA exam. Everything was geared toward commissions. The closest thing to free photography was when we did reportage, when you were set a subject or you devised one of your own. But even then you didn't get the camera out until you were pretty sure what you wanted to photograph. Certainly in my case, I never took pictures without a concept.

Now, with my new camera I could work completely differently. I could let things come to me. I took pictures of friends and photographed things in my immediate surroundings. I took a lot of pictures from moving trains and cars. The shots didn't have to be perfectly in focus; the main thing was that they conveyed a particular atmosphere. The idea of making a book only came at the end.
M J You were saying you took those pictures with no specific intention. But there must have been an intention of some kind—there always is!
I S I wanted to get away from the way I'd always taken photographs up to that point, pursuing set ideas and concepts. My hope was that this different way of looking, of being open to any encounters, would let me develop a new pictorial language. It was about being visually receptive to whatever you happened to come across—using the camera as a notepad. Of course it was a help that I didn't have to earn a living from those pictures.
M J Could you tell us more about the period in your life when you took those pictures?
I S In the autumn of 1970, when I was twenty-three, I moved to England because I had a job at an art school. I taught photography at the Bath Academy of Art in Corsham, way out in the country, two hours from London by car. It was something of a tradition that graduates from our photography course in Zurich would go to England for a time to pass on what they had learnt to the students in Corsham. Most people went for just one semester, but I stayed for two years. Part of the art school was at Corsham

Court, a castle with a real lord, in the middle of beautiful parklands. Only the studios were in barracks on an old military base outside the village—a very strange set-up. Even as a member of staff I didn't have a hook to hang my coat on. If I wanted to see all the students together, to set a piece of work, I had to write a letter a week in advance, which the secretary would copy and distribute to the students. I taught two or three days a week there and spent the rest of my time in London.

When I went back to England after the Christmas vacation in January 1972, I knew I only had another six months there. So I took full advantage of the school's facilities, developing negatives and making contact prints. I made a selection of 9 × 12 cm enlargements and mounted them on card. At the end of the year I had five folders filled with photographs arranged in chronological order.

At the time I was living in south London, between the tube stations Stockwell and Clapham North. The days of Swinging London were long gone; the UK was crippled by strikes and power cuts. In January 1972, for the first time since 1930, the unemployment figures breached the million mark (p. 5). Although I was taking photographs with no explicit intention, there were recurrent themes. Battersea Power Station was within easy reach and I was fascinated by this vast, brick-built structure from the thirties (pp. 67–75). Wherever I went on foot or by car in my neighborhood the power station was always looming into view. It reminded me of Hokusai's *One Hundred Views of Mount Fuji*. Mind you, when I say that themes emerged, it wasn't as though I said to myself, "Okay, so Battersea Power Station is a theme for me, which means I'll spend a month walking around taking pictures at every time of day and night." I tried to remain intention-free.

Another theme turned out to be views from the windows of Madrid House at 88 Bromfelde Road in south London, which I shared with friends (pp. 13, 22, 51, 122, 129, 131). I looked it up on Google Maps the other day and it still looks exactly like it did back then. Not like the area around Battersea Power Station, which is now all built up with apartment buildings.

In mid-1972 I returned to Switzerland. During my time at the School of Applied Arts I'd already developed an interest in film. I went to see a movie almost every day in London. But it wasn't possible for me to start making films in England—I'd have had to enroll in a film school and I didn't have the money for that. I also didn't feel like going to classes again for another four years. By contrast, in Zurich there was already a small network of graduates from the photography course who were making films, people like Fredi Murer (p. 114) and Georg Radanowicz (p. 113); I'd already done the camera work for Georg's portrait of Max Bill in 1968. That gave me a way back into film. Shortly after I arrived back in Switzerland I found work as an assistant on June Kovac's documentary *Wer einmal lügt oder Viktor und die Erziehung*, with Sebastian C. Schroeder on camera (pp. 6 and 7). So now I started working on a film project of my own. I went on taking photographs with my half-frame camera, but by the end of the year it seemed to me that I was starting to repeat certain motifs. Despite having honed my vision abroad, to put it rather grandly, in Zurich and Switzerland there were far fewer things that caught my eye. I started to find my diary shots boring and I increasingly felt the lack of color. I had a stab at color photography but that came to nothing, because slides were too expensive and prints from the negatives were very unsatisfactory. It was only when I got a cell phone that I started to take an interest in color photography again. In a way the shots I was taking back in 1972 prefigured what we do with smartphones today.

M J You were saying that taking photographs with no explicit intention was also a way of leaving behind what you had done before. What sort of things had you photographed before?

I S The two most important works I produced after leaving college were, firstly, a series in 1970, which arose from a trip to the German Democratic Republic (GDR). It told the twenty-year history of the GDR through sculptures and monuments. The trip was organized by the bookseller Theo Pinkus; there were three journalists and myself, as photographer. We traveled through the GDR and worked on various stories. Sil Schmid and I produced a reportage on Swiss nationals living behind the Wall, who wanted to help to build a socialist state—people like the theater director Benno Besson. Wherever we went we saw monuments, not least the Wall itself, which I treated as another monument. I photographed them and this led to a series later on, for which I edited the shots and tinted them. The series was published, with texts by Sil Schmid, in the magazine *Die Weltwoche.*

The other work arose from a task I set myself. I felt that after 1968 it would be good to introduce the bourgeois readers of the journal *Du* to the "youth of today," as a way of breaking down prejudices. The plan was to print one portrait per page, taken in such a way that the head looked really immediate. David Weiss (p. 111) wrote short biographies for all the individuals. *Du* did indeed publish the series, only with four portraits per page, which greatly weakened the impact.

The little Canon helped me to get away from that concept-driven way of working. I started to take pictures of things exactly as they appeared to me in real life. That also helped me as a camera man. A year or two later I did the camera work for Fredi Murer's *Wir Bergler*, in which I was able to draw on certain aspects of the photo diary.

M J What was it that started to frustrate you about photography, and what was the attraction of film?

I S The possibility of telling stories and engaging with the same topic for longer.

M J To what extent are the images in this book part of that transition to film?

I S Actually I've never thought of them in that light.

M J You were talking about telling stories. But isn't that exactly what you were doing with these photographs—creating a chronicle in a book? What was in your mind when you made that first, early version of the book?

I S It was an attempt to bring that project to a conclusion—by making a selection from 3,000 shots and putting them in a particular sequence. A book seemed the best way of doing that.

M J Did you show that version in public at the time?

I S I was constantly showing the pictures to people back then. When I had visitors or went to see someone I'd often get out a folder of photographs or take one with me. In that sense it was always on public view. And the maquette, which I ultimately made in an edition of two with 366 shots (1972 was a leap year), was also actually intended to be published as a book. I knew I'd never find a publisher but I had an idea that I could publish it myself, funded by subscriptions. But after a few attempts to get it off the ground I had to give up. On one hand I got tired of trying to find subscribers, and on the other hand I made a test offset print and was really disappointed by the quality. But offset was the only thing I could have afforded. In the end I submitted it to the Federal Office of Culture here in Switzerland and was awarded a Confederation study grant for applied art.

M J And what made you return to this book?

I S Maybe it comes with age—you go back through your archives to tidy up and to see what could still be used. It was like coming upon a treasure when I found these pictures and started looking at them again after a gap of over forty years, and realized, there's something there.

M J So why did you edit the pictures again rather than just using the first version?

I S The maquette was more like an album, with up to four pictures per page. And the book was divided into four chapters back then. Now there are thirteen chapters. I had around 300 new prints made, in 18 × 24 cm. I went to my editor Anja Bombelli, who's been working on my films for almost twenty years now and who has a wonderful eye for pictorial associations, and together we selected images and put them in the right order. The idea is that these 124 pictures, now in an almost filmic sequence, will suggest possible stories. Significantly enough, the book is still called *At Home and on the Way*, only now preceded by the date: *1972*.

Mein Dank gilt allen, die mich damals und heute in diesem Projekt unterstützt haben:

I want to thank everyone who has supported this project, back then and now:

Anja Bombelli, Adrienne Burrows, Patrick Frey, Frédérique Hutter, Martin Jaeggi, Stephan Kunz, Teo Schifferli, Carmen Sommerhalder

Iwan Schumacher
1972 — At Home and on the Way

Text: Martin Jaeggi
Translation: Fiona Elliott
Copyediting: Miriam Wiesel (German),
Martin Jaeggi (English)
Proofreading: Miriam Wiesel

Manually enlarged prints:
Carmen Sommerhalder, Black-Blanc
Scans: Labo photo, Roger Plaschy

Book design: Teo Schifferli
Printed and bound by Kösel GmbH, Krugzell
Paper: Hello Fat, 135 g
Font: Plain Medium

First edition: Edition Patrick Frey, 2016
Print run: 800 copies
ISBN 978-3-906803-22-7
Printed in Germany

Edition Patrick Frey, Limmatstrasse 268, CH-8005 Zürich
www.editionpatrickfrey.com
mail@editionpatrickfrey.ch

Distribution

Switzerland
AVA Verlagsauslieferung,
CH – Affoltern am Albis
ava.ch

Germany, Austria
GVA Gemeinsame Verlagsauslieferung,
D – Göttingen
gva-verlage.de

France, Luxembourg, Belgium
Les presses du réel, F – Dijon
lespressesdureel.com

United Kingdom
Antenne Books, GB – London
antennebooks.com

Japan
Marginal Press, JP – Tokyo
marginal-press.com

United States
RAM publications + distribution,
USA – Santa Monica
rampub.com

Australia, New Zealand
Perimeter Distribution, AU – Melbourne
perimeterdistribution.com

Rest of the world
Edition Patrick Frey, CH – Zürich
editionpatrickfrey.com